All American History
Student Reader

VOL. I — The Explorers to the Jacksonians

All American History

Uniting America's Story, Piece by Piece

EXPLORATION

REVOLUTION

EXPANSION

COLONIZATION

A full year's curriculum in 32 weekly lessons

CELESTE W. RAKES

Student Reader

Bright Ideas Press

Dover, DE

All American History: Uniting America's Story, Piece by Piece Student Reader
by Celeste W. Rakes
Vol. I of the All American History series

Published by Bright Ideas Press
P.O. Box 333, Cheswold, DE 19936
www.BrightIdeasPress.com

Cover and interior design by Pneuma Books, LLC
Visit www.pneumabooks.com for more information.

ISBN-13: 978-1-892427-12-0
ISBN-10: 1-892427-12-5

Library of Congress Cataloging-in-Publication Data

Rakes, Celeste W.
   All American history / Celeste W. Rakes.
      p. cm.
   Includes bibliographical references and index.
   Contents: v. 1. Uniting America's story, piece by piece : student reader.
   ISBN 1-892427-12-5 (hard cover : alk. paper)
1. United States — History — Textbooks. I. Title.

E178.1.R27 2006
973 — dc22   2005021128

11 10 09 08 07   6 5 4 3

*To my children — Rebekah, Joel, and Daniel — as well as
all the other students in my co-op history classes... this curriculum was developed for you,
and your enthusiastic response to it was the catalyst for its publication.*

TABLE OF CONTENTS

PREFACE

Ten years ago, three other homeschooling moms and I decided to form a co-op and offer classes for our children and for other homeschooled students who would like to participate. My responsibility in the co-op was to teach American history. Although I graduated from college with a degree in history and was certified to teach it, I had never done so in a traditional classroom setting. However, after teaching my own children at home and tutoring others, I had formed some definite ideas about how I wanted to approach teaching this course.

As I began making plans for the class, I spent many hours looking through history curricula (some with which I was very familiar and others that were new to me). Although each program had aspects that I liked, none of them had everything I wanted. Finally, I decided to attempt to develop my own program to use in teaching the class. Those first feeble efforts were the seeds of *All American History*.

ACKNOWLEDGEMENTS

There are many individuals who have been influential in developing my "love of history" as well as important in the nurturing of this particular history project.

My mom and dad — your willingness to share with me many times about "the good ole days" inspired in me a lifelong curiosity about the past and how people lived in days gone by.

My high school history teachers Mrs. Lupold and Mrs. Tollison—your fascinating lectures set me on the course of pursuing the study of history in college. My history professors at Furman University — your mentoring honed my research skills and gave me the keys to a lifetime of reading in the field.

My husband, Jeff—your willingness to support our family has made it possible for us to homeschool these many years and for me to devote countless hours to developing this curriculum for our children and others. You have been a patient and kind encourager and a loving husband and friend!

My longtime friends and now publishers, Maggie and Bob Hogan — your belief in this project is the only reason for its existence. You have been wonderful homeschooling partners, and your friendship has been a tremendous blessing in my life (as well as in the lives of my children and husband).

My new friends at Pneuma Books Heather Armstrong and Nina Taylor — your amazing editorial skills have taken a very rough manuscript (developed over ten years of teaching) and turned it into a polished curriculum. You have stretched and challenged me and enabled me to do more than I thought I could ever do!

My Lord and Savior, Jesus Christ — Your sovereign hand on my life during my years of home-schooling and especially during the preparation of this curriculum has given me great peace and confidence (even when I have felt weak and inadequate). You are my rock, a sure foundation for my life!

INTRODUCTION

In developing my program to teach American history, I had several specific goals in mind. First of all, I knew that I wanted to structure the material both chronologically and thematically. After I had completed my research, I found that I had enough information for eight distinct themes or units. Once I had finished writing those unit studies, I found that I had produced eight lessons for each unit — enough for a two-year program! By organizing my curriculum around these thematic units, I hoped to create a simple and memorable framework for my students to "plug in" the historical information that they learned.

My second goal was to provide my students with the basic factual information that I felt they should learn for each unit. Many history curricula provide a wealth of suggestions for projects and activities but require the teacher or student to gather the information necessary to do them. Although my program offers many opportunities for further exploration, it can still be used effectively without spending countless hours looking for information at the public library or buying a large number of history books to have on hand at home. Those students who want to tackle the research projects in each lesson can easily do so using a computer with Internet access.

In addition to establishing a helpful learning structure and supplying the essential historical information, I also hoped to create a variety of educational experiences for my students to enhance their study and understanding of American history. Too often the study of history means reading a boring textbook, regurgitating the facts from that textbook on a test, and possibly writing the answers to a few homework questions and a report or two. That is not what I wanted history to mean to my children and to my co-op students! I wanted them to experience and believe that history is not boring — that it is the story of real people through the ages

In order to provide a diversity of educational experiences, I attempted to incorporate into my curriculum many study options beyond the mastering of basic historical information. These included:

- reading opportunities (biographies and historical fiction for each unit)
- writing projects (creative writing, as well as the compilation of fact sheets into notebooks on several topics)
- artistic and other hands-on work (original art projects, as well as flags, pictures of historical figures to associate with important events, maps to label, timelines to produce)

I also made a special effort to emphasize the social and cultural aspects of American history, much more so than most history curricula do. My belief is that history comes alive for students when they learn how people in past periods of history lived – what kind of clothes they wore, the houses they lived in, the foods they ate, the games they played, the schools they attended, and so forth. In developing this curriculum, I spent much time researching this aspect of history and trying to make it accessible to the students.

My final goal in creating this history program was to provide opportunities for my students to cement in their minds the important information from each unit. Again, I wanted to develop a variety of methods to accomplish this. The factual information that the students read and discuss includes impact bullets at the end of each lesson, summarizing the main points. Each lesson also has simple review questions that highlight the significant details. Finally, there are several hands-on activities and games for each unit that serve the purpose of review.

All American History

UNIT ONE
THE AGE OF EUROPEAN EXPLORATION

Lessons 1 — 8

By the end of the fifteenth century, several European nations had become swept up into a great burst of westward exploration. Spain, Portugal, England, France, and the Netherlands were the principal countries that competed in this quest. Because of the large number of European explorers during the sixteenth century, this period in history has become known as the Age of European Exploration or the Great Age of Discovery.

Most people living in Europe in 1480 stayed in or near their own villages for most of their lives. They thought of the world as one enormous land mass (they only knew of Europe, Asia, and Africa), broken up by a number of seas and surrounded by one large body of water (which they called the Ocean Sea). Although many educated Europeans believed the world to be round, church maps drawn during this period still depicted a flat earth with Jerusalem at the center. Occasionally, mapmakers also placed monsters on their maps in areas about which they knew nothing; and many believed that the seas were filled with enormous creatures that would swallow them alive.

There were a number of developments in the decades preceding the end of the fifteenth century that helped to spark the great wave of exploration that followed. One important factor was a revival of Greek scientific learning, especially the study of Ptolemy's *Geography* (which held that the world was round). Development of new navigation instruments, seaworthy vessels capable of transoceanic voyages, and improved mapmaking skills also played significant roles in making the Age of European Exploration possible.

Three primary reasons why these European explorers desired to sail westward in the sixteenth century can easily be remembered as the three *g*'s:

- Gold — desire to find a western trade route to the Far East and its treasures
- Glory — desire to conquer land for one's country and gain favor in the eyes of the monarchy
- God — desire to spread one's religion to other areas of the world

European explorations and discoveries during the sixteenth century led to a revolutionary redrawing of the map of the world. They also brought about a dramatic expansion of the world's economy by creating new trade routes and markets. Ready to take huge risks and to go where no European had gone before, these sixteenth-century explorers would ultimately be responsible for bringing about the downfall of old civilizations and paving the way for the rise of new ones in what they came to believe was a New World.

All American History

LESSON I

ATMOSPHERE

THE FIRST AMERICANS

Who were the first people to explore what we call America today? Not Europeans! Historians believe that the first explorers of America were people who migrated from central Asia. These "first Americans" probably crossed the Bering Sea from Siberia to Alaska, either using a raft or walking over a bridge of land that no longer exists. By the time of the Age of European Exploration, there were millions of descendants of these Asian immigrants scattered from Alaska to as far south as Chile.

No one knows exactly when the first Americans arrived. However, we do know that the migrations of these Native Americans continued until they had spread throughout present-day Canada, the United States, Mexico, Central America, and South America. Over time they became organized into hundreds of tribes and family groups. Each group developed its own way of life, depending on the location and type of land where they settled.

Through the centuries, a number of great Native American civilizations grew up in the Americas. These civilizations, such as the Aztec and Inca empires, built large cities, established their own religious

Native Americans fishing
Library of Congress, Prints and Photographs Division [LC-USZC4-4805]

5

beliefs, and developed skills in such disciplines as math, astronomy, and art. However, most Europeans arriving in America during the sixteenth century considered Native Americans to be an inferior, uncivilized race and lusted for their land and its resources with little compassion or guilt.

LEIF (THE LUCKY) ERIKSSON

The first *recorded* European explorer of America was the Viking adventurer Leif Eriksson (spelled various ways—Ericson, Ericsson, Erikson, or Erickson). Son of Erik the Red, Leif was probably born in Iceland, an island that had been colonized by a group of Norwegians sometime between 890 and 930 A.D. Around 982, Leif's father Erik was banished from Iceland for several years because of his violent behavior.

Sailing westward from Iceland, Erik discovered another island, which he named Greenland. This name did not fit the topography of the land, since four-fifths of the island was covered in ice. However, Erik the Red did find good farmland on its south and west coasts. When his period of exile was over, Erik returned to Iceland to recruit others to join with him and his family in colonizing Greenland.

Sometime in 985 – 986, Erik the Red succeeded in persuading a small group of Icelanders to sail with him to Greenland to plant a colony there. In Greenland, Eric established his family on a farm, where his children, including his son Leif, grew to adulthood. Described in Viking sagas as tall and handsome, Leif, like most Norsemen, had long flaxen hair and piercing blue eyes. A skilled seaman and a ruthless warrior, Leif Eriksson was also known as a faithful and generous friend.

As he grew to manhood, Leif heard many stories about King Olav of Norway and his glorious deeds. By 999, Leif had grown eager to meet this celebrated king and made plans to lead an expedition to Norway. While visiting in Olav's court, Leif and his men were introduced to the foundations of the Christian faith. According to some sources, Leif and his companions accepted the Gospel and agreed to be baptized.

Leif Eriksson
Library of Congress, Prints and Photographs Division [LC-USZ62-3028]

Erik the Red
Public Domain

When Leif returned to Greenland, he shared the Gospel with his mother. She became a believer; and after her conversion, she asked her husband Erik to build a church for worship. Although Erik agreed to have this church constructed, there is no record that he visited it when it was completed or accepted the Christian faith as his own.

EVENT

THE FATE OF THE FIRST AMERICANS

At first, many Native American tribes received European explorers and colonists with curiosity and friendliness. In fact, some tribes even helped to save a number of European settlements from starvation. Most Native Americans were fascinated with European materials and skills, which were unfamiliar to them. However, when Europeans seized Native American lands and enslaved them, they became violent. Terrible conflicts and many deaths resulted, and the Europeans usually prevailed. Furthermore, those Native Americans not killed in battle faced the very real possibility of dying from diseases for which they had no immunity. In fact, historians believe that the germs carried by Europeans to the New World had killed 50 to 80 percent of the Native American population within the first hundred years of contact.

As Europeans continued to come to America in the sixteenth century and to plant colonies there in the seventeenth century, they did everything that they could to establish their supremacy over Native Americans. In particular, they sought to increase the natives' dependence upon European manufactured goods, for which they eagerly traded. By taking advantage of this dependency, Europeans were able to secure vast tracts of land in exchange for materials worth very little. As the years passed, more and more Native Americans lost their lives or their freedom at the hands of European explorers and colonists.

ERIKSSON'S EXPLORATIONS

After returning from Norway, Leif began making plans to follow up on the story of a voyage made by Bjarni Herjolfsson in about 985–986. Herjolfsson had apparently sailed past his intended destination, Greenland, and discovered new lands, which were covered in trees and without glaciers. For several days, Herjolfsson had traveled north along this land; he then turned east and made his way to Greenland.

Sometime in 1000 or 1001, Leif decided to buy Herjolfsson's boat. He assembled a crew and set out to retrace Herjolfsson's route. When Leif asked his father to command this expedition, Erik agreed to do so. However, on his way to the ship, Erik fell from his horse and suffered an injury that prevented him from sailing with Leif and his men.

Eriksson's explorations

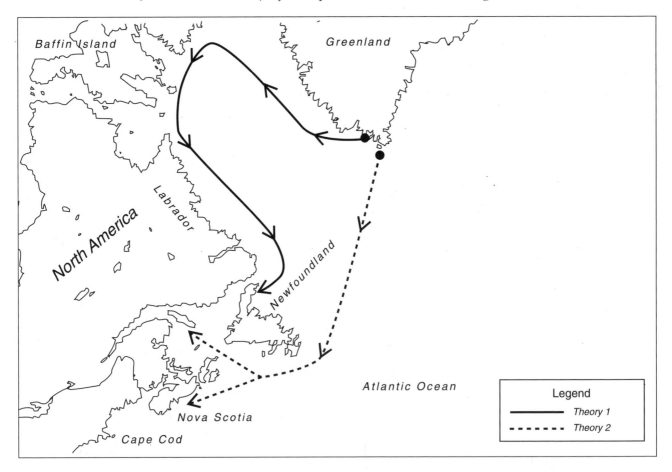

Because Leif and his men left behind no maps, scholars are not certain where they landed during their voyage of exploration. There are several historical theories concerning the location of their three landing sites:

- The first landing site, which they named *Helluland* (Country of Flat Stones), is likely to be present-day Baffin Island or possibly Newfoundland.

- The second landing site, which they named *Markland* (Land of Forests or Woods), is likely to be present-day Labrador or possibly Nova Scotia.

- The third landing site, which they named *Vinland* (Wineland), is likely to be present-day Newfoundland or possibly Cape Cod.

When they landed on Vinland, Leif and his men decided to remain for the winter. There they chopped down trees, built huts, hunted for game, and fished for salmon. They were amazed at the land's abundant resources. They also noticed that the winter days in Vinland were longer than the winter days in Greenland. As they prepared to leave, Leif and his men loaded their ship with lumber and grapes to carry home. On the return voyage to Greenland, Leif succeeded in rescuing fifteen sailors whom he found shipwrecked on a small reef. This daring rescue earned him the nickname Leif the Lucky.

Thorfinn's landing on the shore of Vinland
Library of Congress, Prints and Photographs Division [LC-USZ62-23517]

The year after Leif's return from Vinland, Erik the Red died. Leif's time then became consumed with caring for Erik's lands, and he never personally returned to Vinland. However, other Vikings sought to colonize the area with his assistance. For a period of about twelve years, Vikings apparently traveled back and forth from Greenland to Vinland. Leif's brother Thorvald, his sister Freydis, and his brother-in-law Thorfinn Karlsefni were all involved in exploring and seeking to colonize this new land. (Note: In 1962, the remains of a Viking settlement were found near the northern tip of Newfoundland. Carbon-14 testing

A Viking Ship
Library of Congress, Prints and Photographs Division [LC-USZC4-7646]

of the organic material there dates the settlement at approximately 1000 A.D.)

None of these Viking settlements lasted very long. In fact, there is no recorded evidence of Vikings in Vinland past 1014 A.D. The native people of Vinland, whom the Vikings called Skraelings (which means savage wretches), greatly outnumbered the Norsemen and frequently attacked them. Feeling homesick and frightened, the Vikings loaded their ships with timber and fur and sailed back to Greenland.

Stories about Erik the Red and Leif the Lucky were frequently recounted among the Vikings. Approximately 150 years after Leif's expedition, these stories were written down in the form of heroic poems called *The Saga of the Greenlanders* and *The Saga of Erik the Red*. However, few other Europeans seem to have ever known about the Viking discoveries in America. Consumed with wars, religious crusades, and disease, Europeans had time for little else. For nearly five hundred years after Leif Eriksson, no new European explorers seem to have come to America.

> After the sixteen winters had lapsed, from the time when Eric the Red went to colonize Greenland, Leif, Eric's son, sailed out from Greenland to Norway. He arrived in Drontheim in the autumn, when King Olaf Tryggvason was come down from the North, out of Halagoland. Leif put into Nidaros with his ship, and set out at once to visit the king. King Olaf expounded the faith to him, as he did to other heathen men who came to visit him. It proved easy for the king to persuade Leif, and he was accordingly baptized, together with all of his shipmates. Leif remained throughout the winter with the king, by whom he was well entertained.
>
> —from *The Saga of Erik the Red*

IMPACT

- Historians believe that the first explorers of America migrated from central Asia and eventually scattered from Alaska to Chile.

- A number of great Native American civilizations developed. However, most Europeans arriving in America during the sixteenth century considered these Native Americans to be primitive and inferior and sought to take over their land and other resources.

- Leif Eriksson is the first European known to have discovered land in North America and to have attempted to colonize there. (Five hundred years before Columbus!)

- The Viking colony of Vinland, established by Leif and his men (most likely on Newfoundland or the Cape Cod region), lasted for as long as twelve years. Stories about Leif's expedition were eventually written down by the Greenlanders, but few other Europeans seem to have known about these Viking discoveries in America.

LESSON 2

Marco Polo. . . . . 1254 — 1324 A.D.
Prince Henry the Navigator . . . . 1394 — 1460 A.D.

ATMOSPHERE

MARCO POLO

The Italian merchant and voyager Marco Polo was born into an ambitious upper-class family in Venice. His father Nicolo and his uncle Maffeo were both experienced merchants, who had traveled all over the eastern Mediterranean region. Around the time of Marco's birth, Maffeo and Nicolo set out for Constantinople, a major trade link between the Mediterranean and Black seas. The Polos remained in Constantinople for about six years, looking for trade opportunities.

Then, in 1260, Nicolo and Maffeo ventured farther east when invited by some Mongol officials to join their caravan. They traveled as far as the court of the great Kublai Khan in Cambulac, Cathay (present-day Peking, China). Finally, after being away for fifteen years, Maffeo and Nicolo Polo returned to Venice around 1268. They brought with them a letter from the great Khan to the pope, asking that he send one hundred men of religion, science, and the arts to Cathay.

During the period from 1095 to 1291, several major military expeditions were dispatched by Christians from western Europe to Palestine in an attempt to take the Holy Land back from the Muslim Turks. These expeditions came to be referred to as the Crusades. As a

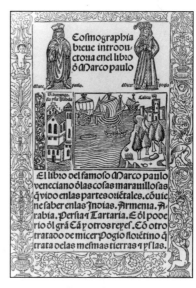

Marco Polo and Poggio
Library of Congress, Prints and Photographs Division [LC-USZ62-68313]

result of the Crusades, many Europeans were introduced to the riches available from eastern Asia. Crusaders returning from the Holy Land to their homes in Europe often brought back with them Asian products, such as rugs, silks, satins, jewelry, gold, silver, perfumes, porcelain, sugar, and spices.

Wealthy Europeans quickly developed an insatiable appetite for these Asian luxury items, and the great demand meant enormous profits for the two groups who monopolized this trade. One of these groups consisted of Asian middlemen, who were responsible for bringing the valuable goods by overland caravan to eastern Mediterranean ports, such as Constantinople. The other group of middlemen included Italian merchants in Venice and Genoa, who were responsible for shipping the Asian products from the eastern Mediterranean region to western Europe. Because both groups of middlemen tacked on additional charges, Asian goods remained high-priced luxuries (sometimes costing western Europeans as much as five hundred times the original price of the items).

PRINCE HENRY THE NAVIGATOR

The Portuguese royal prince and patron of explorers, known as Prince Henry the Navigator, was the third son of King John I and his English wife Philippa. By the time he reached adulthood, Henry had matured and developed into a brave soldier, brilliant scientist, and skilled administrator. In 1415, at the age of twenty-one, Henry joined his brothers in leading the Portuguese army in its conquest of Ceuta, a Muslim stronghold in nearby Morocco. There the prince learned about the riches of West Africa, which was known as the Gold Coast, and began studying its geography and trade. As a member of a strict Catholic religious order, Henry also was interested in spreading the Gospel.

By 1418, Prince Henry had established his own school of navigation, mapmaking, and shipbuilding. Located on St. Vincent Promontory at Sagres, the school had an unobstructed view of the Atlantic Ocean. Beneath the school was a protected bay, which served as Henry's shipyard. The prince recruited ship captains, navigators,

Prince Henry the Navigator
Library of Congress, Prints and Photographs Division [LC-USW3-001435-E]

astronomers, mathematicians, mapmakers, navigational instrument makers, and shipbuilders for his school. Because of the geographical location of Sagres (the southwestern tip of Europe), students at Prince Henry's school were able to experience sailing on both the Atlantic Ocean and Mediterranean Sea.

Under the guidance and leadership of Prince Henry, many sailors were taught navigational skills, navigational instruments were improved, and new seafaring equipment was invented. Much geographical information was collected and distributed, and the techniques of cartography were advanced. However, probably the most revolutionary work carried on at the prince's institute was the development of a new type of sea vessel — the Portuguese caravel.

European shipbuilders had traditionally built sea vessels that were known as square-riggers. These ships had square sails, which were suited for sailing when the wind blew in the direction that the ship was headed. In comparison, the new Portuguese caravels were lighter, more maneuverable ships that sailed more directly into the wind. They were built with a slimmer hull, which made greater speed possible, and a shallow keel, which allowed them to sail into small harbors and narrow inlets. Portuguese caravels were normally rigged with triangular sails but could also be re-rigged with square sails to improve handling in a storm or to gain speed before a following wind. These new sea vessels were safer than square-riggers and able to be run efficiently with fewer crewmen.

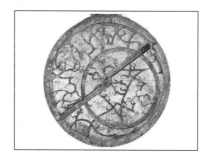

A sixteenth-century astrolabe
Public Domain

Portuguese caravel
Library of Congress, Prints and Photographs Division [LC-USZ6-2330]

EVENT

THE POLOS' EXPLORATIONS

When Marco was about seventeen years old (1271 – 1272), his father and uncle decided to return to Cathay. This time they took Marco with them. In response to the Khan's letter, the pope sent presents for the Chinese ruler but only two priests (not one hundred learned men as the Khan had requested). These priests did not remain with the Polo expedition for long. They turned back for Italy as soon as the first danger arose. Sailing south from Venice to Palestine, the Polos then traveled overland through Turkey, Armenia, Persia, and Afghanistan.

In a journey that took almost four years, they crossed the Pamir Mountains and the Gobi Desert before arriving at the court of the Kublai Khan. The route the Polos traveled was known as the Silk Road, a forty-three-hundred-mile-long trek across the continent of Asia. Because of the presence of bandits and unfriendly rulers, traders in Asian silks and spices did not personally travel the entire length of the Silk Road. Instead, they relied upon a network of trading partners, with no one merchant traveling more than a few hundred miles at one time.

The Polos' journey to China

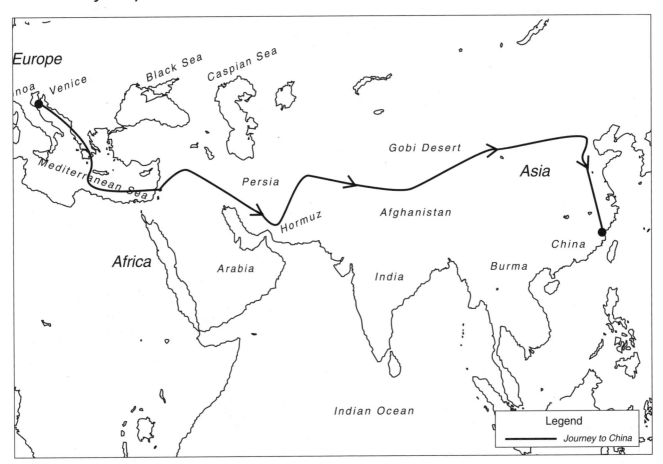

When the three Venetians finally arrived in Cathay, they were warmly received by the Khan. Marco soon became a favorite of the Mongol emperor, who seemed to enjoy the young man's company and to trust him with important responsibilities. Apparently an excellent linguist and negotiator, Marco traveled throughout the Mongol kingdom on special missions for the emperor for seventeen years. During these journeys, the young Italian saw many stunning palaces, costly jewels, and exotic animals, He also heard fabulous stories about Cipangu (present-day Japan), which was supposedly the richest land in the world.

Marco Polo at the Kublai Khan
Public Domain

As Nicolo and Maffeo grew older, they persisted in asking the Great Khan if they might return to their homeland. However, the Khan seemed to care deeply for them and to depend on their loyal service, and he did not want them to leave. In fact, he offered them great treasure and honors to stay in Cathay. Finally, about 1295, the Khan agreed to allow Marco, Nicolo, and Maffeo to return to Venice as part of a mission — accompanying a Mongolian princess pledged to marry the ruler of Persia.

By the time he left the court of the Khan, Marco Polo was about forty years old. He, his father, and his uncle returned to their homeland after twenty-four years with expensive silks, ivory, jade, marble, and porcelain, as well as jewels that they had sewed into their traveling clothes. Sailing from present-day China past Burma and India, the Polos landed at the port of Ormuz on the Persian Gulf. Then they traveled overland to Constantinople and the Black Sea and home to Venice by way of the Mediterranean and Adriatic.

When the Polos returned to Venice, they found the Italian city-state engaged in a long naval war with its rival, Genoa. Marco became involved in this conflict, serving as the captain of a Venetian warship. In 1296 he was captured by the Genoese and thrown into prison, where he remained until about 1299. During his years of captivity, Marco spent many hours sharing with the other prisoners fantastic stories about his travel adventures. One of these fellow prisoners was a man named Rustichello. An Italian romance writer of some distinction, Rustichello suggested to Marco that his stories should be written down. Marco agreed to dictate his travel stories to Rustichello, who called the resulting volume *A Description of the World.* Later retitled *The Travels of Marco Polo,* the highly entertaining book became quite popular.

Recopied by hand many times, *The Travels of Marco Polo* contained valuable information about the geography, animal and plant life, and politics of Asia, although some claimed that Polo's stories were just tall tales. In fact, much of what Polo recounted was true; but his interpretation of certain people, places, and events was influenced by his personal prejudices. Also, some of his information came from tales of other travelers in the court of the Khan and not his eyewitness account. Nevertheless, his book contained much

The Polos' journey from China back to Venice

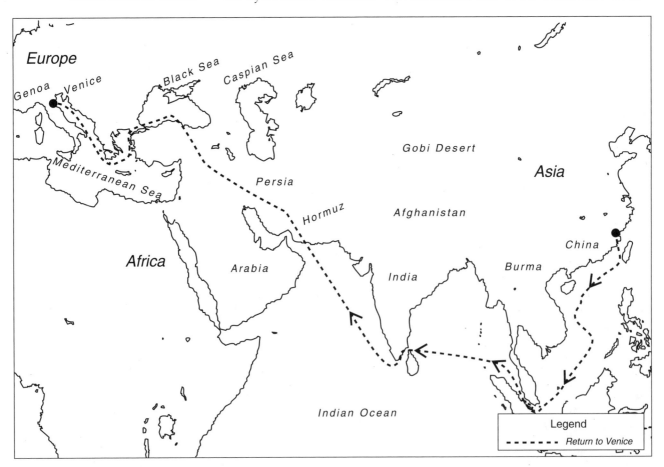

true information about the advanced civilization he found in eastern Asia.

> Imperadori getlteman, king and duci and all other people that you want to know the various generations of people and the diversities of the regions of the world, you read this book where troverrete all the greatest large maraviglie and diversitadi of people of Erminia, Persia and Tarteria, India and many others province. And this will tidily count you the book siccome to messere Marco Polo, savio and city nobleman of Vinegia, counts to them in this book and same it saw. But still v' à of those things which elli did not see, but udille from worthy persons of faith, and but the seen things he will say of view and the others for heard, acciò that ' l our book is veritieri and sanza niuna menzogna.
>
> —from *The Travels of Marco Polo*

Marco Polo was married at age forty-five. He and his wife had three daughters, and he resumed his career as a Venetian merchant. During the remaining years of his life, he talked constantly of Asia and the incredible profits to be earned by trading there. Because of this, he became known in Venice as Marco Millions. When urged on his deathbed to confess to the lies and exaggerations in his book, Polo swore that he had told the truth.

After the invention of the printing press, Polo's book was distributed to many other countries and was translated into several different European languages. His careful observations and elaborate details captured the imagination of people throughout Europe and inspired a number of European explorers in the centuries that followed the publication of his book. Christopher Columbus studied *The Travels of Marco Polo* from cover to cover and made certain that the book accompanied him on his first voyage across the Atlantic in 1492.

After the Polos' travels, many merchants began using the land route to China. However, by the early 1400s the Muslims had started to gain power in the eastern Mediterranean region. By 1453 they had taken over Constantinople, the main trade city on the land route between Europe and Asia. This, in effect, closed the land route to Asia for European merchants and explorers. Therefore, by the late 1400s, Europeans were actively looking for another trade route to the Far East.

EXPLORATIONS SENT FROM PRINCE HENRY'S SCHOOL

Historians have referred to Prince Henry as the explorer who stayed home. Although Henry never personally participated in any of his school's expeditions, for forty years he financed and sent out Portuguese sea captains in caravels to explore the western coast of Africa. His goals in sponsoring these expeditions were to expand Portuguese trade, discover a new sea route around Africa to Asia,

Explorations of Prince Henry's students

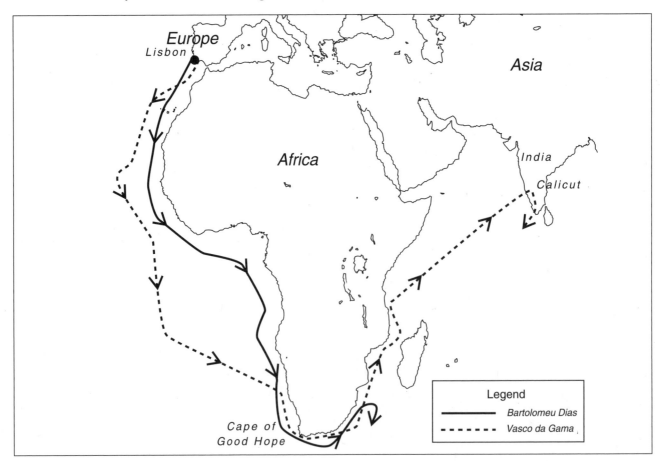

Legend
———— Bartolomeu Dias
- - - - - Vasco da Gama

create much-needed maps of the coast of western Africa, find Christian allies in the struggle to defeat the Muslims, and search for gold and other treasures.

Year after year, beginning in 1420, sailors from Henry's school ventured farther and farther south down the Atlantic coast of Africa. Some of their discoveries included the Azores, the Madeiras, and the Cape Verde Islands. Prince Henry's navigators claimed all the land they encountered for Portugal and often returned home with sugar, ivory, gold, and eventually slaves. However, Henry had great difficulty persuading his captains to sail south of Cape Bojador, a slight bulge on the African coast south of the Canary Islands. According to superstition, beyond this point was an area known as the Great Sea of Darkness. In this region the sun was supposedly so close to the earth that it burned people's skin black. It was said that the seawater boiled there, ships caught on fire, and monsters devoured sailors.

Over the years, Prince Henry sent out at least fifteen expeditions that failed to sail south of Cape Bojador. Finally, in 1434, a Portuguese sea captain named Gil Eannes succeeded in his second attempt to round Cape Bojador. He accomplished this by sailing his ship out to sea before reaching the cape and not turning eastward until he had passed it, thus avoiding the treacherous currents and fierce northeast winds beside the shore. Once the legend was found to be false, the barrier of fear was broken and Portuguese expeditions began pressing further and further south of Cape Bojador.

By the time Prince Henry died, the Portuguese had reached Cape Palmas (present-day Liberia). His student Bartolomeu Dias rounded the Cape of Good Hope in 1487 and found himself on the eastern coast of Africa. Although his men were frightened and insisted that they turn back, Dias had proven that there was a sea route around Africa. Then, from 1497 to 1499, another Portuguese sea captain named Vasco da Gama successfully sailed around Africa all the way to India and returned to Portugal with spices and other luxury items.

Vasco da Gama
Library of Congress, Prints and Photographs Division [LC-USZ62-105882]

Throughout his lifetime, Prince Henry shunned the limelight. When he died, he left no books or monuments. However, the advances of his school in ship design and navigational techniques

---

made possible the successful voyages of Columbus and others that followed. The expeditions that Henry financed and sent out led to the establishment of a Portuguese sea route to Asia, as well as a Portuguese overseas empire. Truly, the activities of Prince Henry the Navigator marked the beginning of the great Age of European Exploration.

IMPACT

- Marco Polo was one of the first Europeans to travel across Asia into present-day China.

- Marco Polo was the author of an influential book, *The Travels of Marco Polo,* that inspired other European explorers in their search for another trade route to the Far East.

- Prince Henry the Navigator was the founder of a ground-breaking school of navigation, mapmaking, and shipbuilding, where a new type of sea vessel (the caravel) was created. These vessels were used by explorers during the Age of European Exploration.

- Prince Henry sponsored and sent expeditions that claimed western Africa for Portugal and led to the establishment of a Portuguese sea route to Asia.

LESSON 3

Christopher Columbus. . . . . 1451 — 1506 A.D.
Amerigo Vespucci . . . . 1454? *or* 1451? — 1512 A.D.

ATMOSPHERE

CHRISTOPHER COLUMBUS

The Italian navigator and explorer Cristoforo Colombo was born in Genoa, a prosperous Mediterranean seaport. The oldest of five children, Christopher was expected to learn the family trade — wool weaving. However, his true ambition was to become a sailor. By the time he was fifteen, he was already working as a cabin boy on ships trading in the Mediterranean Sea.

In 1476, a Genoese ship on which Columbus was sailing was attacked by pirates and sunk off the coast of Portugal. Although Columbus was wounded in the attack, he managed to swim six miles to safety, using an oar to stay afloat. All of the other men perished in the attack. When Columbus came safely ashore in Portugal, he was convinced that God had saved him so that he might accomplish great things for Him.

Columbus then moved to Lisbon, the busiest seaport in Portugal and the home of his brother Bartolomeo. The two brothers worked together as chartmakers. During his years in Lisbon, Christopher learned to read and write in Portuguese and Spanish, examined many geography and history books, studied math and astronomy, and read

Christopher Columbus
Library of Congress, Prints and Photographs Division [LC-USZ62-103980]

the Bible and *The Travels of Marco Polo*. He also worked as a sailor for Portuguese sea captains. It was during this period of his life that Columbus married a noblewoman named Felipa, whose father was a Portuguese explorer involved in the discovery of the Madeiras. Felipa's mother passed on to Christopher her husband's sailing charts, logs, and maps.

Through his reading and studying, Columbus decided that the best route for reaching Asia and the Spice Islands (the Moluccas) was to sail west, not east as the Portuguese were doing. He calculated that Cipangu (Japan) was located approximately 2,400 nautical miles due west of the Canary Islands and that Cathay (China) was another 1,500 miles west. These distances are more than four times what Columbus thought they were. A distance of 2,400 nautical miles is actually an accurate estimate of the distance between the Canaries and the West Indies. Columbus also did not realize that he would have to travel across two oceans, instead of one, to reach Asia.

Ferdinand and Isabella
Library of Congress, Prints and Photographs Division [LC-USZ62-105452]

In 1484, Columbus approached King John II of Portugal to ask for money to finance a westward expedition. The Portuguese king refused Columbus's request, deciding instead to continue sending ships down the western coast of Africa. The same year, Christopher moved to Spain, now a widower with a five-year-old son named Diego. Determined to find support for his expedition, Columbus (known in Spain as Cristobal Colon) set out to persuade the Spanish rulers, King Ferdinand and Queen Isabella, to provide the money for it. At the time, the Spanish were fighting the Moors, who held Granada, and they were not in a position to think about financing anything else.

Columbus waited three years in Spain; then he traveled back to Portugal to see if King John had changed his mind. However, that year (1487) the Portuguese explorer Bartolomeu Dias had successfully rounded the Cape of Good Hope, so the Portuguese king again refused Columbus. When King Henry VII of England also turned down the opportunity to finance Columbus's expedition, Christopher returned to Spain and waited for several more years.

During this period in his life, Columbus entered into a relationship with a woman named Beatriz, with whom he had a second son named Fernando.

Finally, at Christmas in 1491, Isabella summoned Christopher to the royal court to discuss the possibility of an expedition. During his meeting with the Spanish monarchs, Columbus insisted that they grant him three promises: one tenth of all the riches that he brought back, governorship of all the lands that he visited, and the title Admiral of the Ocean Sea. The governorships and the title would be passed on to his heirs. Ferdinand adamantly refused the requests, and Columbus left. However, Isabella soon sent a messenger after Columbus with the news that she and Ferdinand had agreed to sponsor his westward expedition. They decided that Columbus's journey would pose a small risk with the possibility of great returns, so Ferdinand and Isabella signed a contract with the Italian navigator on April 17, 1492. In addition to the Spanish monarchy's desire for monetary gain, Queen Isabella was a devout Catholic interested in spreading the Gospel to other lands.

AMERIGO VESPUCCI

The Italian merchant and navigator Amerigo Vespucci was born in Florence, very close to the time that Columbus was born in Genoa. During his youth, Vespucci was educated by his uncle, a Dominican priest and Platonic philosopher. Amerigo Vespucci was trained in Latin, physics, astronomy, mathematics, literature, cosmography, and navigation.

Vespucci spent the early days of his career working for the firm of Lorenzo de Medici. Over time he became a trusted confidante to the rulers of Portugal and Spain. By the early 1490s, Vespucci had moved to Seville and become connected with a company that equipped ships for long voyages. Vespucci supposedly met Christopher Columbus and may have helped that explorer prepare for his third expedition in 1495. Like Columbus, Vespucci believed in the possibility of reaching Asia by sailing west.

Amerigo Vespucci
Library of Congress, Prints and Photographs Division [LC-USZ62-102761]

EVENT

COLUMBUS'S EXPLORATIONS

First Expedition (1492 – 1493)

On August 3, 1492, Columbus set sail from Palos, Spain, with about 120 men on three small wooden ships. The *Nina* and the *Pinta* were caravels, captained by two brothers, Martin and Vicente Pinzon. The *Santa Maria* was a larger, square-rigged vessel called a *nao*, captained by Columbus. Before sailing, Columbus took his men to church to pray for their safety. He wrote that he sailed "in the name of our Lord, Jesus Christ, to the regions of India, to see the Princes there and the peoples and the lands and to learn of their disposition, and of everything, and the measures that could be taken for their conversion to our Holy Faith."[1]

After three days at sea, the *Pinta*'s helm broke, and the three ships stopped at the Canary Islands to have it repaired. They resumed their voyage a month later on September 6, heading west with strong east trade winds that pushed them straight across the Atlantic. Columbus navigated by dead reckoning, using a compass and a crude astrolabe to guide him. After traveling thirty-three days without sight of land, most of the crew became frightened and demanded that they turn back for home. Columbus refused to go back and on October 10, he asked that they sail on for three more days.

On October 11, the expedition spotted the faint light of a fire ahead. On the following day, the lookout on the *Pinta* shouted, "Tierra, tierra!" (land, land). Since Columbus knew that they had sailed at least 2,400 nautical miles (the distance that he thought lay between Europe and Japan), he decided that they had reached an island in the East Indies. Columbus named the island on which they landed San Salvador (Holy Savior). Most historians believe he landed on present-day Watling Island in the Bahamas. When Columbus, the Pinzons, and a large group of men went ashore, Columbus fell to his knees and thanked God. Then they planted the cross of the Spanish king and queen and the Spanish flag.

The *Santa Maria*
Library of Congress, Prints and Photographs Division [LC-D4-22452]

Columbus and his men discovered dark-skinned people living on San Salvador. He named them Indians because he thought that they had reached the Indies. However, these natives called their island Guanahani and themselves Tainos. Columbus and his crew gave the Tainos cloth, red caps, and glass beads, which they had brought with them from Spain. In return, the Indians gave Columbus and his men animal skins, shells, green parrots, corn, pumpkins, pineapple, sweet potatoes, tobacco, arrows, and balls of cotton. When Columbus asked the Tainos where they had gotten the little gold ornaments that they wore, they told him about a larger island where there was gold. Although Columbus believed that they were talking about the island of Cipangu (Japan), they actually were probably referring to present-day Cuba.

From San Salvador, Columbus and his crew sailed east. By October 28 they had reached Cuba. The natives there told Columbus that there was gold inland and pearls in the sea. On December 6, Columbus's expedition landed on a third island, which he named La Isla Española, later known as Hispaniola (present-day Haiti and the Dominican Republic). There he found natives with gold, which he exchanged for some small gifts. On Christmas Eve the *Santa Maria* ran aground north of Hispaniola. Columbus had his men dismantle the ship and use the wood to build a fort. He left thirty-nine of his crew members there with supplies and weapons to establish the first Spanish colony in the New World — La Navidad (Christmas). These men were never seen by Europeans again.

On March 15, 1493, Columbus, his remaining two ships, his crew, and several Indians whom he had brought back with him landed in Palos, Spain. They were met by great crowds at the dock. Columbus became a hero—recognized for his courage and for his skills as a navigator. King Ferdinand and Queen Isabella were eager to finance a second westward expedition and gave Columbus secret orders to map as much of the land he explored as possible. Their desire was to establish Spanish claims to all of it. The Spanish monarchs also authorized Columbus to create a permanent Spanish trading colony and to seek

Landing of Columbus
Library of Congress, Prints and Photographs Division [LC-USZ62-105062]

to convert the natives to Christianity. In the next decade, Columbus made three more westward expeditions.

Second Expedition (1493 – 1496)

During this second voyage, Columbus discovered that the colony at Navidad had not survived. He founded a new colony on Hispaniola named Isabella; but it would also fail due to mosquitoes, disease, and problems with the natives. Columbus and his men explored present-day Puerto Rico, Jamaica, Martinique, and Guadeloupe during this expedition. However, they failed to find any gold, silver, or gems. When he returned, Columbus received a cool reception at court and the title Admiral of the Mosquitoes.

Third Expedition (1498 – 1500)

Although royal interest in his expeditions had weakened, Columbus was given several ships to venture westward again. On this third expedition, he and his crew took a more southerly route, thinking they would come upon lands where more gold would be found. They explored Trinidad and reached the South American mainland, sailing along the coast of Venezuela. During this trip Columbus was arrested in Hispaniola by an inspector sent there by the Spanish king and queen. He returned to Spain in chains but soon gained his release by order of Ferdinand and Isabella.

Fourth Expedition (1502 – 1504) and Final Years

During his final westward expedition, Columbus explored the coast of Central America from Honduras to Panama. He continued to hope that he would discover a passage or a strait leading to the Indian Ocean. During this voyage Columbus finally discovered some gold mines. However, by this time his health was poor and his reputation was irreparably damaged.

Two years after his final expedition, Columbus died with little attention from the Spanish people. Isabella was already dead, and Ferdinand was no longer open to seeing Columbus. The Spanish king was disappointed that Columbus had brought back little treasure and had not succeeded in opening a trade route to the Far East. Columbus himself insisted that he had made it to China and would have reached Japan if he had had more time.

Columbus's logbooks from his first and third voyages have survived through the years, as well as a number of his letters and accounts of his second voyage written by three crew members. Although Columbus himself never acknowledged having found a New World, by the early 1500s it had become apparent to a growing number of people that his voyages had revealed the existence of a new land.

Columbus's explorations

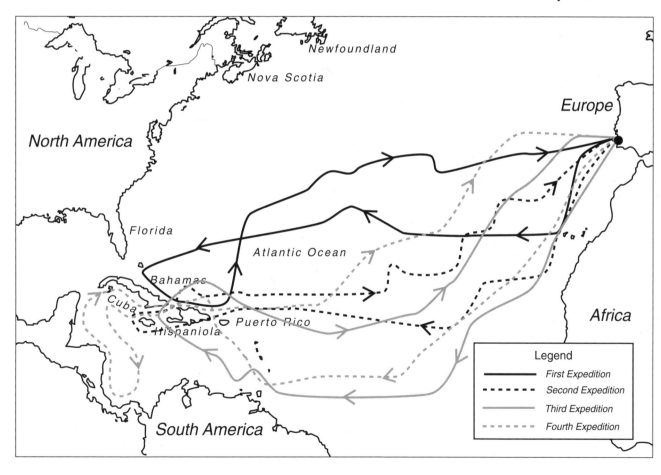

VESPUCCI'S EXPLORATIONS

Amerigo Vespucci claimed to have made four voyages of exploration to the New World. However, there has been enormous confusion among historians concerning Vespucci's claims.

First Expedition (1497 – 1498)

According to Vespucci, he was part of an expedition that explored the South American mainland from 1497 until 1498. Soon after his death, scholars began to question this claim. Historians have found no substantial evidence that he was involved with an expedition during this time period.

Second Expedition (1499 – 1500)

Although Vespucci claimed to have led this expedition, historians believe it was led by the Spanish navigator Alonzo Ojeda and that Vespucci traveled with Ojeda as a merchant and astronomer. Alonzo Ojeda had sailed with Columbus on his second voyage. This expedition set out from Cadiz, Spain, and followed Columbus's sea routes. It apparently reached present-day Venezuela (which means Little Venice) and traveled along its coast before returning to Spain.

Third Expedition (1501 – 1502)
and Fourth Expedition (1503 – 1504)

Again, Vespucci claimed to have led these expeditions, but historians believe they were led by Portuguese sea captains. The groups sailed from Lisbon to explore Brazil and much of the east coast of South America. After these voyages, Vespucci was convinced that they had found a New World.

Final Years

In 1502 or 1503 Vespucci wrote letters to Lorenzo de Medici, describing his voyages to what he believed to be a new continent. This account was published in 1503 or 1504 under the title of *Mundus Novus* (New World) and was widely read all over Europe. This publication helped establish Vespucci as a famous explorer and as the first

Lorenzo de Medici
Library of Congress, Prints and Photographs Division [LC-USZ62-112535]

person known to write about the belief that a new continent had been discovered.

In 1507, Martin Waldseemüller, a German mapmaker, included Vespucci's letters in his book *Introduction to Cosmography*. Waldseemüller's world map showed a narrow continent between Europe and Asia that blocked the way to Asia. Just beyond that continent's borders, in an unknown sea, was an oblong island that he marked Cipangu. Waldseemüller decided to name the narrow continent America (the Latin form of Amerigo) after Amerigo Vespucci. Columbus died the year before Waldseemüller's map came out. In a later version of his map, Waldseemüller decided to remove the name America. However, the name had already caught on and soon became applied to all land in the Western Hemisphere.

By 1505, Vespucci had become a Spanish citizen. He lived in Seville and worked as a chief navigator for the Spanish government agency regulating commerce. His title was pilot major of Spain, which was a

Waldseemüller's world map
Library of Congress, Prints and Photographs Division [G2300 1507.W3 Vault]

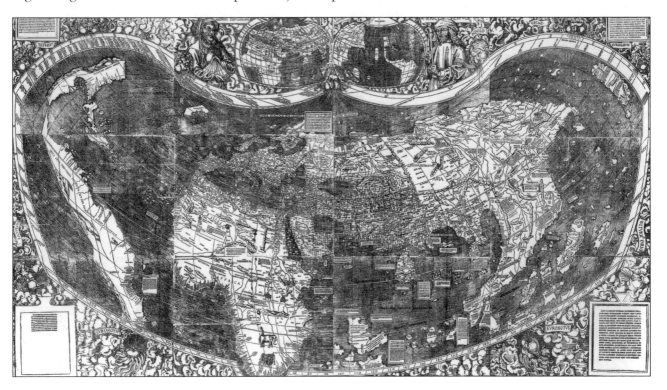

reward from the king. He held this job from 1508 until his death from malaria in 1512.

IMPACT

- Christopher Columbus was the first European to discover the Bahamas, Cuba, Hispaniola, Central America, and the northern coast of South America.

- Columbus also discovered a trade route across the Atlantic using winds that blow from east to west. (These winds are called trade winds, and they are still used by sea captains today.)

- Columbus began a chain of events that would lead to the settlement of the New World. Columbus showed others that a long sea voyage was possible and gave Spain an unexpected advantage in the coming race for riches and colonies.

- Amerigo Vespucci was one of the first believers in the discovery of a new continent — a New World.

- The name that the new continent became known as — the Americas — is the Latin form of Vespucci's given name, Amerigo.

LESSON 4

ATMOSPHERE

JOHN CABOT

The Italian navigator Giovanni Caboto was born in the same country (Italy) and probably in the same year (1451) as Christopher Columbus (Cristoforo Colombo). Very few details of his early life are known. He may have been born in Genoa or Naples, but by 1461 Cabot was living in Venice. After living in Venice for fifteen years (the prescribed period of residence to obtain citizenship), he was naturalized on March 28, 1476.

While living in Venice, John Cabot spent much time at sea, sailing to lands in the eastern Mediterranean region. By the early 1480s, he had become known among Venetian merchants as an experienced mapmaker, navigator, and seaman. Like Columbus, Cabot believed that a better route to the riches of the Far East lay to the west, not to the east. He was eager to join Columbus in searching for that route, believing that an even shorter way could be found farther north.

During this period of his life, Cabot married a Venetian woman named Mattea. Together they would have three sons — Sebastiano, Ludovico, and Sancto. In the early 1490s, Cabot moved his family to

Pope Alexander VI
*Library of Congress, Prints and Photographs
Division [LC-USZ62-101870]*

Bristol, England. There he worked for Venetian merchants, buying wool and cloth from the English and selling Venetian glass, silks, and spices.

The year after Columbus returned from his first expedition (1493), Pope Alexander VI attempted to settle a fierce territorial dispute between King Ferdinand of Spain and King John II of Portugal. At that time, the pope issued a bull, which decreed the establishment of a Line of Demarcation. This line was drawn 100 leagues (1175 miles) west of the Cape Verde Islands (off the coast of Africa in the Atlantic) and extended from the North Pole to the South Pole. Land discovered east of the Line of Demarcation belonged to Portugal, and land discovered west of it belonged to Spain.

Portuguese atlas showing Line of Demarcation
Library of Congress, Maps Collection
[g3200m gct00052]

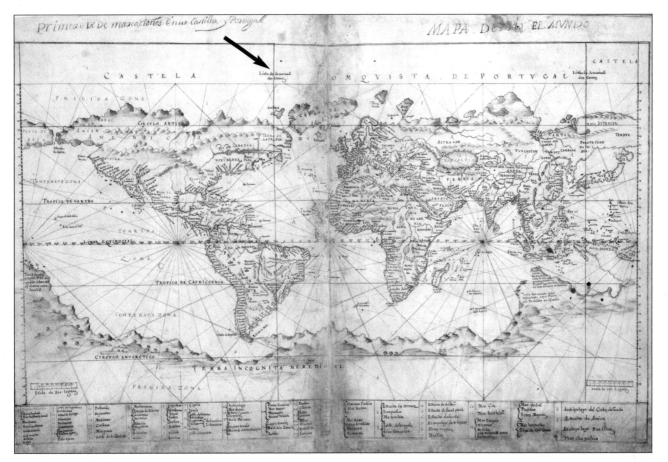

When Portugal objected to the location of the Line of Demarcation, negotiations resumed. The resulting Treaty of Tordesillas moved the Line of Demarcation further west by 270 leagues. This change meant that Portugal would be able to claim Brazil. Although England had not been included in these negotiations, the English king and English merchants had become very interested in joining Spain and Portugal in their search for a western route to Asia.

Thus, when John Cabot knew that neither the Spanish nor the Portuguese were willing to sponsor his northwestern expedition, he turned to the English. He was pleased to find a group of Bristol merchants willing to provide him with several ships for a voyage of exploration. In addition to this assistance, Cabot and his sons were also granted letters patent by the English King Henry VII, which gave them the right to seek out any land previously unknown to all Christians and to claim all discoveries for England.

VASCO NUÑEZ DE BALBOA

Spanish adventurer and conquistador Vasco Nuñez de Balboa was born in Jerez de los Caballeros to a poor noble family. At some point before early adulthood, Vasco moved to the port of Moguer, located on the Atlantic coast of southwest Spain. This city became important after 1492 as a place for ships to take on supplies and sailors before heading west across the Atlantic. As Balboa listened to some of these sailors tell stories about their voyages, he grew eager to join them in their expeditions.

OTHER SPANISH CONQUISTADORS

The main thrust of early Spanish exploration in the New World was in Central and South America, not North America. During a thirty-year period (1520 – 1550), the Spanish would conquer more territory than the Romans had conquered in five hundred years and carve out a Spanish empire that lasted for three hundred years.

This wave of conquest was led by men referred to as conquistadors. Dreaming of gold and jewels, these Spanish adventurers generally came

Montezuma
Library of Congress, Prints and Photographs Division [LC-USZ62-43530]

Battle with the Peruvians
Library of Congress, Prints and Photographs Division [LC-USZ62-104357]

from noble Spanish families. Many of them were younger sons who knew that they would not inherit their family fortunes. Most of them were arrogant and ruthless. They believed they were superiors, bringing civilization to the natives, with the right to steal, enslave, and kill.

Although some had the blessing of the Spanish king, others did not. The conquistadors often fought among themselves for the riches that they discovered and for royal recognition. The two great civilizations conquered and plundered by Spanish conquistadors were the Aztec civilization of Mexico and the Inca civilization of Peru.

EVENT

CABOT'S EXPLORATIONS

In 1496, Cabot sailed west from Bristol with one ship. He only traveled as far as Iceland before he was forced to turn back to England, due to poor winds, a shortage of supplies, and problems with his crew. The following year, in early May of 1497, Cabot again sailed from Bristol with one ship, the *Matthew* (possibly named for his wife, Mattea). His son Sebastian was one of the eighteen to twenty crew members on board.

The *Matthew* headed north up the coast of Ireland and then turned west. Cabot's plan was to reach Cathay (China) by using a more northern route than the one used by Columbus. They sailed across the Atlantic in thirty-three days, first sighting land on June 24, 1497. Since no original maps or logbooks from this voyage have survived, the exact location of their landfall is unknown. Scholars have guessed Newfoundland, Labrador, or Nova Scotia.

John Cabot
Library of Congress, Prints and Photographs Division [LC-USZ62-3029]

After anchoring the *Matthew*, Cabot and a few members of his crew traveled ashore in a small boat. They raised a crucifix and planted the banners of King Henry VII, the pope, and St. Mark (the patron saint of Venice). Cabot was convinced that he and his men had found an island off the coast of northeast Asia. This area soon became known as the "new founde land."

For about a month, Cabot and his crew sailed along the Canadian coastline, exploring and naming many capes and islands. They apparently encountered no other people during this time. However, they did discover abundant codfish and swarms of mosquitoes. When they explored inland, they found trees that had been cut, land cleared for farming, traps for small animals, and remains of campfires. Apparently, this "new founde land" had been inhabited not too long ago.

In July of 1497, the *Matthew* crossed back to England in fifteen days. Cabot boasted that he had found a new route to Asia. Although he returned with no spices or treasures, he was welcomed home as a hero by his sponsors. He also impressed King Henry VII with his report of a good land with a mild climate and excellent fishing areas.

As a reward for his successful expedition, Cabot was granted ten pounds by the English king, as well as the title the Great Admiral.

Cabot's explorations

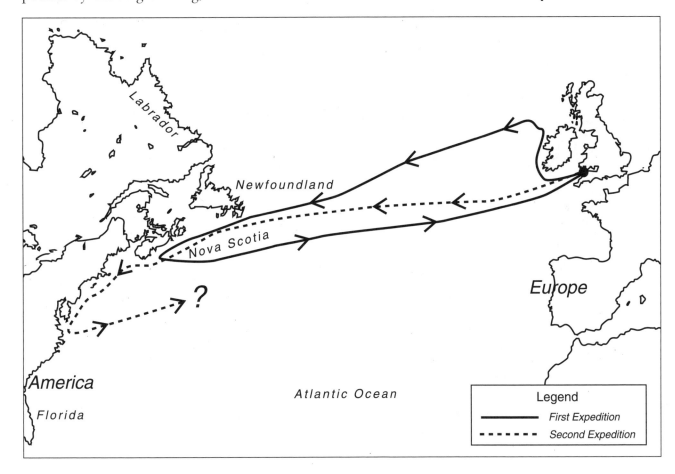

Later, the king also gave him a pension of twenty pounds a year and a second royal charter. This charter provided Cabot with the promise of one ship to use for his next voyage of exploration, permission to start a colony in Cipangu (Japan), and authorization to establish a trading center for the shipping of spices to England.

The following year in May, John Cabot left Bristol, England, with five ships (one financed by the king and the other four by English merchants) and a crew of two hundred. His vessels were well stocked with food and gifts to trade. Unfortunately, no one knows for certain exactly what happened to Cabot and most of the men with him on this voyage. One of the expedition's ships returned to Ireland for repairs, and the four other ships may have sailed as far south as Delaware Bay. However, there is no conclusive evidence that these ships ever returned to England. There are also no surviving journals or ship logs written by Cabot or any of his crew members on this voyage.

One of John Cabot's contemporaries wrote some years later that "he (Cabot) is believed to have found the new lands nowhere but on the very bottom of the ocean."[2] After John's disappearance, his son Sebastian, who was also an accomplished navigator and mapmaker, continued to lead voyages in search of a western route to Asia.

BALBOA'S EXPLORATIONS

In 1500 or 1501, Balboa sailed from Spain as part of an expedition led by Rodrigo de Bastidas. Bastidas had supposedly been inspired by Columbus to believe that pearls and gold could be found along the northern coast of South America and in the Gulf of Uraba. His expedition made it to their destination, but Bastidas did not have enough men, food, and supplies to start a colony there. However, some sources believe that Bastidas and Balboa were able to trade European goods for a large quantity of pearls and gold from natives in the area.

When Bastidas's expedition set sail again, their ship apparently started to leak. Arriving at the Spanish colony of Hispaniola, he and his men were forced to abandon their ship. Balboa was left with nothing and spent the next several years attempting to make a living on

Vasco Nuñez de Balboa
Library of Congress, Prints and Photographs Division [LC-USZ62-31872]

the island by farming. He was not successful and became deeply in debt. In 1510, Balboa decided to try to escape his creditors, stowing away with his dog Leoncico on a ship headed to the newly established Spanish colony at San Sebastian (located at the lower end of the isthmus of Panama on the Gulf of Uraba).

Commanded by Martin de Encisco, the ship on which Balboa was a stowaway had been sent from Santo Domingo to help the struggling San Sebastian colony. When Balboa was discovered on board, he was allowed to stay. The relief expedition found the settlement burned to the ground and the original group of eight hundred Spanish colonists reduced to only sixty by sickness, starvation, and Indian massacres.

Balboa's explorations

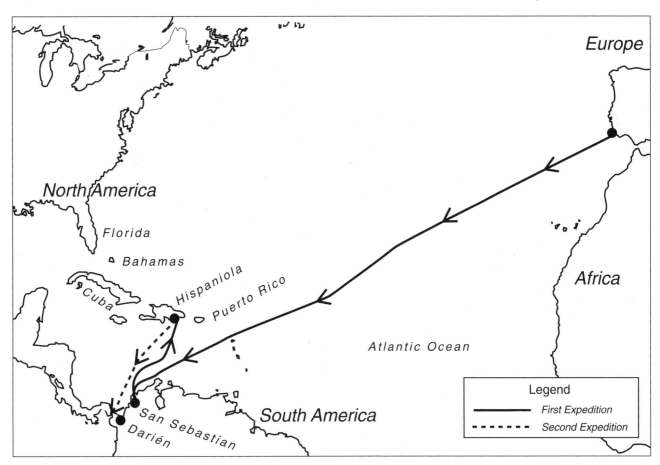

Because of his previous experience exploring the area, Balboa was able to suggest a new site west of the Gulf of Uraba for relocation of the San Sebastian colony. This area, located on the bank of a river that the natives called Darien, had more plentiful food resources and more peaceful natives. By 1511, the Spanish colony of Santa Maria de la Antigua del Darien, which became simply known as Darien, was beginning to flourish.

Eventually, Balboa made a bid for leadership of this group. He encouraged the colonists at Darien to reject Martin de Encisco's authority and to accept his governorship of the colony. For the next two years, Balboa thrived in this position. He amassed a fortune in gold and jewels, made friends with many of the surrounding Indians, and married the daughter of the local Indian chief.

Balboa's Indian allies in Darien told him stories about a great sea a few days' travel to the south and west. These natives reported that more gold and other wealth could be found in the land beyond this sea (present-day Peru). Balboa decided that he wanted to lead an expedition from Darien in search of this land — not only to find the reported treasures but also to impress the Spanish king and thus strengthen his claim as governor.

On September 1, 1513, Balboa set out from Darien with between one hundred and two hundred Spanish colonists and a number of Indian guides (as many as a thousand, according to some sources). Another Spanish explorer, Francisco Pizarro, was part of Balboa's group. The expedition sailed to San Blas on the east coast of Panama and from there journeyed overland for twenty-five days through swamps, dense jungles, and mountains. They fought mosquitoes, snakes, and several native tribes along the way before reaching the west coast of Panama.

Finally, in late September, alone at the top of a tall cliff, Balboa sighted a large sea, just as his Indian guides had promised. What we now call the Pacific Ocean, he called the Mar del Sur (South Sea). When others from his group joined Balboa, they sang together the *Te Deum* (a Catholic hymn of thanksgiving), erected a cross, and claimed the land for Spain. Then they descended the mountain and pushed on to the edge of the ocean, which they also claimed with all adjacent lands for Spain. After spending a month amassing gold, Balboa and his men returned to Darien. Because they had loaded treasure in place of provisions, some of his group almost starved to death on the way back.

In June of 1514, an elderly nobleman named Pedro Arias de Avila (known as Pedrarias the Cruel) arrived in Darien from Spain with twenty ships and fifteen hundred men. Pedrarias had been sent by the Spanish king to take Balboa's place as governor of Darien. However, when the Spanish monarch received news of Balboa's expedition to the Mar del Sur, he commissioned the adventurer to serve under Pedrarias as governor of a new area on the north coast of Panama. Balboa agreed to take on this challenge and worked to establish the colony of Acla in northern Panama. He also began to consider forming an expedition to conquer the land that is present-day Peru.

By 1517, Pedrarias had become increasingly jealous of the still popular Balboa. After working up false charges of treason against the explorer, he had Balboa arrested and executed in early 1519. Balboa proclaimed his innocence and loyalty to the end, but he and four of his friends were beheaded.

OTHER CONQUISTADORIAN EXPLORATIONS

Hernando Cortés and the Aztecs of Mexico

In 1519, Hernando Cortés set out to conquer the Aztecs. He had heard of the Aztec's wealth from other Spanish explorers. When Cortés and his force of five hundred soldiers arrived on the Mexican coast, he gave orders that all ships but one be sunk. That ship was sent back to Spain to give a report to the king. Leaving the coast, Cortés and his men marched inland until they reached the Aztecs.

Greeted by the Aztec king Montezuma, Cortés was given gifts of gold and silver. Montezuma believed that Cortés was a legendary Aztec god, who had disappeared across the Atlantic and had returned. The Aztecs were terrified of the Spanish horses and guns, which they had never seen. Over a period of several years, Cortés and his men killed thousands of these Aztecs, including Montezuma.

Hernando Cortés
Library of Congress, Prints and Photographs Division [LC-USZ62-33515]

By August of 1521, Mexico had officially become a Spanish colony. Cortés sent many ships back to Spain loaded with gold and silver, making it the wealthiest country in the world. After seven years of governing Mexico, Cortés had become so powerful that the Spanish government grew concerned and ordered him back to Spain, where he died in poverty in 1547.

Francisco Pizarro and the Incas of Peru

The daring adventurer Francisco Pizarro had traveled to America with Diego Columbus and served in expeditions with Balboa and Cortés. Pizarro used Panama as a base in several attempts to find a southern kingdom with a ruler reportedly so wealthy that he used gold for

Cortés's inland trek to the Aztecs

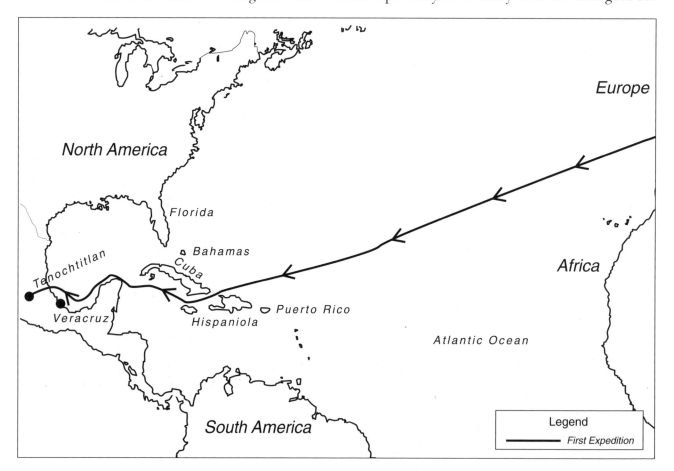

stones. Pizarro continued to push south and eventually discovered the city of Tumbes (located in present-day Ecuador). In this beautiful city, Pizarro found gold vases, jewels, gold and silver temple walls, and beautiful fabrics. He also was given information about the land of the Incas, the Empire of the Sun, where gold and silver were said to be plentiful.

When Pizarro returned to Panama, he received no encouragement from the governor there, who considered the conquistador's trips down the coast to be fruitless and dangerous. So Pizarro traveled to Spain to seek assistance for his quest, where he was arrested and jailed for debts that he had incurred in Panama. He was eventually freed by Cortés, who won him an audience with the king.

Pizarro's route from Panama to Peru

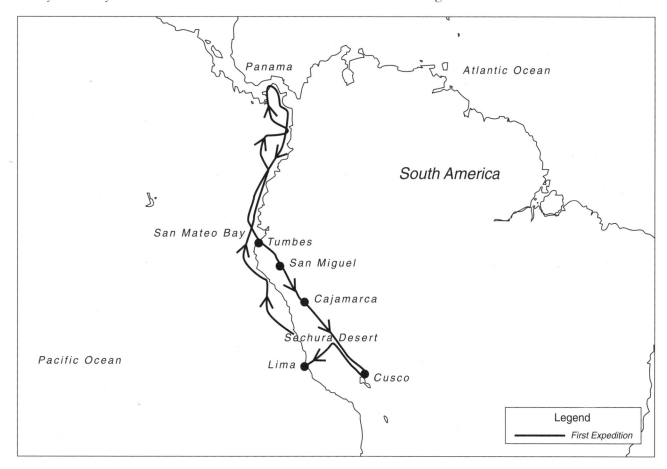

Francisco Pizarro
*Library of Congress, Prints and Photographs
Division [LC-USZ62-104354]*

Finally, Pizarro received royal authority for his conquest of the Inca Empire.

In 1532, Pizarro was joined by Hernando de Soto and almost three hundred men in a terrifying march to the Empire of the Sun. The group took the Inca king Atahualpa captive through deception and eventually had him strangled. In a short period of time, Pizarro and his men ravaged the countryside, enslaving the natives and destroying their civilization. Although Pizarro became incredibly wealthy, he did not have long to enjoy his wealth. He was killed by other Spaniards in 1541 and buried secretly to prevent his remains from being mutilated and publicly displayed.

IMPACT

- John Cabot established England's claim to an empire in North America.

- Cabot explored lands in the Northwest Atlantic (the coast of Newfoundland, Labrador, and Nova Scotia), where many islands, straits, and lakes today are named for him.

- Cabot reported the abundance of fish off the banks of Newfoundland and Labrador, which led to an end of English dependence on Icelandic dried fish.

- Vasco Nuñez de Balboa was the first European to sight the waters of the Pacific Ocean from an American shore.

- Balboa proved to be the source of inspiration for Spanish exploration and conquest along the western coast of South America.

- From 1520 – 1550, Spanish conquistadors carved out a Spanish empire in Central and South America that would last three hundred years.

- Two great civilizations were conquered and plundered during this wave of Spanish conquest. Hernando Cortés and his men took over the Aztec Empire in Mexico, and Francisco Pizarro's expedition overcame the Inca Empire in Peru.

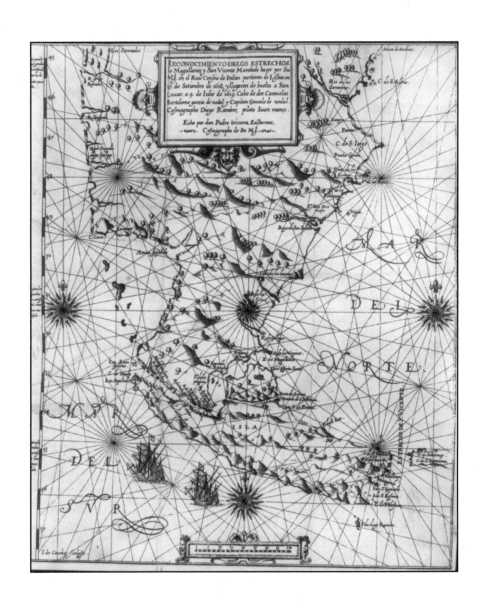

LESSON 5

ATMOSPHERE

JUAN PONCE DE LEON

Spanish soldier and explorer Juan Ponce de Leon was born in San Servos, Spain. The son of a nobleman, he served as a page to the Spanish knight Don Pedro Núñez de Guzmán, a friend of the royal family. Little more is known about the early life of this Spanish adventurer.

A well-trained soldier, Ponce de Leon fought alongside Don Pedro in the Spanish fight to regain their land from the Moors. He also sailed with Columbus on his second voyage in 1493.

Nine years later, he joined an expedition to Hispaniola led by its newly appointed governor, Nicolas de Ovando. When they arrived on the island, the Spaniards found the natives in a state of revolt. In the fighting that followed, Ponce de Leon played an important role. After the Spanish subdued the natives, Ovando rewarded Ponce de Leon by appointing him to be his lieutenant, with headquarters in a town in the eastern part of the island. There he was told by the natives about great wealth to be found on the nearby island of Borinquen (present-day Puerto Rico).

Juan Ponce de Leon
Library of Congress, Prints and Photographs Division [LC-USZ62-3106]

Ferdinand Magellan
Library of Congress, Prints and Photographs Division [LC-USZ62-92885]

**King Charles I
(Roman Emperor Charles VI)**
Public Domain

Eventually, in 1508, Ponce de Leon was granted a commission to explore Borinquen. He proceeded to conquer the island and claim it for Spain. From 1509 until 1512, he served as governor of this new Spanish colony, making a fortune in land, slaves, and gold. Ponce de Leon lost his position as governor when Christopher Columbus's son, Diego, asserted his right to make official appointments in the West Indies.

FERDINAND MAGELLAN

Portuguese navigator and explorer Ferdinand Magellan was born in the northern Portuguese town of Sabrosa. By the age of twelve, Ferdinand was serving as a page in Lisbon at the court of King John II. After the king's death in 1495, Ferdinand went to work for the India House, a government trading company that outfitted ships for voyages. During his time in Lisbon, Magellan supposedly met both Vasco da Gama and Christopher Columbus.

In 1505, at the age of twenty-five, Magellan enlisted as a soldier for Portugal. A year later, he sailed with the Portuguese first admiral, Francisco de Almedia, and his fleet on an expedition to establish a Portuguese viceroyalty in India. During his eight years in the Orient, Magellan participated in many military and exploratory expeditions. He traveled as far east as Malacca (near Singapore) and the Moluccas (the Spice Islands). While stationed in Morocco in 1513, he was severely wounded. Magellan emerged from his time in the military a tough and determined man, who had been hardened by adversity.

As a result of his years in the Orient, Magellan became interested in the search for a westward route to the Far East. He believed that a passageway existed through a narrow channel or strait in the southern part of America. Because the Portuguese king was not interested in his plans to search for that strait, Magellan traveled to Spain. King Charles I of Spain (later Roman emperor Charles VI) agreed to send Magellan to search for a southwest passage to the Far East and to bring back spices from the Moluccas.

As part of his contract with Magellan, the Spanish king granted him five ships, as well as funds for the expedition. Several wealthy

Spanish families also lent money to Magellan for his venture. In return for their financial investments, both Charles and the noblemen were promised a large share of any profits from the voyage. The wealthy Spaniards also insisted that three of Magellan's ships be commanded by Spanish captains. These men, who were not loyal to Magellan, constantly plotted against him during their time at sea. In addition to returning with treasure, the explorer hoped to prove that the Spice Islands were on the Spanish (not the Portuguese) side of the Line of Demarcation.

GIOVANNI DA VERRAZANO

Italian navigator Giovanni da Verrazano was born into a wealthy, aristocratic family. His family's castle, Castello Verrazano, was located thirty miles south of Florence.

As a young adult, Giovanni moved to Dieppe, France. He pursued a maritime career there, making several voyages to the eastern Mediterranean region and probably also visiting Newfoundland. During this time, Verrazano captured two of Cortés's Spanish galleons laden with gold.

Giovanni da Verrazano
Library of Congress, Prints and Photographs Division [LC-USZ62-30427]

EVENT

DE LEON'S EXPLORATIONS

In 1512, as compensation for the loss of his Borinquen governorship, Ponce de Leon was granted a royal license to discover and settle the island of Bimini. According to Native American legend, Bimini was the location of great riches, as well as a fountain of youth. This legendary spring was said to have waters that restored one's health and youth.

On March 3, 1513, Ponce de Leon's expedition to Bimini set sail with three ships — the *Santa Maria*, the *Santiago*, and the *San Cristobal*. The ships sailed northeast through the Bahamas with stops at Grand Turk Island and San Salvador. By early April the expedition had landed on the east coast of the Florida peninsula. Because their

Model of a Spanish galleon
Library of Congress, Prints and Photographs Division [LC-USZ62-103297]

arrival occurred during Easter week, Ponce de Leon named their landing site Tierra de Florida (Land of Flowers). The word *Florida* was a reference to the Easter feast, which was known as *Pascua de Florida*. Soon, the name Florida became attached to the entire area, which Ponce de Leon claimed for the Spanish. Most authorities believe that the expedition from Borinquen landed just north of present-day St. Augustine. The natives in the region were quite unfriendly, attacking the Spanish and wounding several of them.

Because Ponce de Leon believed that the Florida peninsula was an island, he attempted to sail around it. After failing to find an opening in the land, he decided to proceed south along the east coast of Florida. During this leg of his journey, Ponce de Leon discovered the Bahama

Ponce de Leon's explorations

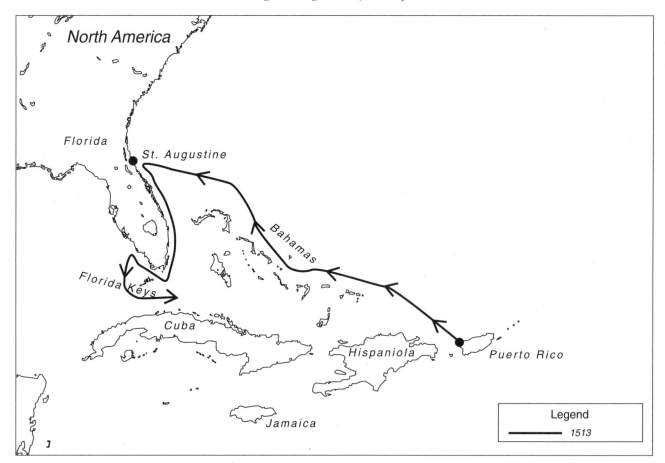

Channel, which would provide a new sea route from the West Indies to Spain. He also was the first European to make observations about the Gulf Stream. Sailing around the southern tip of Florida, the expedition traveled north along the west coast of the peninsula, probably making it as far north as Pensacola before returning south. Near present-day Tampa, the group suffered another violent attack by the natives of the region. Retracing his route, Ponce de Leon and his men returned to Borinquen, arriving in late September of 1513.

From 1513 to 1517, Ponce de Leon made several trips back to Spain to meet with Spanish royalty. Then from 1517 to 1520, he explored and conquered Guadeloupe and Trinidad for Spain. In 1521, Ponce de Leon made the decision to return to Florida to establish a Spanish colony. With a group of about two hundred men, fifty horses, a number of domestic farm animals, and various farm implements, he sailed from Borinquen and landed on the west coast of Florida, probably near Tampa. However, the Native Americans in the area again proved to be unfriendly. They brutally attacked the Spanish. Many of Ponce de Leon's men died, and he himself suffered a severe leg injury from an arrow.

The expedition left Florida for Cuba, where Ponce de Leon died from his injury. His men then took his body to San Juan (Puerto Rico) for burial. There his tomb bears this epitaph: "This narrow grave contains the remains of a man who was a lion and much more so by his deeds." Juan Ponce de Leon literally means "John of the Lion's Paunch" in Spanish. Although Ponce de Leon never found the fountain of youth or planted a colony in Florida, he did pave the way for further Spanish exploration in the southeastern part of North America.

Seeking the fountain of youth
Library of Congress, Prints and Photographs Division [LC-USZ62-2977]

MAGELLAN'S EXPLORATIONS

On September 20, 1519, Ferdinand Magellan set sail from Sanlucar, Spain, with a motley crew of 250 – 270 men and five old ships — the *Santiago,* the *San Antonio*, the *Conception*, the *Trinidad*, and the *Victoria*. The expedition sailed south into the Atlantic Ocean and reached the Canary Islands in just seven days. By November, Magellan and his men had arrived in Brazil and continued south along the east coast of South America.

At the end of March of 1520, Magellan decided to winter in the harbor of San Julian. He and his men spent the next five months there, contending with frigid weather and a lack of fresh food supplies. During this time, Magellan was forced to put down the first of several mutinies among his crew. Also, during a May reconnaissance expedition, the *Santiago* hit a shoal and wrecked in rough waters seventy miles south of San Julian. Finally, in August the remaining ships were able to continue their voyage.

During a storm in October, Magellan and his crew discovered an opening in the coastline, which proved to be the entrance to a strait

Magellan's explorations

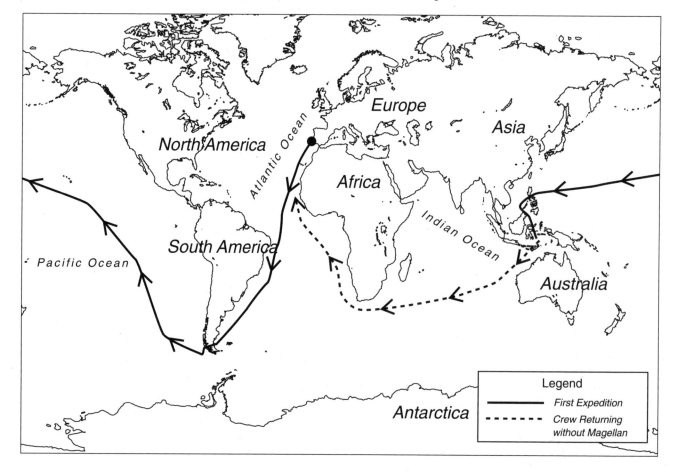

located near the tip of South America. For thirty-eight days the expedition twisted and turned through the more than three-hundred-mile strait, which Magellan named the Strait of All Saints (the name was later changed to the Strait of Magellan). As they sailed at night, the crew frequently viewed fires from distant native camps, which led them to name the area Tierra del Fuego (land of fire).

Unfortunately, at some point during this thirty-eight-day journey, the captain of the *San Antonio* secretly deserted and sailed his ship back to Spain, taking with him most of the expedition's provisions. This was a severe blow to the remaining three ships. When Magellan and his crew finally reached the open sea, the explorer gave it the name Mar Pacifico (Peaceful Sea), because its waters seemed so calm compared to the stormy waters that they had just endured. He and his men believed that their voyage was finally near its end.

Sailing north along the western coast of Chile and then westward across the Pacific, Magellan and his crew spent the next ninety-eight days without sighting land. During this time, nineteen men died, and many others almost starved to death. They ate rats, sawdust, maggots, and leather in an attempt to stay alive, and they struggled with scurvy. On January 24, 1521, the expedition sighted a little island that was quite barren, and on February 4 they spotted another island with no place to drop anchor. Finally, in early March, the group reached Guam, where they found fresh fruits, vegetables, and water.

From Guam, Magellan and his men traveled on to Cebu, an island in the southern Philippines. Magellan hoped to stay in Cebu for a while to rest and repair the remaining three ships. During this time the explorer preached the Gospel to the natives of the island, and many of them underwent conversions. The king of the island, however, was primarily interested in using Magellan to acquire more power and convinced him to lead a raiding party on another island named Mactan. There, on April 17, 1521, Magellan and his band of between fifty and sixty men were quickly overwhelmed by thousands of natives. During the ensuing battle, Magellan was killed by a poisoned arrow in his foot and a spear through his heart. Forty of his men died with him.

Map of the Strait of Magellan
Library of Congress, Prints and Photographs Division [LC-USZ62-71977]

Magellan's crew left his body behind in the Philippines. They also burned his ship, the *Conception*, because there was not enough crew left for three ships. The remaining two ships in the expedition reached the Moluccas in November of 1521, where they loaded rich cargos of spices. However, on the way back to Spain, the *Trinidad* was captured by the Portuguese. Only the *Victoria* and its eighteen surviving crew members, captained by Juan Sebastian del Cano, made it all the way back to Spain in 1522. This ship had sailed around the world and had returned with a cargo that more than paid for the expedition (533 hundredweight of cloves).

Magellan's expedition proved that it was possible to reach the Indies from Europe by sailing west. However, the voyage turned out to be twice the expected distance, and del Cano received recognition as its hero instead of Magellan. Finally in 1524, a Venetian nobleman named Antonio Pigafetta, one of the expedition's survivors, wrote a popular account of the voyage. With the publication of Pigafetta's story, Magellan's role in the first circumnavigation of the world was recognized.

King Francis I
Library of Congress, Prints and Photographs Division [LC-USZ62-18182]

In this port they refitted the ship. Here the captain-major made Alvaro re Mesquita, a Portuguese, captain of one of the ships the captain of which had been killed. There sailed from this port on the twenty-forth of August four ships, for the smallest of the ships had been already lost; he had sent it to reconnoiter, and the weather had been heavy, and had cast it ashore, where all of the crew had been recovered along with the merchandise, artillery, and fittings of the ship. They remained in this port, in which they wintered, five months and twenty-four days, and they were seventy degrees less ten minutes to the southward.

—from Pigafetta's account of Magellan's voyage

VERRAZANO'S EXPLORATIONS

In 1524, King Francis I of France commissioned Verrazano to lead an expedition to the New World. By 1520, the Spanish had discovered Florida, and the English had claimed Newfoundland. However, the area between Florida and Newfoundland was unexplored. Since Magellan's expedition had established that America was indeed a separate continent, the French were hopeful that a Northwest Passage to Asia could be found in this unexplored area — a passage that would be shorter than traveling around the Cape of Good Hope or through the Strait of Magellan.

Provided with four ships for his expedition, Verrazano planned to follow a route somewhat north of the route used by Columbus on his first journey. The expedition set sail in late 1524 or early 1525, financed by several wealthy Frenchmen and Florentine businessmen. Two of his vessels shipwrecked soon after their departure. A third ship was sent back to France with treasure obtained from privateering. Thus,

Verrazano's explorations

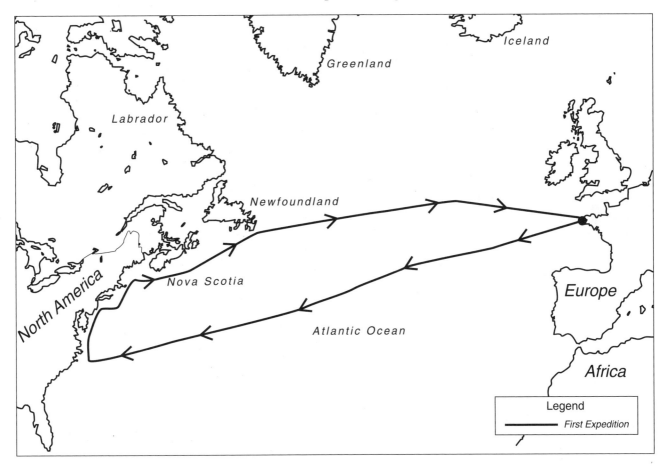

only the flagship *La Dauphin* (*The Dolphin*) with a fifty-member crew actually crossed the Atlantic. Giovanni's brother, Girolomo, who was a mapmaker, was also a member of this crew.

Verrazano probably first touched land in America on or about March 1, 1525, at a point south of Cape Fear, North Carolina. From there he sailed about 150 miles south along the coast of South Carolina. Eventually, Verrazano turned back north because he did not want to encounter the Spanish in Florida. Not far from his original landfall, Verrazano anchored the ship well out to sea and sent a smaller boat to shore for a pleasant meeting with the natives.

Sailing farther north, Verrazano coasted along the Outer Banks of North Carolina. As he explored the area, he decided that the sea that lay beyond the Outer Banks (Pamlico Sound) was the Pacific Ocean and that North America was just a narrow strip of land between the Atlantic and Pacific. For years afterward, mapmakers, beginning with Girolomo Verrazano, showed Pamlico Sound as part of the Pacific Ocean.

The French expedition continued northward, probably stopping at Kitty Hawk, North Carolina, and sailing past Virginia, Delaware, and New Jersey. Because Verrazano kept quite a distance from the coastline until New Jersey, he missed the entrances to the Chesapeake and Delaware bays. However, the Frenchmen did become the first Europeans known to have seen New York Bay. They anchored in the narrows, later named after Verrazano and presently spanned by the Verrazano Narrows Bridge.

Traveling on toward the east, Verrazano and his men discovered Block Island and then sailed into Narragansett Bay, where they anchored at Newport Harbor for several weeks to avoid bad weather. Since the Wampanoag in the region were very friendly, Verrazano and his men traveled inland to trade with them. The descendants of these Wampanoag would befriend the Pilgrims a century later (in the 1620s). The French crew sailed on through Vineyard Sound and Nantucket Sound and rounded Cape Cod. Reaching the coast of Maine, they passed Cape Breton and Newfoundland before returning to Dieppe, France, on July 8, 1525.

Verrazano Narrows Bridge
Library of Congress, Prints and Photographs
Division [NY, 24-BROK, 57-9]

After his return to France, Verrazano sought to organize a second expedition to America. However, because France was at war, he could find no financial backers. Finally in the spring of 1527, Verrazano was able to set sail again. During this expedition he traveled to the coast of Brazil and returned to France with a cargo of valuable tropical lumber.

A year later in 1528, Verrazano again sailed westward across the Atlantic. He supposedly reached the coast of Florida and then followed the chain of the Lesser Antilles. On one of these islands (probably Guadeloupe), Verrazano anchored a distance away from shore, as was his habit. According to a number of sources, Verrazano traveled ashore to meet the island's natives and found them to be quite unfriendly. In fact, the cannibalistic Carib tribe supposedly killed the explorer and ate him.

IMPACT

- Juan Ponce de Leon was the first European to discover Florida, the Bahama Channel, and the Gulf Stream.

- De Leon colonized Borinquen (Puerto Rico) and served as its first governor; many places in Puerto Rico (including Ponce, the second-largest city) bear his name.

- Ferdinand Magellan was the first man to prove that the world is round and that the Far East could be reached by sailing west from Europe.

- Magellan's explorations proved to be the source of information concerning the true size of the Pacific Ocean and the distance between Asia and America (much greater than he had thought). This also led to a more accurate world map.

- Giovanni da Verrazano, the first European to discover New York Bay and Narragansett Bay, established the French right to claim territory in North America.

- Verrazano became the source of the first documented geographical descriptions of most of the eastern coastline of North America as well as information on several Native American tribes living along this coast.

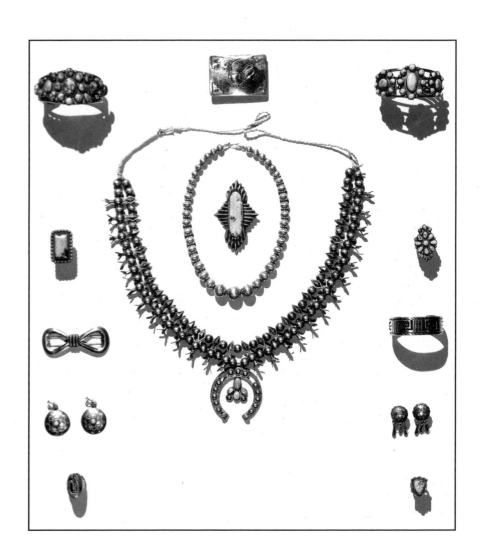

LESSON 6

ATMOSPHERE

JACQUES CARTIER

French navigator and master mariner Jacques Cartier was born in Saint-Malo, a seaport in the Brittany region. Historians know little about his youth, except for the fact that he was a member of a prominent and well-respected family.

In early adulthood, Cartier married the daughter of an important city official and studied at the French center for navigators in Dieppe. As a master pilot, he made voyages across the Atlantic Ocean between the years of 1524 and 1527 and possibly accompanied Verrazano on his expedition to the Atlantic coast of North America.

HERNANDO DE SOTO

Spanish conquistador Hernando de Soto was born in the town of Jerez de los Caballeros, near the Portuguese border. Growing up in a family of minor nobility, Hernando traveled to the Spanish colony of Darien at the age of nineteen with Pedrarias the Cruel. There he witnessed the execution of Balboa.

When he was twenty-four, Hernando de Soto took part in the Spanish conquest of Nicaragua. For a while he lived in Nicaragua,

Jacques Cartier
Library of Congress, Prints and Photographs Division [LC-USZ62-9097]

Hernando de Soto
Line drawing courtesy of Amy Pak

Francisco Vasquez de Coronado
Library of Congress, Prints and Photographs Division [LC-USZ62-38775]

intent upon making his fortune and becoming a hero. In 1532 – 1533, de Soto traveled with Pizarro to Peru, where he participated in the fight to conquer the Incas. During the time that he spent as part of these Spanish expeditions, de Soto was involved in enslaving large numbers of natives in the search for wealth. As a soldier, Hernando de Soto gained a reputation for stubbornness, toughness, and bravery.

By the time de Soto returned to Spain in 1535 or 1536, he was wealthy from Inca gold. He settled in Seville, married Pedrarias's daughter, and could easily have retired to a life of luxury. However, de Soto soon grew restless and bored with Spanish court life. By 1537, he had received an appointment from Emperor Charles V to serve as the governor of Cuba with rights to conquer and settle Florida — what the Spanish called the North American mainland.

FRANCISCO VASQUEZ DE CORONADO

Spanish conquistador Francisco Vasquez de Coronado was born into a wealthy noble family in Salamanca, Spain. Because he was not the eldest son in the family, Francisco did not inherit his family's estate. In 1535, at the age of twenty-five, he was appointed to serve on the staff of Antonio de Mendoza, the Spanish viceroy to New Spain (Mexico). Four years later, Coronado was appointed governor of the province of New Galicia in northern Mexico. For two years he served well in this post, putting down both a slave revolt and an Indian uprising. During this time he also married Beatriz Estrada, the rich and beautiful daughter of the colonial treasurer.

In the 1540s, the Spanish were still searching for gold in the New World. Viceroy Mendoza was especially intrigued by stories he frequently heard about the Seven Cities of Cibola. According to reports, these fabulously wealthy cities of gold were located in an unknown land to the north of Mexico beyond the desert. In 1540, Mendoza commissioned Coronado to find the Seven Cities of Cibola. The Spanish viceroy provided half of the money needed for the expedition. Coronado's wife, the wealthiest Spanish heiress in Mexico, provided the rest.

EVENT

CARTIER'S EXPLORATIONS

In the 1520s, France had twice the population of Spain and Portugal combined and six times the population of England. However, the French had long been overshadowed by these other European nations in the sending out of transatlantic expeditions. In 1533, King Francis I of France persuaded the pope to amend the Treaty of Tordesillas to pertain only to land that had already been discovered. A year later, King Francis commissioned Jacques Cartier to lead an expedition with the purpose of discovering and claiming for France lands rich in gold and other treasures and to find a Northwest Passage to Asia. By 1534, Europeans had explored much of the east coast of North America, but no explorer had yet penetrated the continent.

First Expedition (1534)

On April 20, 1534, Cartier left Saint-Malo with two small ships and approximately sixty Frenchmen. He and his men reached North America in twenty days. They first sailed south along the coasts of Labrador and western Newfoundland. Because Cartier found this region so desolate, he called it the "land God gave to Cain."

Next, the expedition sailed clockwise around what appeared to be a great inland sea. They sailed through the Strait of Belle Isle into the Gulf of St. Lawrence and crossed over to the shores of the Gaspé Peninsula, just missing the entrance to the St. Lawrence River. On this peninsula, Cartier raised a thirty-foot cross and claimed the land for France in the name of King Francis I.

While exploring the Gaspé Peninsula, Cartier and his men met over three hundred Iroquois. In an attempt to establish a friendship with the native people, the French gave them gifts—beads, knives, caps, colorful coats, and other goods. The Iroquois, in turn, told the French about a kingdom, which they called Saguenay, located further inland and rich in gold and minerals. During their stay on the peninsula, Cartier attempted to keep careful records of the area's trees, vegetables, fruits,

Iroquois Indians
Library of Congress, Prints and Photographs Division [LC-USZ62-56198]

---

and grains because King Francis was interested in whether it would be a good site for colonization.

When Cartier and his men left the Gaspé Peninsula to return to France, they took with them two of the sons of the Iroquois chief Donnaconna. Some sources contend that Cartier kidnapped them, while others maintain that they left with the chief's blessing. These Iroquois would learn French and return to North America with Cartier as interpreter-guides. When Cartier returned to France, he was warmly received by the king, although he had returned without gold or news of a Northwest Passage.

Second Expedition (1535 – 1536)

In late spring of the following year, Cartier set sail again for North America. He returned with three ships and approximately 110 men. During this expedition, the Frenchman and his men found the opening to the St. Lawrence River and attempted to travel west on the river in a search for the kingdom of Saguenay.

However, Cartier and his men were only able to sail as far inland as the Native American village of Stadacona (present-day Quebec) before the swiftly flowing water made it impossible for them to continue. From Stadacona the Frenchmen used several smaller boats to go further upriver to the village of Hochelaga. Located next to Hochelaga was a mountain, which Cartier named Mont Real (Royal Mountain).

Cartier and his men returned to Stadacona to spend the winter of 1535 – 1536. During these intensely cold months, twenty-five of the Frenchmen died from scurvy. Finally, a brew of white cedar, rich in ascorbic acid, was found to combat the condition. In mid-1536, Cartier returned to France with Donnaconna the Iroquois chief, and nine other Iroquois. He returned without gold and without discovering a Northwest Passage, and this time the French king was not as pleased with the explorer.

Third Expedition (1541 – 1542) and Final Years

In early 1541, the French king commissioned Jean-Francois de la Rocque, sieul de Roberval, as the leader of a third expedition to North

Gulf of St. Lawrence
Library of Congress, Prints and Photographs Division [LC-USZ62-45582]

America. Cartier was made Roberval's subordinate. The king supplied Roberval with ten ships, four hundred sailors, and three hundred soldiers for the purpose of establishing a French colony in the St. Lawrence Valley. There were also several women on board. However, Roberval was unprepared to leave by late spring, so Cartier sailed ahead to North America with five ships.

Cartier established a French settlement named Cap Rouge near present-day Quebec and also continued to explore the St. Lawrence River until the rapids he encountered prevented further progress. By this time the Iroquois in the region had become less trustful of the French and began attacking the French base sporadically. As a result of Indian attacks and scurvy, a number of Frenchmen on this expedition died.

Cartier's explorations

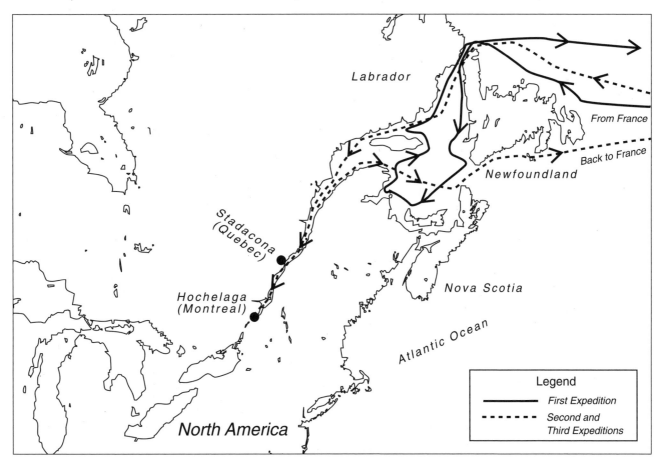

When Cartier finally encountered Roberval in Newfoundland, he was headed back to France. Although Roberval ordered Cartier to return to Cap Rouge with him, Cartier refused to obey and returned to France before the end of 1542.

Roberval and his men remained another year but eventually evacuated the St. Lawrence River settlement, discouraged by the harsh winter, scurvy, and violent river rapids. When these Frenchmen returned to their homeland, they took back with them what they thought to be diamonds and gold. However, they eventually discovered that their treasures were only quartz and iron pyrite.

For the remaining twelve years of his life, Cartier lived in Saint-Malo. In 1545 he published an account of his three expeditions, which was the first detailed documentation of European exploration in North America. Cartier's information provided mapmakers with reliable knowledge of large parts of eastern Canada. This enabled them to produce maps that would be quite useful to the French explorers, traders, and missionaries that followed Cartier.

DE SOTO'S EXPLORATIONS

Before leaving Spain, de Soto recruited over six hundred trained men for his expedition and gathered supplies that included over two hundred horses, fighting dogs, and a herd of pigs for food. He apparently sold property to help finance his expedition. De Soto's wife sailed with him as far as Cuba but did not venture with him and his men as they traveled on to Florida's west coast. By the end of May 1539, their expedition had probably landed near Tampa Bay.

For the next four years, Hernando de Soto and his men would travel in search of gold and other treasure. They covered over four thousand miles of wilderness, exploring parts of Florida, Georgia, South Carolina, North Carolina, Tennessee, Alabama, Mississippi, Arkansas, Oklahoma, and Texas. In the process, they often brutally attacked and plundered Native American villages, seizing local chiefs and holding them for ransom. This behavior led to ongoing skirmishes with the natives — the Cherokee, Seminole, Creek, Appalachian, and Choctaw. It also meant that the natives who did not resist often told the Spanish what they wanted to hear — that great wealth existed in some faraway location.

As they pushed toward the interior of the continent, de Soto was firmly resolved to find treasure or perish. However, the constant war with the Indians, long marches, mosquitoes, snakes, and increasing disappointment over not finding treasure finally led de Soto's men to plot to abandon him and sail to Mexico or Peru. De Soto learned of their plans and managed to thwart them. He continued to drive his men on, promising them glory and gold.

By the spring of 1542, Hernando de Soto had become sick with a fever, probably malaria. He finally died on May 21, 1542. His men were very concerned that the natives, whom de Soto had treated brutally,

de Soto's explorations

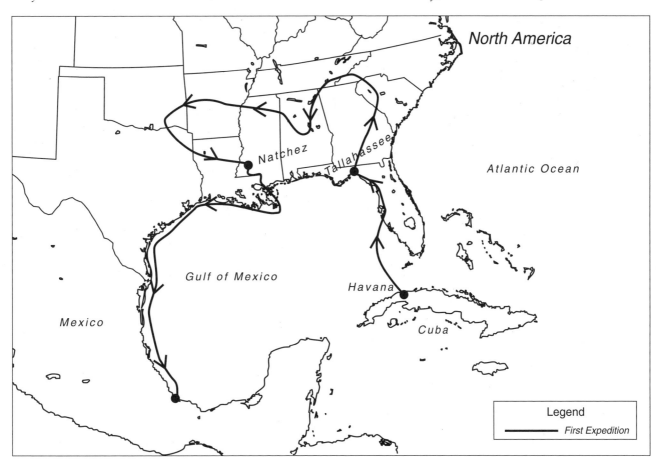

not learn of his death. Therefore, they hollowed out the trunk of a large tree and placed their leader's body in it. Then they lowered the trunk into the Mississippi River near Natchez, Mississippi. De Soto and his men were the first Europeans known to have seen and crossed the Mississippi River, which they called el Grande.

The survivors of the expedition headed west in the hope of finding Mexico. Instead, they arrived in Texas and quickly grew discouraged by the vastness of the land. Finally, they decided to march back to the Mississippi River, where they built boats and then floated down the river. As they made their way down the Mississippi, they often stopped at Native American villages and took whatever they needed. After entering the Gulf of Mexico, they eventually reached a Spanish settlement on the east coast of Mexico (which the Spanish called New Spain). Only 311 of the original 600 men survived their four years of exploration.

Hernando de Soto died a disillusioned, disappointed, and financially ruined man. His failure to find riches halted Spanish exploration of the interior of eastern North America for the next one hundred years, and his hostile relations with the Native Americans would be harmful to future European explorers and missionaries in the region. However, survivors of de Soto's expedition went on to write accounts of Florida, which were useful to those founding the first permanent Spanish settlement on the continent of North America — St. Augustine — in 1565.

CORONADO'S EXPLORATIONS

Coronado's expedition to search for the Seven Cities of Cibola was well financed and carefully planned. The expedition included five priests, an army of more than three hundred Spanish soldiers, and approximately three hundred armed Indian allies. There were also hundreds of Indian and African slaves, more than five hundred horses, and an enormous provision and baggage train. Coronado eventually split the expedition into several different groups that traveled in different directions from 1540 until 1542.

Laying out of St. Augustine
Library of Congress, Prints and Photographs Division [LC-USZ62-1659]

As Coronado began this expedition, he had high hopes for its success. He had been told that the land he would be traveling through was flat and that he would find abundant supplies of food and water there. The opposite was true. However, despite these travel obstacles, Coronado and his men explored much of the land that is now part of the southwestern United States, including Arizona, New Mexico, Texas, Oklahoma, and Kansas.

One of these expeditions was the first European group known to have seen the Grand Canyon (and the last for the next two hundred years). Another group discovered the Continental Divide, which runs north and south through the Rockies. Coronado's men were also the first Europeans to travel up the Rio Grande River and see the

Coronado's explorations

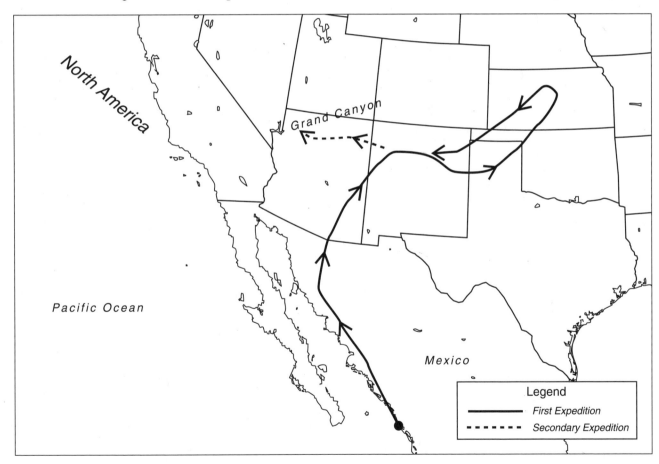

Grand Canyon
Library of Congress, Prints and Photographs
Division [LC-USZC4-4412]

Turquoise jewelry
National Archives print [61-2811]

Painted Desert. At one point in 1541, one of Coronado's groups was very close to de Soto's expedition, which was located in eastern Oklahoma at the time.

Finally, in 1542, Coronado and his men returned to New Spain after traveling over six thousand miles. Only one hundred of the original three hundred soldiers made it back. Some had been killed by Indians, and others had died from disease. Others had left to explore on their own. Both Coronado and Mendoza felt that the expedition had been a complete failure. Instead of the golden cities of Cibola, Coronado and his men had found only poor Pueblo, Hopi, and Zuni agricultural villages full of houses made of sun-dried mud.

The native tribesmen encountered during Coronado's expeditions were generally peaceful and industrious people — weavers of cotton cloth, makers of turquoise jewelry and beautiful pottery, and skilled farmers. However, they were not willing to convert to Christianity and resisted other efforts by the Spanish to "civilize" them. Coronado and his men raided these tribal villages when they were starving and looking for food, set the natives' homes on fire when they were angered, and enslaved or killed many of them.

Although Coronado had fallen out of favor with Mendoza, he was not initially removed from his post as governor of New Galicia. Eventually Coronado was tried on charges of corruption, negligence, and cruelties against Indians under his authority. Some sources believe Coronado was removed from his post at this point.

By this time, the attitude of the Spanish court toward conquistador activities had begun to change under pressure from certain priests. In 1542, the Spanish king decreed new laws to protect Native Americans in Spanish colonies, and inquiries into conquistador activities began. After Coronado's trial was over, the disillusioned explorer returned to Mexico City. There he died in 1544, several decades before his chronicle describing his expedition was published. He left a widow and eight children.

IMPACT

- Jacques Cartier was the first European to discover the Gulf of St. Lawrence and the St. Lawrence River. These discoveries and the names he gave them became established features on European maps.

- Cartier became the first European to use the name Canada for this region. (This word originated from the Iroquois name Kanata, which referred to a village near Quebec.) Cartier used this name to refer to all the land farther west along the St. Lawrence River.

- The French used Cartier's discoveries as an axis for their colonial empire in North America and as an impetus for further exploration.

- Hernando de Soto was the first European to successfully explore Florida and the southeastern United States, which established Spanish claim to this area.

- De Soto was also the first European to cross the Mississippi River.

- Francisco Vasquez de Coronado was the first European to explore the southwestern region of the United States, which established Spanish claim to this vast new territory. His reports on his expedition provided important information on the geography and ethnography of the North American Southwest, which were not appreciated during his time as they are now.

LESSON 7

Sir Francis Drake. . . . . 1540 — 1596 A.D.
Sir Walter (Ralegh) Raleigh . . . . . . 1552? *or* 1554? — 1618 A.D.

ATMOSPHERE

SIR FRANCIS DRAKE

Francis Drake — English navigator, privateer, and explorer — was born in Devonshire, twenty miles north of the seaport of Plymouth. His father worked as a sailor before his children were born, and most of his twelve sons also became seamen. A devout Puritan, Drake's father labored both as a farmer and as a preacher. In 1549, the family was forced to leave Devonshire during a time of great religious upheaval, and they lost all of their property. They moved to Kent and lived for a time in an old abandoned ship.

As a young boy of twelve or thirteen, Francis went to sea as a captain's cabin boy and spent several years sailing the North Sea and the Bay of Biscay. By his early twenties, he had become the captain of a small ship. During the 1560s, he made a number of voyages to the Caribbean. Known as the Dragon, Drake was fearless in raiding Spanish and Portuguese ships and ports. He paid no attention to the Line of Demarcation, and he worked secretly for Queen Elizabeth I, who provided him with money and ships and shared in the treasures that he seized. Drake and other English sea captains who made daring raids for the queen were referred to as sea dogs.

Sir Francis Drake
Library of Congress, Prints and Photographs Division [LC-USZ62-38479]

Queen Elizabeth I
Library of Congress, Prints and Photographs Division [LC-USZ62-53515]

In 1567, Drake participated in an expedition with his distant relative, the famous British admiral Sir John Hawkins. Their objective was to raid Spanish settlements in the West Indies and Central America. At Veracruz, however, the Spanish succeeded in sinking most of the English ships. Although Drake escaped, he lost almost all that he possessed. Drake never forgave the Spanish for his losses at Veracruz and for their cruel treatment of the English prisoners there. Most of the rest of his life was devoted to relentless warfare against the Spanish—plundering their settlements and destroying their ships.

In 1577, Drake proposed to the English queen that he sail into the Pacific to raid Spanish ships carrying silver along the coast of Chile and Peru. Queen Elizabeth and a number of English noblemen agreed to invest in Drake's proposed venture. Their intent was to weaken Spain (Spain had amassed a vast empire in the New World) and to make England richer. The queen also hoped that Drake would discover new lands for England and even find the Northwest Passage.

SIR WALTER RALEIGH

Sir Walter Raleigh was an English navigator, soldier, explorer, historian, poet, courtier, and politician. One of the most colorful personalities of Elizabethan England, Raleigh was born in Devonshire in the mid-sixteenth century. By the time he reached adulthood, he was a six-foot tall, handsome, spirited individual. Although Raleigh was known for his courtly manners, he also could be quite haughty and impatient.

In 1569, Raleigh volunteered to fight in the Huguenot (Protestant) army in France in one of that country's religious wars. Raleigh was a fervent Protestant, and he had grown up hating Catholicism. In 1572, he attended Oxford University, and in 1575, he studied law at Middle Temple in London. There are no records indicating that he graduated from either institution. By 1580, Raleigh was in Ireland, helping to suppress a rebellion there. During this period of his life, he also apparently traveled on several voyages of exploration with his half-brother, Sir Humphrey Gilbert.

When Raleigh returned to England from Ireland, he immediately was drawn into court life. Because he was so charming, he soon

Sir Walter Raleigh
Line drawing courtesy of Amy Pak

became a favorite of Queen Elizabeth I and eventually she knighted him. During the years of his friendship with the queen, Raleigh composed poetry for Elizabeth and received from her a wine monopoly, valuable properties in Ireland, and an appointment as captain of her guard. A famous story also relates that Raleigh supposedly laid his velvet coat over a mud puddle so that the queen would not have to dirty her satin shoes.

EVENT

DRAKE'S EXPLORATIONS

First Expedition (1577 – 1580)

In December of 1577, Drake's expedition sailed from Plymouth, England, with five ships—the *Marigold*, the *Elizabeth*, the *Swan*, the *Christopher*, and the *Pelican*. More than 160 crewmen sailed with Drake. Initially, most of the crew members were told that they were sailing to Alexandria, Egypt, to trade on the Nile because of their fears concerning passage through the Strait of Magellan. Before reaching the strait, Drake abandoned his two supply ships, the *Christopher* and the *Swan*. Furthermore, after months of harsh weather and rough sailing, Thomas Doughty, a courtier of the queen, convinced Drake's exhausted crew to mutiny against him. Drake put down the rebellion by arresting Doughty and executing him. Before leaving the waters of the Atlantic, Drake rallied his men and unified his command with a remarkable speech, and he renamed the *Pelican* the *Golden Hind*.

Replica of the *Golden Hind*
Courtesy of Southwark Photo Library

As Drake crossed the Strait of Magellan, he and the crew on the *Golden Hind* were separated from the two other remaining ships. The *Marigold* sank, killing the entire crew, and the captain of the *Elizabeth* decided to return to England. During their passage through the strait, Drake and his crew were able to establish that Tierra del Fuego was an island, not a continent (as many had believed following Magellan's voyage).

Sailing up the coast of Chile and Peru, Drake and his crew took a Spanish galleon filled with silver and other treasures by surprise. They also pirated several Spanish settlements for food and treasure. The *Golden Hind* continued sailing northward, and some sources believe that Drake's ship traveled all the way to Vancouver before turning south again. Near San Francisco, Drake stopped to repair his leaking ship. He claimed the area for Queen Elizabeth, naming it Nova Albion (New England). In 1936, a brass plaque was discovered near San Quentin Bay, north of San Francisco, which some authorities believe was erected by Drake.

Drake's circumnavigation of the globe

Drake decided to return home by sailing around the world as Magellan had done. He hoped to avoid running into the Spanish,

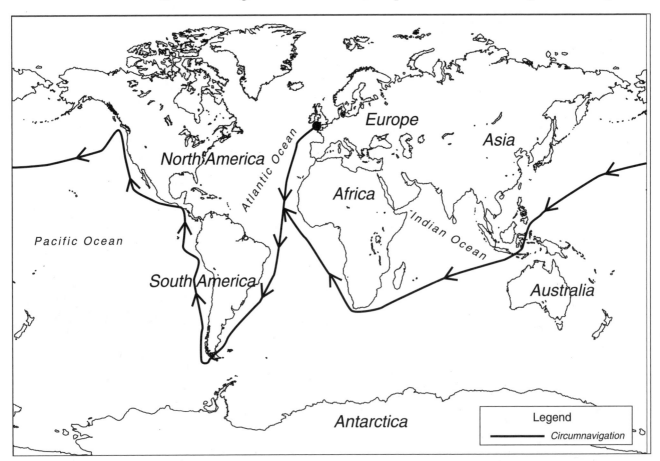

whom he had angered. Thus, Drake and his men sailed westward across the Pacific Ocean, stopping at the Philippines and the Spice Islands, where they loaded a rich cargo. They continued to sail westward across the Indian Ocean, turning south to travel around the southern tip of Africa and then north up the west coast of that continent. On November 3, 1580, the *Golden Hind* reached Plymouth, England, completing its circumnavigation of the globe. Its journey around the world had taken three years and covered thirty-six thousand miles.

Drake returned to England with riches that showed a 5,000 percent increase on his backers' investment. With this treasure, the queen was able to raise a large army and build a fleet of warships. The following year, Queen Elizabeth honored Drake by dining with him on board the *Golden Hind* and rewarding him with a large sum of money and knighthood. Timber taken from the *Golden Hind* was later made into a chair that was kept at Oxford University.

Second Expedition (1585) and Third Expedition (1587)

In the early 1580s, Drake spent two years serving as mayor of Plymouth and two years serving in the House of Commons. Then in 1585, Queen Elizabeth sent Drake on an expedition with a fleet of twenty-five ships and two thousand men to capture Spanish treasures in the West Indies. During this expedition, Drake and his men burned Santo Domingo and St. Augustine and returned home with tobacco and potatoes. Two years later, Drake led a famous attack, known as the "singeing of the King of Spain's beard," on Cadiz and Coruna. During this daring raid, the English sank or captured between twenty and thirty Spanish ships, destroying supplies intended for the Spanish Armada (fleet).

Defeat of the Spanish Armada

In 1588, Sir Francis Drake, now a British vice-admiral, played a major role in the English defeat of the Spanish Armada. To stop the activities of the English sea dogs, King Philip of Spain sent his fleet of more than 130 ships up the English Channel to crush the English fleet. Drake was supposedly bowling when news came of the

The Spanish Armada
Library of Congress, Prints and Photographs Division [LC-USZ62-49872]

Armada's impending attack on the English. According to English legend, Drake was so sure of England's victory that he finished his game before putting out to sea.

One of history's greatest naval battles raged on for more than a week in the English Channel. At first Drake allowed the Armada to proceed without an English attack while a high wind turned into a full-blown storm. When the Spanish commanders became seasick, their ships were driven past Flanders, Belgium. At this point Drake proceeded to attack the Spanish fleet with light English ships, vessels that could turn quickly in any direction and sail under Spanish guns without being hit. The supposedly invincible Armada was completely routed by the English navy. Many of the Spanish ships were sunk, and thousands of Spanish sailors died. Only fifty-four of Philip's ships returned to Spain. The era of English sea power had begun, and Spain was no longer feared as a great naval power.

At the time of his death, Sir Francis Drake was a figure of international importance—known throughout the world as a daring and ruthless sea captain and privateer. During a voyage in the West Indies, Drake died of dysentery near the coast of Panama. He was buried at sea.

RALEIGH'S EXPLORATIONS

By the early 1580s, Raleigh was quite interested in leaving England and sailing to the New World to see the land explored by the English there. However, the queen would not allow him to lead colonizing expeditions to America in person. Although Elizabeth issued Raleigh a patent to start a colony in the New World, she insisted that he send two captains to search for a site rather than going to America himself.

When these captains returned to England in 1584, they reported finding an island named Roanoke off the coast of North Carolina that would be suitable for colonization. The region in America given to Raleigh in his royal charter was named Virginia in honor of Elizabeth I, Virgin Queen of England.

In 1585, Raleigh sent his first group of English colonists to Roanoke under the leadership of Sir Richard Grenville. Although he personally did not take part in the colonizing expedition, he found one hundred men who were willing to go. However, these colonists were primarily interested in becoming wealthy from treasure in the New World and returning to England to live, not in beginning a colony and living in the New World. They also did not realize how dangerous the American wilderness really was and how much work it would take to live there. This first expedition to Roanoke quickly ran out of food. When the colonists tried to force the Indians to give them food, trouble ensued. A year later, this first group returned to England with Sir Francis Drake, who had stopped by Roanoke to visit with them.

Explorations commissioned by Raleigh and Raleigh's actual explorations

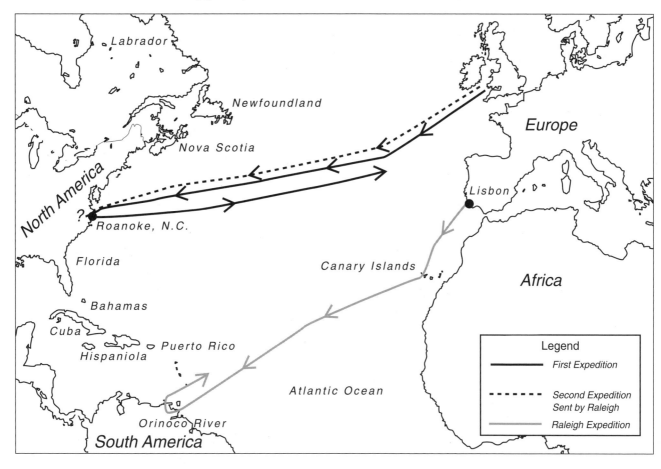

Among this first group of colonists was Raleigh's confidante, Thomas Harriot, who published *A Briefe and True Report of the New Found Land of Virginia.*

In 1587, Raleigh sent another expedition to Roanoke, this time with about 150 men, women, and children. Raleigh had decided that families would be more interested in settling down and making a life in the New World. The second group of colonists repaired the houses left by the first group. On August 18, 1587, Virginia Dare, grandchild of the colony's governor, John White, was born. She was the first English child known to be born in the New World. Eventually, Governor White decided to return to England for needed supplies. Before he left, he instructed the colonists to carve a message on a tree if they had to leave the island. He told them to put a cross above the message if they were in trouble.

About the time White returned to England, all English ships were commissioned into service to deal with the invading Spanish Armada. White was forced to stay in England for three years before he was allowed to return to Roanoke. When he finally returned to the island in 1590, White discovered that all the English colonists that he had left there had vanished. He found *Cro* carved on a tree and *Croatoan* (the name of the natives who lived on a nearby island) carved on one of the posts surrounding the fort. However, there were no crosses carved on the tree or the post. John White returned to England without finding the missing colonists. Although Raleigh sent other ships to search for the lost colony, no trace of it was ever found. Meanwhile, he decided to sell his patent rights to a merchant company and to give up his attempt to establish an English colony in Virginia.

Some of the Roanoke colonists who returned to England brought back tobacco. Raleigh became convinced that tobacco was good for coughs and often smoked a pipe. He popularized its use in England and Ireland, creating a demand for the tobacco leaf that has continued through the centuries.

By 1592, Raleigh was no longer a court favorite — due to the queen's discovery of his secret love affair with one of her maids of honor, Elizabeth Throckmorton. For a time, Elizabeth threw both Raleigh and Bess, whom he had married, into the Tower of London. When he was released from prison, Raleigh sat in Parliament and became connected with a poetic group known as the School of Night. This group, which included Thomas Harriot and Christopher Marlowe, was known for its skepticism. In fact, many Englishmen considered these poets to be atheists.

Finally in 1595, Queen Elizabeth allowed Raleigh to leave England on an expedition to search for the legendary Lost City of Gold, El Dorado. Raleigh's group traveled to Lisbon, to the Canary Islands, and on to Trinidad, an island off the coast of Venezuela. They sailed up the Orinoco River in Venezuela but never found El Dorado. A year later, Raleigh published a book about this trip — *The Discovery of Guiana*.

After Elizabeth I died and her cousin James I ascended the English throne, Raleigh's political situation became quite tenuous. James suspected Raleigh of trying to prevent his ascension to the throne and revoked the numerous offices and privileges given to him by Elizabeth. In 1603, Raleigh was accused of treason by King James and sentenced to death. Fortunately for Raleigh, public opinion turned in his favor, and his death sentence was suspended. Instead, he was banished to the Tower of London. During his time in prison, Raleigh's wife and son were often permitted to live with him and he was visited by scholars and poets. He also worked on a book, *The History of the World*, for Henry, the Prince of Wales.

After more than a decade in the Tower, Raleigh was released in 1616 and allowed to leave England to lead another expedition to search for gold in South America. Although King James ordered Raleigh and his men not to invade Spanish territory, some of the men disobeyed the king's orders and attacked the Spanish in the area. When Raleigh returned to England, James ordered his execution under the original sentence of treason. In 1618, Sir Walter Raleigh was beheaded. Fearless to the end, he joked with his executioner and gave the signal for the ax to fall. Supposedly, he said, "This is a sharp medicine, but it is a sure cure for all diseases."[3]

Christopher Marlowe
Public Domain [Some question exists as to whether the sitter for this portrait was actually Marlowe, but it is presumed so.]

IMPACT

- Sir Francis Drake was the first Englishman to visit the west coast of North America and to sail in the Pacific and Indian oceans, leading to increased English interest in that part of the world.

- Drake was the leader of the second expedition to sail around the world.

- Drake was a commander in the English defeat of the Spanish Armada, which led to the decline of Spain as a world colonial power.

- Sir Walter Raleigh was the first individual known to attempt establishing an English colony in North America.

LESSON 8

ATMOSPHERE

HENRY HUDSON

Little is known about the personal life of the English navigator and explorer Henry Hudson. Even the date of his birth is uncertain. Some sources believe that Henry began sailing as a cabin boy at the age of sixteen. Whatever his training and experience, by 1607 Hudson had gained a reputation as an experienced and skilled navigator.

SAMUEL DE CHAMPLAIN

French navigator and mapmaker Samuel de Champlain was born in Brouage, a small seaport on the Bay of Biscay. His father and uncle, apparently experienced sea captains, were responsible for teaching Samuel navigational skills. As a young adult, Champlain joined the French army and served until 1598. From 1599 to 1601, he sailed on voyages to Mexico, Panama, and the West Indies.

Henry Hudson
Library of Congress, Prints and Photographs Division [LC-USZ62-128969]

The Hudson River
Library of Congress, Prints and Photographs Division [LC-USZ62-43584]

Hudson's third and fourth expeditions

EVENT

HUDSON'S EXPLORATIONS

Between 1607 and 1611, Hudson made four voyages to America — three for the English and one for the Dutch. During these expeditions he explored parts of the Arctic Ocean and a large part of northeastern North America. His goal was to find a passage to the Far East. Although Hudson was a competent navigator and a courageous leader, he also could be headstrong and often mismanaged his crews. By playing favorites and allowing morale to suffer dangerously, he made himself susceptible to mutinies.

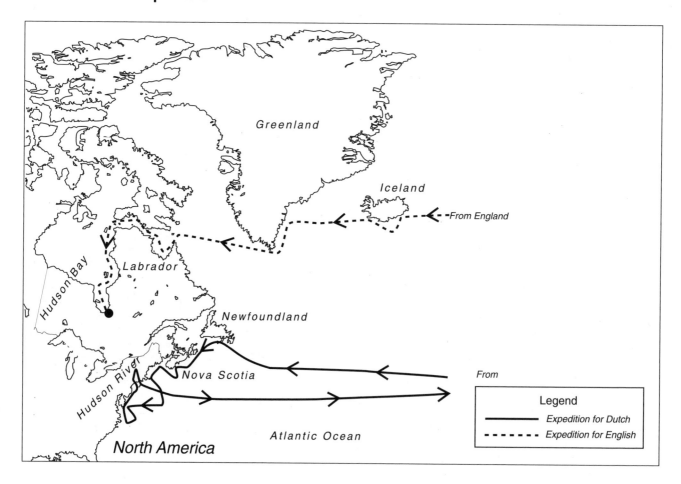

First Expedition (1607)

Hudson's first expedition, as well as his second, was sponsored by the English Muscovy Company. Hudson's grandfather was one of this company's founders, and several of his uncles and cousins were company agents or sailors.

On his first voyage of exploration, Hudson was accompanied on his ship, the *Hopewell*, by his young son, John, and ten crew members. His goal for this trip was to find a passage to the Far East by going straight across the North Pole. Traveling northeast along the shoreline of Greenland, Hudson sailed farther north than any previous explorer. He was amazed by the number of walruses and whales that they saw, but numerous icebergs finally forced them to head back home.

Icebergs
Library of Congress, Prints and Photographs Division [LC-USZC4-8296]

Second Expedition (1608)

The following year, Hudson left on another expedition sponsored by the Muscovy Company. They prepared the *Hopewell* for the voyage by strengthening its hulls, installing thicker masts, and stocking more provisions. Exploring the Arctic Ocean northeast of Norway, Hudson and his men were once again prevented from going farther by large numbers of massive icebergs. Hudson was forced to return home without succeeding in his goal to find a shortcut to China and Japan.

Third Expedition (1609)

Invited to Amsterdam by the Dutch East India Company in the fall of 1608, Hudson was hired by that company to continue his search for a shorter route to the Orient. Sailing on the *Halve Maan* with about twenty Dutch and English sailors, Hudson made use of maps made by the Amsterdam cartographer Jodocus Hondius. He and his men traveled first to Newfoundland, then to the Kennebec River in Maine, and finally farther south to the Hudson River. The Dutch and English sailors were not able to communicate well with each other, and fights often arose among the crew members. They also grumbled about the cold weather and their seasickness, which some sources believe was the reason that Hudson headed south.

Replica of the *Halve Maan*
Library of Congress, Prints and Photographs Division [LC-USZ62-72068]

Although Henry Hudson was not the first European to discover the Hudson River, he was the first to sail up that river for any distance. He explored the river inland almost as far as Albany, looking for a passage to Asia. During this expedition, Hudson also entered the Chesapeake Bay and sailed into Delaware Bay, dropping anchor off Cape Henlopen. As a result of Hudson's third voyage, the Dutch laid claim to land in North America.

Fourth Expedition (1610) and Final Years

Hudson was once again commissioned by a company of English merchants to find a passageway to Asia across the northern part of the

Champlain's explorations

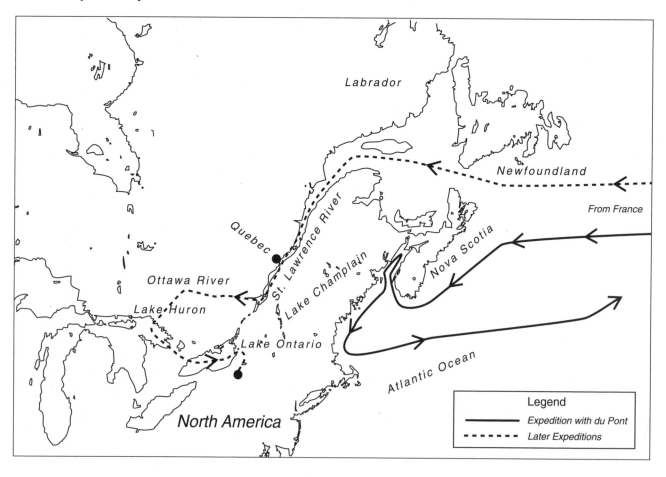

world. Sailing on the *Discovery*, Hudson traveled to Iceland, then to Greenland, and through icebergs to North America.

Entering what is now called the Hudson Strait, south of Baffin Island, he maneuvered around the edges of Hudson Bay and James Bay. Hudson's hope was that this strait would lead to an ocean. In reality it only led to a bay.

Forced by ice to spend the winter in the area, Hudson and his men had little to eat at first. Eventually they began catching ducks and sea birds, but many of the crew remained sick from scurvy. Disheartened by sickness, bitterly cold weather, and food shortages, the crew eventually mutinied. Hudson, his son, and seven others were placed in a small boat without food and water and set adrift. They were never heard from again, and no attempt was ever made to search for them. The surviving members of the expedition returned to England. Some sources believe that they were sent to prison for mutiny; others maintain that they were never punished.

Split Rock on Lake Champlain
Library of Congress, Prints and Photographs Division [LC-USZ62-69181]

CHAMPLAIN'S EXPLORATIONS

During the period from 1603 to 1612, Champlain visited America on five different occasions. In 1603 he joined a French fur-trading expedition led by Francois Grave du Pont. Champlain served as a geographer for this group, which explored the Gaspé Peninsula, the Gulf of St. Lawrence, and the St. Lawrence River as far as the Lachine Rapids. When he returned to France, Champlain brought pelts and dried fish with him, ensuring good profits for the expedition's investors.

A year later in 1604, Champlain returned to North America with another French expedition. The purpose of this trip was to continue the search for the Northwest Passage and to look for a site suitable for a permanent French settlement. From 1605 to 1607, Champlain was involved in exploring and charting the coast from the Bay of Fundy south as far as Cape Cod and Martha's Vineyard. As a result of his careful surveying, Champlain was able to produce accurate maps of the region. He has been called the first cartographer of New England.

In 1608 Champlain founded and named the first permanent French settlement in the New World at Quebec. From this settlement

Samuel de Champlain
Line drawing courtesy of Amy Pak

Algonquin man
Library of Congress, Prints and Photographs
Division [LC-USZC4-4603]

Engraving of Huron Indians
Library of Congress, Prints and Photographs
Division [LC-USZ62-57966]

he made many excursions into the unknown west and discovered Lake Champlain on the border of New York state and Vermont. Champlain also established a fur-trading post at Montreal and reached Lake Huron and much of the region near Lake Ontario. These French settlements in the New World became known as New France. During his years in North America, the French explorer returned several times to France to raise money for Quebec and to bring over more families.

Sometime around 1609, Champlain decided to befriend the Huron and Algonquin tribes, believing that this would prevent Indian attacks on Quebec and make it easier for the French to trade furs and to explore. This friendship led to the French decision to ally with the Huron in their battles with the Iroquois, who lived in nearby New York. The result was 150 years of bitterness and hostility between the French and the Iroquois.

In 1629, Quebec was captured by the English. Champlain was taken to England as a prisoner but eventually allowed to return to France. He spent much of his time in captivity writing about his explorations. In 1633, Quebec became free of English control, and Champlain returned to the New World. He continued to serve as governor of New France until he died of a stroke on Christmas Day in 1635.

IMPACT

- Henry Hudson was the first European known to sail up the Hudson River.

- Hudson was the reason the Dutch presence was established in North America and the English claimed the Hudson Bay area.

- Hudson's name was given to an important bay, strait, and river in North America; and he contributed significantly to the geographical knowledge of the northeastern region of North America.

- Samuel de Champlain became known as the father of New France. He was a successful colonizer and administrator.

- Champlain produced an extensive body of writing about New France as well as excellent maps of the area.

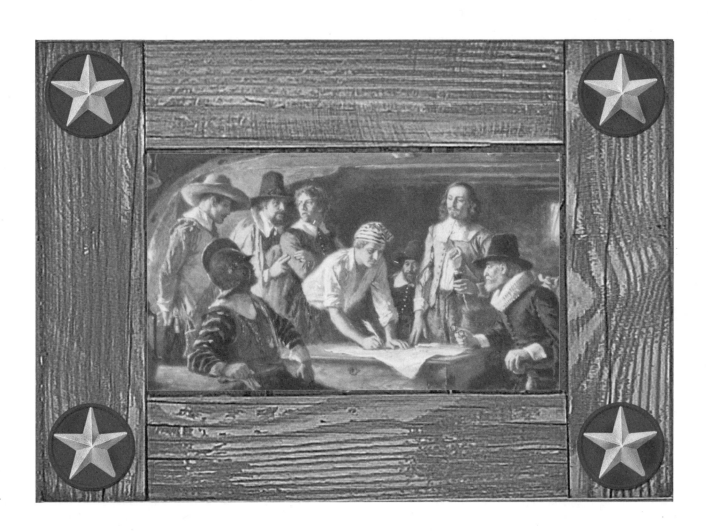

UNIT TWO
THE PERIOD OF COLONIZATION

Lessons 9 — 16

At the beginning of the seventeenth century, England, Spain, France, the Netherlands, and Sweden all claimed land in North America. Over the next one hundred years, English colonies developed along the Atlantic coast from Maine to Georgia. The Spanish held on to Florida, while seeking to extend north into Georgia and the Carolinas. Swedish and Dutch colonies were planted in New York, New Jersey, and Delaware. However, by 1670 these mid-Atlantic colonies had been taken over by the English. After the French established their first North American settlement at Quebec, they proceeded to take control of most of eastern Canada.

As more and more settlers came to North America, disputes arose over territorial boundaries. Wars were fought to settle these claims. By the end of the seventeenth century, the two countries with the most territory in North America were England and France. In the mid-eighteenth century these two nations fought for control of North America in the French and Indian War (1754 — 1763). When England won this war, it gained control of French Canada.

By 1750, the English had established thirteen colonies on the eastern seaboard of North America. These colonies were divided into three distinct regions:

- New England colonies: Massachusetts, Rhode Island, Connecticut, and New Hampshire
- Middle colonies: New York, New Jersey, Pennsylvania, and Delaware
- Southern colonies: Virginia, Maryland, North Carolina, South Carolina, and Georgia

Although a family could move from one English colony to another without major readjustment, there *were* differences among individual colonies and even greater distinctions among the three regional groups.

There were two primary motives behind the establishment of English colonies in America — economic and religious. Several of the thirteen colonies were established as havens for religious groups undergoing persecution in the homeland. Other colonies were formed primarily as a means to make a profit. Most of these colonies were founded and developed by joint stock companies, chartered by the English crown, and made up of private investors. The English monarchy, merchants, and businessmen looked upon the colonies as a source of valuable raw products and as a market for English goods. With widespread unemployment in England and a population increase, colonization also provided a place for the poor and surplus population to be sent to start a new life.

After 1680, England ceased to be the chief source of immigrants coming to America. Thousands of refugees were arriving from all over Europe, seeking to escape the ravages of war or poverty. From 1690 until 1775, the population of the thirteen colonies doubled every twenty-five years, reaching 2.5 million on the eve of the American Revolution. Only then was the word *American* first used to refer to these European immigrants living in the thirteen colonies on the Atlantic seaboard.

All American History

LESSON 9

The Virginia Colony . . . . EST. 1607 A.D.

ATMOSPHERE

VIRGINIA CHARTERS

Until the early seventeenth century, England had not been in a strong position to establish colonies in America. Because they were frequently at war with other European nations, the English had not been able to spare the ships or money needed to start settlements in the New World. However, in 1604 England finally signed a peace treaty with Spain, freeing it to begin thinking seriously about colonizing in America. At that time the only European colony on the continent of North America was the Spanish colony at St. Augustine, founded in 1565.

In the early 1600s, the English king, James I, issued a joint charter to two stock companies — the Plymouth Company and the London Company. This official royal document authorized these two companies to settle the area in America that the English called Virginia. The Virginia Company of London was given permission to settle southern Virginia, the land south of the Chesapeake Bay. The Virginia Company of Plymouth received the right to colonize northern Virginia, the land north of the Chesapeake Bay.

Captain John Smith
Library of Congress, Prints and Photographs Division [LC-USZ62-55182]

During December of 1606, an expedition planned by the London Company set sail from England to Virginia. Commanded by Captain Christopher Newport, the expedition consisted of three small wooden ships: the *Godspeed*, the *Discovery*, and the *Susan Constant*. More than one hundred English men and boys were on board, along with food, tools, and supplies.

The last English attempt at colonization in America had been the settlement sponsored by Sir Walter Raleigh at Roanoke (1587 – 1590). Even fifteen years later, the English still came to America with the hope of finding some of those missing from Roanoke's Lost Colony. There was also a continuing desire to look for a Northwest Passage to Asia as well to search for gold and other valuables (like the Spanish had found in some of their American colonies).

On the voyage across the Atlantic, the three English ships were battered by winter storms. There was also much unrest among the colonists on board, who were crammed together and often hungry. A feisty soldier-adventurer named Captain John Smith was accused of mutiny and arrested. His enemies wanted to hang Smith, but Captain Newport refused to allow them to do so. By the time the three ships reached Virginia, at least thirty-four people had died at sea.

Finally, after a four-month voyage, the expedition sighted land in April 1607. Sailing into the Chesapeake Bay, the three ships anchored near an elbow of beach. The English named this site Cape Henry, in honor of Prince Henry (the oldest son of King James I). The colonists planted a cross at Cape Henry and thanked God for their safe arrival. Then Captain Newport opened a sealed metal box, which had been placed into his care by the London Company. This box contained the names of seven colonists chosen by the company to serve on the colony's local governing council. One of the names on the list was John Smith, who was still under arrest.

The box from the London Company also contained instructions for the council to choose a site for settlement many miles inland in order to provide for the colony's protection against possible Spanish attacks. To follow these instructions, the English explored the Chesapeake Bay area for several weeks. Unable to find a suitable location, they left the mouth of the bay and sailed up a nearby river, which they named the James River in honor of King James. Looking for a naturally defensible location, the English finally discovered a peninsula sixty miles from the mouth of the bay. They decided to plant their colony there, and they named it James Towne (again to recognize their king).

EVENT

ESTABLISHMENT OF JAMESTOWN

The colonists immediately set to work building rough huts for shelter. By June of 1607, they had also constructed a tiny triangular fort, surrounded by a fence of wooden stakes (for protection against the Native Americans in the area). A group of about thirty colonists had already been attacked by a small band of natives back at Cape Henry. Inspired by the success of the Spanish colonists in finding gold in the New World, many of the first settlers at Jamestown were eager to begin searching for gold. Their hope was to find gold quickly and easily and then return to England. The colonists didn't even bother to plant crops because they were so preoccupied with hunting for gold.

John Smith's map of Virginia
Library of Congress, Prints and Photographs Division [LC-USZ62-116706]

Many of the first colonists at Jamestown were ill equipped to survive the physical and emotional hardships of settling in the wilderness. At least a third of the colonists were gentlemen, with no experience in farming, hunting, fishing, or trapping. The English also continued to fight among themselves and received little incentive from the London Company to work hard. Each settler was given the same pay, no matter how much he worked, and no one was allowed to own property.

Unfortunately, the location chosen for Jamestown was not a favorable one for colonization. During the summer, the peninsula turned into a swamp and became a breeding ground for mosquitoes. The mosquitoes caused malaria, which along with dysentery killed many of the first colonists. The peninsula also did not have a good supply of fresh water or fertile soil, and it had served as a hunting ground for a nearby tribe. By winter, the colonists' supplies had run out, and many of them began to starve. When a supply ship with more colonists arrived in January of 1608, fewer than forty colonists were still alive. And no gold had been found!

By the fall of 1608, the Jamestown colonists had elected Captain Smith president of their council. He had demonstrated his courage and resourcefulness by leaving the settlement to go on scouting expeditions for food and badly needed supplies. Smith made friends with the native Algonquian and learned to plant corn the Indian way, to hunt, to fish, and to dig a well to get pure water. A natural trader, Smith was also able to obtain food for the Jamestown settlers by taking blankets, shovels, and axes to the Algonquian villages. As

The Virginia Colony

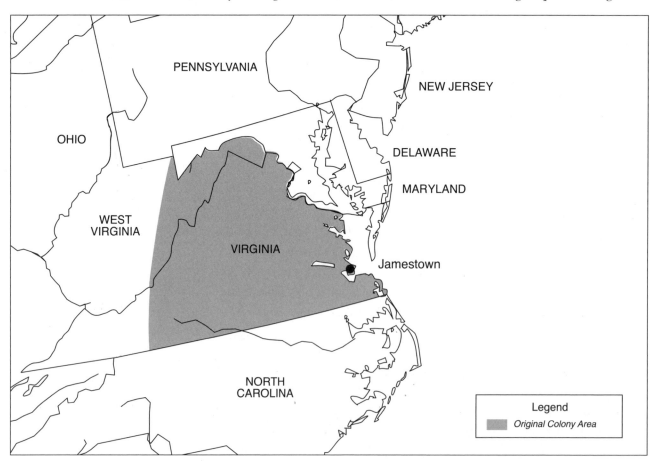

the leader of the Jamestown colony, Smith insisted that every person contribute to the work necessary for the settlement to survive. Smith's rule was "he that will not work shall not eat." As a result of John Smith's organizational and motivational leadership, only twelve out of two hundred of the colonists died during the second winter (1608 – 1609).

Unfortunately, in the fall of 1609, Smith left Jamestown and returned to England. Most sources maintain that the reason he returned was because he had been badly burned. Smith's departure brought an end to the colony's harmonious relationships with the Algonquian. The Algonquian chief, Powhatan, and his people began to look at Jamestown with increasing fear and anger, resenting the loss of their hunting grounds. They began attacking the fort at Jamestown periodically, and they refused to trade with the settlers. After Smith returned to England, the London Company replaced the colony's council with a governor.

Chief Powhatan
Line drawing courtesy of Amy Pak

By the end of 1609, over four hundred new English settlers had arrived in Jamestown. To attract new colonists, the London Company had advertised free passages to America for those willing to put in seven years of unpaid labor. English immigrants who took advantage of this offer were known as indentured servants. Some of these indentured servants were individuals who had held high social positions in England but had fallen into hard times. Others were prisoners released from jail on condition that they go to the colonies.

The winter of 1609 – 1610 became known as the starving time in the history of Jamestown. During these months there was rampant death in the colony, due to starvation, dysentery, and malaria. In order to survive, colonists ate cats, dogs, horses, rats, and snakes and chewed on shoe leather. In late spring of 1610, two English ships arrived in Jamestown to find the colony in a state of disaster. Many of its buildings had been burned to the ground to keep the settlers warm, and only sixty of its people (10 percent) had survived.

Since many of the passengers on the two English ships had also died (from yellow fever), both groups decided to return to England rather than stay in Jamestown. In June, the group of Jamestown survivors boarded the English ships and floated down the James River with the passengers who had decided to sail back to the homeland. They had traveled less than fifteen miles when they encountered a new expedition of English ships arriving with supplies and three hundred new colonists. Also on board was the new governor of the settlement, Lord De La Warr.

Under De La Warr's leadership, Jamestown was rebuilt. The new governor also established military rule in Jamestown. Men were ranked from private to captain and marched to work and to church two times a day. Anyone who disobeyed De La Warr's orders was punished. Eventually, some of the Jamestown settlers became so unhappy that they ran away to live with the Algonquian, and others escaped on passing ships. Finally, in 1616, the London Company ended the harsh military rule in Jamestown because the company was having trouble finding people willing to immigrate to the colony.

POCAHONTAS

In 1616, John Smith wrote that the Algonquian princess Pocahontas helped the colony avoid famine and death. This daughter of Powhatan, chief of the Algonquian nation, was named Matoaka at birth but nicknamed Pocahontas, which meant Little Wanton (playful and hard to control). The first meeting of Pocahontas and John Smith became a legendary story, the subject of controversy among scholars. Soon after the establishment of Jamestown in 1607, Smith was taken captive and brought to the official residence of Powhatan. There, according to the legend, Pocahontas (ten or eleven at the time) saved Smith from being clubbed to death by her father. Some scholars believe that this incident was actually part of a traditional Algonquian mock execution and salvation ceremony and that Pocahontas's actions were part of the ritual. Other Native American scholars maintain that this entire incident likely never happened, especially because it was used by the English to justify waging war on Powhatan's people.

Apparently, Pocahontas frequently visited Jamestown in the early years of the settlement. She brought messages from her father and

Pocahontas (Rebecca)
Library of Congress, Prints and Photographs Division [LC-D416-18753]

accompanied natives who wanted to trade food and furs for the colonists' trinkets and hatchets. When relations between the colonists and the Algonquian deteriorated, Pocahontas's visits became less frequent. Then, in 1612, Pocahontas (seventeen at the time) was apparently kidnapped by Captain Samuel Argall and held for ransom. After receiving the English demands, Powhatan sent some of the ransom and asked that his daughter be treated well. Pocahontas was taken to Jamestown and then moved to a new settlement at Henrico, where she enjoyed relative freedom. She was educated in Christianity and fell in love with an English colonist, John Rolfe.

In 1613, Pocahontas was released. When she returned to her father, she asked Powhatan for permission to marry Rolfe, and he gave his consent. Pocahontas was baptized, given the Christian name Rebecca,

Marriage of Pocahontas to John Rolfe
Library of Congress, Prints and Photographs Division [LC-USZ62-5242]

and married Rolfe on April 5, 1614. Their union resulted in a spirit of peace and goodwill between the colonists and the Native Americans for a time. In 1616, Pocahontas, her husband, and their son Thomas traveled with a group of English and Algonquian to London to secure further financial support for the Virginia settlement. The arrival of Pocahontas in London was well publicized, and she was presented to King James I and the rest of London society. She also saw John Smith again, whom she had believed to be dead. In March of 1617, Pocahontas became ill from pneumonia, or possibly tuberculosis, and died as she and her family were beginning their journey back to America.

A PROFITABLE AND PRODUCTIVE JAMESTOWN

The London Company had become quite unhappy that Jamestown was not making money. Because the company was suffering financial troubles, it needed its colony to produce a profitable export. Finally, in 1612, Jamestown discovered a cash crop that would guarantee its economic survival. That year, John Rolfe developed a way to grow a mild, high-quality tobacco in Jamestown that would sell well in England.

The year 1619 was a significant year in Jamestown's early history because approximately ninety English women were brought over from the homeland as potential brides for men in the colony. These women had been carefully screened and determined to be of good moral character. Because a successful suitor was required to pay 120 pounds of tobacco for his bride, these women were called tobacco brides. Now family units could be formed in Jamestown, providing even more motivation for the men to build permanent homes and develop a stable community.

A second major development in 1619 was the establishment of a general assembly for Jamestown, known as the House of Burgesses. The governor was instructed to divide the colony into eleven districts; each district would elect two burgesses, or representatives. This group of twenty-two burgesses would then meet to make laws for the colony. Although these laws could be ignored by the governor, this first representative assembly in the English colonies marked the beginning of self-government in colonial America.

The final significant event in 1619 was the sale of African slaves (by a Dutch trader) to the London Company for the first time. In the beginning, Virginia farmers treated the Africans shipped to their colony in the same way that they treated white indentured servants. After a period of bondage, the Africans were given their freedom. However, by the second half of the seventeenth century, the Virginia Colony had passed laws that eliminated this custom. Planters had found that crops were grown most efficiently on plantations that employed large labor forces, and black slavery became established as a lifelong condition.

The first meeting of the Assembly of Virginia
Library of Congress, Prints and Photographs Division [LC-USZ62-890]

FIRST MEETING OF THE ASSEMBLY IN VIRGINIA.

By 1622, Powhatan, the Algonquian chief, had died. The new chief, Opechancanough, pretended to be friendly with the Jamestown settlers but secretly planned to drive them out in a well-organized attack. In March, the native tribesmen attacked the colony and within a few hours slaughtered over three hundred colonists. Jamestown was nearly destroyed, and the London Company never recovered from the massacre. By 1624, King Charles I had revoked the London Company's charter. Jamestown became a royal colony with the English king responsible for managing the colony's daily affairs.

THE BACON REBELLION

As Virginia became established as a colony, wealthy tobacco planters controlled the coastal tobacco lands called the Tidewater. When indentured servants were freed, they were given land to settle in the interior of Virginia. There they faced increasing attacks from Native Americans. The governor of the colony repeatedly refused to help defend the frontiersmen against these attacks. When the governor failed to offer them protection, the frontiersmen accused him and the wealthy tobacco planters of being more interested in protecting their fur trade with the natives than in helping to protect their fellow colonists.

After a particularly destructive Native American attack in 1676, a young frontier planter named Nathaniel Bacon asked Governor Berkeley for a commission that would allow him to go to war against the Indians. When the governor refused, Bacon went ahead anyway and led a frontier army against the natives. Although Governor Berkeley denounced Bacon as a traitor, he did not stay to confront the frontiersman as Bacon and his followers moved toward Jamestown. The governor fled, and Bacon and his men burned the city to the ground. Soon afterward, Bacon died from a fever and the rebellion ended. Although Bacon had become a legendary hero, twenty of his followers were hanged by Berkeley without a trial. The Virginia House of Burgesses responded to Bacon's Rebellion by passing legislation to curb the political power of the wealthy landowners and to increase popular participation in government. Although most

Nathaniel Bacon
Library of Congress, Prints and Photographs Division [LC-USZ62-91133]

of these measures were soon repealed, the principle of representative government had begun to take root in the Virginia Colony.

IMPACT

- Jamestown, established by the Virginia Company of London in 1607, was the first permanent English colony in North America. It was located on a peninsula sixty miles from the mouth of the Chesapeake Bay.

- The first Virginia colonists, eager to find gold quickly and return to England, were ill equipped to survive life in the wilderness. The organizational and motivational leadership of Captain John Smith was instrumental to their survival.

- After enduring several periods of starvation and many other hardships, the Virginia colonists were finally able to discover a cash crop that guaranteed their economic success — a high-quality tobacco developed by John Rolfe.

- The pivotal year of 1619 brought tobacco brides, African slaves, and the House of Burgesses (a representative assembly) to the Virginia Colony.

- Bacon's Rebellion in 1676 led to increased popular participation in the government of the Virginia Colony.

LESSON 10

The Massachusetts Colony . . . . EST. 1620 A.D.

ATMOSPHERE

THE PURITANS

Religion did not play an important role in the development of the Jamestown colony. Most of the early colonists there were members of the English state church, the Church of England (the only religion allowed under the colony's charter). However, settlers of other faiths were allowed to live in peace in Jamestown, and there was little religious persecution there. In the establishment of the Massachusetts Bay Colony, religion was a crucial factor.

During the reign of Henry VIII, England had officially become Protestant. Most of the English were members of the Church of England, which was headed by the king and called the established church. A group in England known as the Puritans believed that the Church of England had kept too many Catholic rituals and requirements and wanted these removed from the state church. Within this group of Puritans was a smaller group who wanted to separate from the Church of England and form a completely new church. They called themselves Saints, but their enemies called them Separatists.

In the early 1600s, King James I began to persecute the Separatists, imprisoning them to keep them from practicing their religion. A

A Puritan woman
Library of Congress, Prints and Photographs Division [LC-USZC4-4290]

group of Separatists from Scrooby, a village in northeastern England, decided to flee to Holland. They eventually settled in the university town of Leiden, where they were allowed to worship as they pleased and establish their own church. However, after almost a decade of living in Holland, the Separatists became restless. Coming from a rural background, they did not enjoy living in a city with its factory work and worldly temptations. They also were concerned that their children were forgetting their English language and heritage. Finally, they became worried that England might go to war with Spain and that Holland would be recaptured by the Spanish.

Thus, a group of about one hundred Separatists from Scrooby petitioned the Virginia Company of London, asking to be allowed to settle in Virginia. They had read John Smith's *Description of New England* and had decided that they wanted to immigrate to America to plant a colony in which they could establish the ideal church. After two years of negotiations, the Virginia Company granted the Separatists a patent to start a colony in northern Virginia. Although King James I refused to give the group a charter, he indicated that he would not interfere if the Separatists returned peacefully to England in order to sail to America.

THE MASSACHUSETTS BAY COMPANY

During the 1620s, Puritans in England continued to be harassed by King James I and his successor Charles I. A group of these Puritans began meeting together at Cambridge University, which many of them had once attended. They decided that they no longer wanted to live in England without religious freedom, and they began planning to sail to America to establish a holy community in the wilderness.

Influential Puritans in Parliament persuaded King Charles I to grant a royal charter to twenty-six Puritan investors — first called the New England Company but soon changed to the Massachusetts Bay Company. John Winthrop, a Puritan lawyer, was elected to serve as the first governor of the Massachusetts Bay Colony. In a sermon that Winthrop preached to the Puritan settlers in 1630, he used the Biblical reference of a "city upon a hill" to describe their colony.

John Winthrop
Line drawing courtesy of Amy Pak

The word Massachusetts came from an Indian word meaning "at the big hill."

EVENT

ESTABLISHMENT OF PLYMOUTH

On September 16, 1620, 102 English passengers set sail for Virginia on the *Mayflower*. There were men, women, and children on board. Almost half of those sailing were Separatists, headed to America for freedom to practice their religion. The Separatists were willing to work hard to help their colony succeed, and they were not motivated by the

The Massachusetts colony

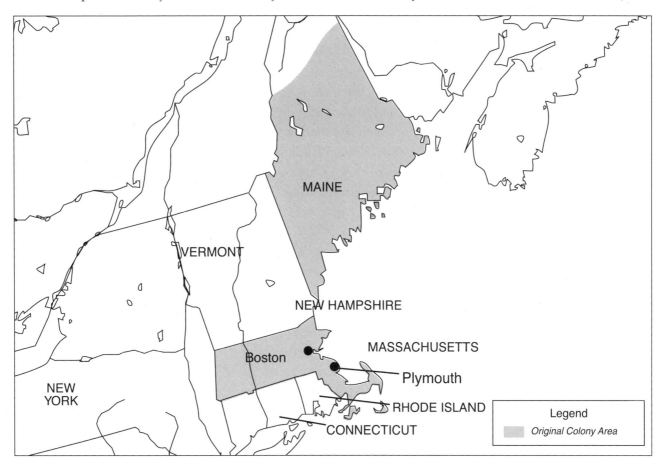

MAINE

VERMONT

NEW HAMPSHIRE

MASSACHUSETTS

Boston

Plymouth

RHODE ISLAND

NEW YORK

CONNECTICUT

Legend
Original Colony Area

The *Mayflower*
Library of Congress, Prints and Photographs
Division [LC-USZ62-3046]

expectation of finding gold and other riches. The other members of the group, whom the Separatists called Strangers, had left England because of problems at home or because of a desire for adventure. Most of the men on board were lower-class tradesmen, not wealthy or well-born gentlemen. Together, these Separatists and Strangers became known as the Pilgrims. Because the Separatists did not insist upon forcing their religious beliefs on the Strangers, the two groups were able to respect each other and work together to plant a new colony.

Crossing the Atlantic on the *Mayflower* took sixty-five days. The ship was quite small and crowded. Each adult was assigned a space of seven feet by two-and-a-half feet below deck; children were given even less. No passengers were allowed on deck, which meant they were forced to live in a dark, foul-smelling place for over two months. Their supply of fresh food eventually ran out during the voyage. However, the Pilgrims had brought lemon juice, beer, and onions with them to prevent scurvy. Many in the group became sick, but only one person died during the voyage. A baby boy, named Oceanus Hopkins, was born as the Pilgrims sailed to America.

Due to navigational errors and a storm that blew them off course, the Pilgrims did not land near Jamestown as planned. In early November, they landed at the tip of Cape Cod at a place named Provincetown, which they recognized from John Smith's maps. The captain of the *Mayflower* refused to sail south down the coast toward Virginia because he felt that it would be dangerous to do so with winter approaching. Before the Pilgrims disembarked, Susan White gave birth to the first English child born in New England — Peregrine White.

Because the *Mayflower* had landed out of the jurisdiction of their Virginia patent, some of the passengers claimed that they no longer had to obey company rules. In order to establish order, the Pilgrims drew up an agreement, which became known as the Mayflower Compact, and asked every adult male to sign it. The forty-one Saints and Strangers who signed the compact pledged to covenant themselves together into a "civil body politic" and to obey the "just and equal" laws of the community. They also pledged their loyalty to King James I. The structure of the Mayflower Compact eventually became a cornerstone for the Declaration of Independence and the U.S. Constitution.

In the name of God, Amen. We, whose names are underwritten, the Loyal Subjects of our dread Sovereign Lord King James, by the Grace of God, of Great Britain, France, and Ireland, King, Defender of the Faith, &c. Having undertaken for the Glory of God, and Advancement of the Christian Faith, and the Honor of our King and Country, a Voyage to plant the first colony in the northern Parts of Virginia; Do by these Presents, solemnly and mutually in the Presence of God and one another, covenant and combine ourselves together into a civil Body Politick, for our better Ordering and Preservation, and

Signing of the Mayflower Compact
Library of Congress, Prints and Photographs Division [LC-USZC4-7155]

Miles Standish
Library of Congress, Prints and Photographs Division [LC-USZ62-83802]

Squanto
Line drawing courtesy of Amy Pak

Furtherance of the Ends aforesaid; And by Virtue hereof do enact, constitute, and frame, such just and equal Laws, Ordinances, Acts, Constitutions, and Offices, from time to time, as shall be thought most meet and convenient for the general Good of the Colony; unto which we promise all due Submission and Obedience. In WITNESS whereof we have hereunto subscribed our names at Cape Cod the eleventh of November, in the Reign of our Sovereign Lord King James of England, France, and Ireland, the eighteenth and of Scotland, the fifty-fourth. Anno Domini, 1620

—from the *Mayflower Compact*

A London merchant, John Carver, was elected as the first governor of the new colony at Plymouth. Captain Miles Standish, a Stranger hired to be in charge of building the settlement and dealing with the Indians, set out with exploring parties across the Cape Cod Bay. Standish and his men sailed around the cape to an area named Plimoth (later spelled Plymouth) on Smith's map, where he found a protected harbor. Carrying their muskets and swords, Standish and his party went ashore at Plymouth. There they found a good supply of fresh water and fields that had already been cleared. They did not find any people. Believing this was the place that God had prepared for them, the Pilgrims landed at Plymouth on December 21.

BUILDING A COMMUNITY AT PLYMOUTH

The Pilgrims began building their colony on a snowy Christmas Day in 1620. The location for their settlement was not ideal — a bleak, windy coastal area with thin, rocky soil. The colonists used wood to build their houses and cut reeds to thatch their roofs. The largest building planned by the Pilgrims was their church, which would also serve as a meeting place and a fort. Day after day that first winter, the colonists worked in the cold. Food was scarce because they had arrived too late to plant crops. Too weak to fight off illness, half of the settlers died by the end of the winter. However, the Pilgrims refused to give up and continued to work tirelessly when they were able to do so.

In the early spring of 1621, the Pilgrims were surprised when a Native American walked into their settlement and said, "Welcome, Englishmen." His name was Samoset, and he had learned English from fishermen and traders who had come to the area. Samoset introduced the Pilgrims to Massasoit, chief of the Wampanoag tribe, with whom Governor Carver signed a treaty of peace that would last for fifty years. When Carver died of a stroke in April, he was replaced as governor by William Bradford. Bradford would continue to treat the Wampanoag with respect and fairness. As long as Massasoit lived, the Wampanoag treaty with the Pilgrims was not broken.

Another Native American who befriended the early Plymouth settlers was Squanto. This great benefactor to the Pilgrims had been

The Pilgrim fathers holding their first meeting for public worship
Library of Congress, Prints and Photographs Division [LC-USZ62-17892]

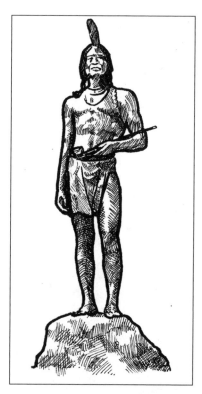

Massasoit
Line drawing courtesy of Amy Pak

kidnapped years earlier by a passing English ship and taken to Europe as a slave. When he finally returned to New England, Squanto found that his people, the Patuxet, had been wiped out by the plague. The Pilgrims believed Squanto to be a special instrument sent to them by God to help them. He taught them how to plant corn, tap maple trees, catch fish, and trap beavers.

While waiting for their first crops to come in, the Pilgrims almost ran out of food. At one point, they were supposedly down to a daily allotment of six kernels of corn per person. When a summer drought threatened their crops, the colonists set aside a day of prayer and fasting. By the end of the day, a gentle rain had begun to fall; the rain continued for the next ten days. After their first harvest in 1621, the Pilgrims invited the Wampanoag tribe to a three-day feast of thanksgiving. Massasoit accepted the invitation, and he and ninety braves came to feast with the fifty surviving colonists. The Pilgrims provided turkeys, geese, ducks, and swans. Only four married women had survived the first winter, and these four oversaw the preparations for this thanksgiving feast.

Near the end of 1621, a ship named the *Fortune* arrived in Plymouth with thirty-five new settlers. However, the *Fortune* had failed to bring food and other badly needed supplies. Nevertheless, the Pilgrims shared what they had with the newcomers. Two years later, two other ships landed at Cape Cod with ninety more colonists. Some of these new settlers were the wives and children of men already in the colony. By 1637, the population of the Plymouth settlement had grown to 549. William Bradford served as the colony's governor for more than thirty years (until 1657) and documented these early years at Plymouth in his book *Of Plimoth Plantation.*

They began now to gather in the small harvest they had, and to fit up their houses and dwellings against winter, being all well recovered in health and strength and had all things in good plenty. For as some were thus employed in affairs abroad, others were exercised in fishing, about cod and bass and other fish, of which they took good store, of which every family had their portion. All the summer there was no want; and now began to come in store of fowl, as winter approached, of which this place did abound when they came first (but afterward decreased by degrees). And besides waterfowl there was a great store of wild turkeys, of which they took many, besides venison, etc. Besides they had about a peck a meal a week to a person, or now since harvest, Indian corn to the proportion. Which made many afterwards write so largely of their plenty here to their friends in England, which were not feigned but true reports.

—from *Of Plimoth Plantation*

Statue of William Bradford
Library of Congress, Prints and Photographs Division [LC-USZ62-35644]

Through hard work and perseverance, the Pilgrims were eventually able to buy out the patent from the Virginia Company of London. Eight Pilgrims — including Miles Standish, William Bradford, John Alden, and William Brewster—formed a holding company to put up the money. This step enabled them to become masters of their own economic fate. However, Plymouth never obtained its own charter and remained a small settlement that prospered modestly from fur trading, fishing, and farming. In 1691, Plymouth became part of Massachusetts Bay and ceased to be a separate colony.

ESTABLISHMENT OF MASSACHUSETTS BAY

By late March of 1620, the Massachusetts Bay Company had four ships ready to set sail for America. By the end of the summer at least fifteen ships and one thousand men, women, and children had made the trip from England to Massachusetts. Unlike the Pilgrims who settled at Plymouth, this group of colonists represented all levels of English society—indentured servants, unskilled workers, craftsmen, yeoman farmers, traders, merchants, lawyers, and gentlemen. The Puritans selected the harbor of Boston as the location of their new colony.

About two hundred of the Puritans died during their first winter in America. Two hundred more decided to return to England the following spring. However, from the very beginning, the colony at Massachusetts Bay seemed destined to prosper. Its colonists were hard-working, ambitious people, who were dedicated to making their settlement a success. Within a year they had established seven towns along the Charles River, including Boston, Watertown, Charlestown, and Dorchester. The dominant structure in each of these towns was the meetinghouse, which served as a church, town hall, and social center. These meetinghouses were usually placed at one end of a field called the common or the green, and then houses were built all around the field. The Massachusetts Bay Company offered prospective settlers free land, and the region's population grew quickly.

The land in Massachusetts was not as fertile as the land around the Chesapeake Bay. Its rocky soil was able to grow tobacco, but the quality of the tobacco was poor. However, flax grew well, and the Puritans planted corn and other vegetables. They also quickly developed a fishing industry, and their dried codfish became an important item of international commerce. As the colonists cleared forests, they built ships to use in trading with England, and soon bustling shipyards dotted the coast.

Under the terms of the Massachusetts Bay charter, the government of the colony was in the hands of the governor, eighteen magistrates, and a General Court. The General Court eventually split into two houses: an upper house consisting of the governor and his assistants and a lower house consisting of two representatives per town. The town's freemen elected these representatives. Eventually, the General Court ruled that freemen must be members of an approved Puritan church. Thus, for over fifty years, no man in Massachusetts could vote unless he belonged to an accepted Puritan congregation (women did not have the right to vote). Although the Puritans believed in religious freedom for themselves, they did not extend that freedom to others.

As Puritans continued to be persecuted in England, increasing numbers of them made their way to America. During the decade of the Great Migration (1630 – 1640), some twenty thousand men and women (many of them Puritans) left England for America. In time, over fifty villages sprang up in the Massachusetts area. However, this wave of immigration declined once Puritans were no longer being persecuted in England. In fact, after the mid-seventeenth century, there would be very little additional European immigration into New England until after the American Revolution.

THE PEQUOT WAR AND KING PHILIP'S WAR

During the colonial period, Massachusetts settlers, along with colonists in nearby Connecticut and Rhode Island, were involved in two major conflicts with New England Indian tribes: the Pequot War (1636 – 1637) and King Philip's War (1675 – 1676). The Pequot War was waged in the Mystic Valley of Connecticut, and King Philip's War took place in eastern Massachusetts (as well as in part of Rhode Island). Both conflicts were fought because the Native Americans of the region resented the English colonists' encroaching upon their lands.

Metacom (King Philip)
Library of Congress, Prints and Photographs Division [LC-USZ62-62742]

During the early years of the Massachusetts Bay Colony, the Wampanoag chief, Massasoit, had asked the Massachusetts General Council to give his two sons, Wamsutta and Metacom, English names. The Council picked the names of two ancient Greek kings — Alexander and Philip. When Massasoit died in 1661, he was succeeded by his son Alexander. However, Alexander soon died, and his young brother Metacom (Philip) became chief.

Philip was a proud, courageous leader, who despised the English for humiliating his people and taking their land away. In 1675, he secretly urged other tribes to join with him and his people in an alliance to drive the English colonists out of New England. During the two years of warfare that followed, more than fifty colonial villages were attacked by this Indian coalition, resulting in the deaths of thousands of colonists and natives. Eventually, however, Philip and his men began to run out of food and to suffer defeats. In the summer of 1676, Philip was captured and killed by an Indian loyal to the English. His head was chopped off and sent as a trophy to Plymouth, where it was displayed on a pole for some twenty-five years. His wife and children and other captured natives were sold into slavery in the West Indies. By the end of King Philip's War, the Wampanoag and Narragansett tribes had been almost completely destroyed.

Sir Edmund Andros
*Library of Congress, Prints and Photographs
Division [LC-USZ62-30882]*

THE DOMINION OF NEW ENGLAND

When Charles II ascended the English throne in 1660, he revoked the Massachusetts Bay charter. The king accused the Massachusetts colonists of exceeding the limits of their charter, engaging in acts of religious intolerance, and violating the Navigation Acts. In 1686 Charles's successor, James II, moved to consolidate New England, New York, and New Jersey into one unit called the Dominion of New England. Appointing Sir Edmund Andros as royal governor over all of the Dominion, the king gave Andros dictatorial powers that allowed him to govern in an oppressive way. James also made no provision for a representative assembly or trial by jury.

In 1689, after the overthrow of James II in the Glorious Revolution, Bostonians called a town meeting for the purpose of dissolving the government of the Dominion of New England. They forced Andros to resign as governor and sent him to England to be tried. Then, in 1691, King William and Queen Mary made Massachusetts (including Plymouth) a royal colony. As a colony of the crown, Massachusetts had a governor, appointed by the monarchy, who was given the right to disapprove of any law passed by the General Court. However, the colonists were allowed to keep the lower house of the General Court, and voting rights were extended to all qualified male property owners.

IMPACT

- Religion played a crucial role in the establishment of the first two permanent English settlements in Massachusetts — Plymouth (established by Separatists fleeing persecution in 1620) and Massachusetts Bay (established by Puritans fleeing persecution in 1630).

- The Mayflower Compact was signed by all the adult males preparing to disembark at Plymouth, and it became a cornerstone of the Declaration of Independence and the U.S. Constitution. The colony established at Plymouth prospered under the leadership of Governor John Winthrop and Captain Miles Standish and with the assistance of Native Americans, such as Massasoit and Squanto.

- The Massachusetts Bay Colony, first established at Boston harbor, was referred to by its governor, John Winthrop, as being like a "city upon a hill." This colony seemed destined to prosper from the beginning and within a year had established seven towns along the Charles River.

- During the colonial period, the Massachusetts settlers, along with colonists in nearby Connecticut and Rhode Island, were involved in two major conflicts with New England Indian tribes — the Pequot War (1636 – 1637) and King Philip's War (1675 – 1767).

LESSON II

ATMOSPHERE

THE LACONIA COMPANY

In 1622, King James I gave two English merchants, Sir Fernando Gorges and John Mason, the right to start a colony in the northern part of New England. Their land grant was called the main (Maine) because it was located on the mainland of a coast dotted by islands. It included New Hampshire and part of what became the state of Maine. Mason and Gorges formed the Laconia Company and sent two groups of settlers to the main. These settlers did not come to America to escape religious persecution; they came to make money.

RHODES OR ROODT EYLAND

Historians have two theories concerning the origin of the name, Rhode Island. Some believe that the explorer Verrazano returned to France after exploring New England and described for the king a triangular island in the Narragansett Bay. Verrazano supposedly told the French king that this island reminded him of the Greek island of Rhodes in the Aegean Sea. Other sources attribute the colony's naming to a Dutch explorer, Adriaen Block. When Block

1614 Map by Adriaen Block
Public Domain

127

explored the Narragansett Bay, he is said to have found an island with red clay along its shore. He called that island *Roodt Eyland*, which means Red Island in Dutch.

The first known European colonist to settle in Rhode Island was William Blackstone, a minister of the Church of England. Blackstone had left England in 1623, becoming the first and only settler at that time of Shawmitt, later renamed Boston. This minister was apparently a hermit, who enjoyed reading and tending his orchard. When the Puritans arrived in Massachusetts in 1630, Blackstone left the area and traveled fifty miles southwest of Boston through the wilderness to present-day Rhode Island. There he built a farm that he called Study Hill, planted another orchard, and resumed his reading.

The New Hampshire, Rhode Island, and Connecticut colonies

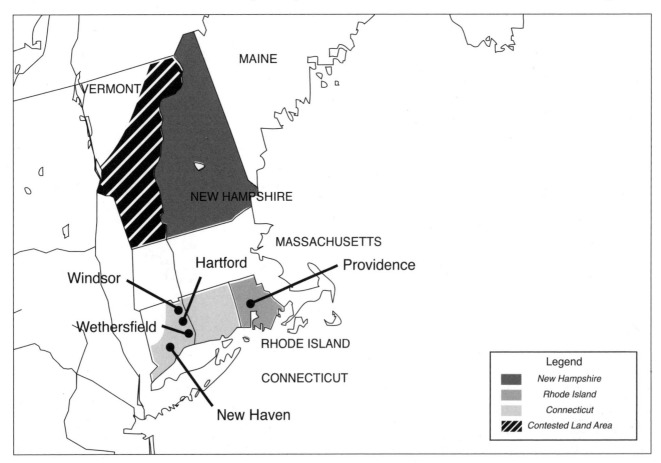

MAINE

VERMONT

NEW HAMPSHIRE

MASSACHUSETTS

Hartford   Providence

Windsor

Wethersfield

RHODE ISLAND

CONNECTICUT

New Haven

Legend

New Hampshire

Rhode Island

Connecticut

Contested Land Area

FUR TRADERS AND PILGRIMS

During 1633, three different groups arrived in what became known as Connecticut—a name derived from a Mohican word that means "at the long tidal river." The first group traveled from New Netherlands to establish a fur-trading post on the Connecticut River. This post, manned by a few soldiers and traders, never became part of a permanent Dutch settlement in the area.

Three months later, an English group from Plymouth sailed past the Dutch fort on its way to establish its own trading post at Windsor. These Pilgrims had been invited to the Connecticut Valley by two Indian chiefs who hoped to trade with them and gain their help in driving out the warlike Pequot tribe. In addition to the Dutch and the Pilgrims, a Massachusetts fur trader named John Oldham also came to Connecticut in 1633 and established a small outpost at Wethersfield.

EVENT

ESTABLISHMENT OF NEW HAMPSHIRE

The first group of English settlers arrived in the area in 1623. This group, led by David Thomson, came over to America on the *Jonathan* and included no women or children. These settlers had been given adequate provisions and quickly began cutting timber and catching fish, both of which they shipped to England. This fishing and timbering settlement, begun by the Laconia Company, was located about fifty miles north of the location where Boston would later be settled. It prospered and grew in a modest way. However, the much-desired fur trade never materialized from this group.

Eventually, the Laconia Company folded and Gorges and Mason divided their holdings at the Piscataqua River. Mason's claim became known as New Hampshire after Mason's home in Hampshire, England. The land held by Gorges would eventually become the state of Maine. Gorges's claim was taken over by Massachusetts and remained part of Massachusetts until Maine entered the Union as the twenty-third state.

John Wheelwright
Public Domain

Two Puritan towns, Exeter and Hampton, were established in this area around 1640. Exeter was founded by a Puritan minister, John Wheelwright, who had been banished from the Bay colony due to his religious beliefs. Since the first settlers in New Hampshire had been members of the Church of England, their religious differences with those in the new Puritan towns kept the settlements from uniting. However, the New Hampshire settlers soon realized that they were not strong enough to stand alone against attacks from the Native Americans or French Canadians. In 1641, they appealed to Massachusetts for help, and for the next thirty-nine years they would remain under Massachusetts's authority. Finally, around 1680, Charles II declared New Hampshire to be a royal colony separate from Massachusetts.

After the establishment and collapse of the Dominion government, the New Hampshire towns could not agree on a draft for a new plan of government. Thus, in 1690, New Hampshire once again asked Massachusetts for temporary annexation. Only two years later, the English monarchs William and Mary re-established New Hampshire as a separate royal colony. However, in the years that followed, New Hampshire would continue to struggle with internal disputes, bitterly cold winters, rocky soil unsuitable for farming, bloody frontier wars with Native Americans, and boundary disputes with Massachusetts.

ESTABLISHMENT OF RHODE ISLAND

In 1631, a Puritan minister named Roger Williams and his wife arrived in the Massachusetts Bay Colony. A gifted and charismatic young man, Williams was at first welcomed by the leaders of Boston. He spent time getting to know the Native Americans in the area, showed great compassion toward the suffering, and attracted many followers. However, Williams also did not hesitate to speak out for religious liberty and freedom of conscience, and the Puritan leaders in Massachusetts soon decided that he was too stubborn and opinionated.

According to Roger Williams, the Massachusetts Bay Colony had no legal title to its land. His opinion was that the land still belonged to the natives of the region because the Puritans had not paid them for it. Williams also maintained that persecuting others in the name of Christianity was sinful, and he called the forced conversion of Indians to Christianity inhumane. Finally, Williams preached that state and church should be separate — that the government should not support any one church and that the church should have no say in the government.

The Puritan leadership in Massachusetts did not know how to handle Roger Williams. Even Governor Winthrop, Williams's lifelong friend, often disagreed with him. In 1635, Massachusetts passed a law that made church attendance mandatory and imposed a tax that would be used to support the church. When Williams condemned this as government interference in religious matters, he was brought

Roger Williams
Library of Congress, Prints and Photographs Division [LC-USZ62-15057]

before the General Court, tried as a danger to the government, and banished from the colony. However, before Williams could be shipped back to England, he escaped into the forest, leaving his wife and two daughters behind.

When Williams left Massachusetts Bay in January 1636, he headed south to a Wampanoag village on Narragansett Bay, just outside the jurisdiction of Massachusetts. Williams had already established a friendly relationship with these Native Americans and knew some of their language. During his first winter away from Massachusetts Bay, this minister's Wampanoag friends helped him to survive, sharing with him their wigwams and food.

By the spring of 1636, several of Williams's friends had joined him. This small group from the Massachusetts Bay Colony eventually settled on a peninsula located between two rivers flowing into the Narragansett Bay. They called their settlement Providence Plantations. This location was an excellent site for a settlement. It was situated on a hill that was dry and well drained. There was an excellent harbor, clear water, timber, and game nearby. In June, Williams bought this land from the Native Americans. However, since he had not received a patent from the king or a land company, Williams's claim to this land was illegal as far as England was concerned.

Soon Williams's wife and daughters, people from his church in Salem, and other rebels joined him. With these Massachusetts outcasts, Williams signed a compact that recognized the principle of majority rule and the separation of church and state. Although voters were required to be male property owners, the right to vote did not depend on church membership. Williams and his followers built a village of thatched-roof houses and planted gardens and fruit trees. Every settler was given five acres for a garden and six acres for a cornfield. Every settler was allowed to practice his faith freely. In fact, Williams welcomed all to Rhode Island — Catholics, Quakers, Jews, and even atheists. Providence was described as the place where "all the cranks of New England" went. Truly, it offered something unique — complete religious freedom.

A second Massachusetts outcast who came to Rhode Island was Ann Hutchinson. Like Williams, she was forced to leave the Puritan colony because of her "unorthodox" beliefs. Hutchinson was not afraid to attack legalism in the church, and she was convinced that an individual could come into direct contact with God through personal contemplation. She was accused of being a heretic, tried, and exiled.

Hutchinson was married with fourteen children, and she was the sister-in-law of John Wheelwright, who helped to settle New Hampshire. According to Governor Winthrop, Ann had a "ready wit and bold spirit." Hutchinson and her followers left for Providence in 1638. Roger Williams helped her group to buy land from the natives and form a settlement at what is now Portsmouth. After Anne's husband died in 1642, she moved on to the New Netherlands colony, where she was killed by Indians. In addition to Portsmouth, two other towns were founded in Rhode Island in the early colonial period—Newport and Warwick.

In 1643, four New England colonies — Plymouth, Massachusetts Bay, Connecticut, and New Haven — formed the New England Confederation as a means of common protection against Indian attacks. However, because of its tolerance for religious dissenters, these colonies did not ask Rhode Island to join them. Not only did they not invite Rhode Island to join the confederation, they also threatened to cut off trade with the colony and to ruin it economically. Roger Williams worked diligently to keep the four Rhode Island towns working together in the face of this threat.

To ensure Rhode Island's legal title to its land, Roger Williams traveled to England to meet with the king. He returned with a patent and charter on March 24, 1644. Almost twenty years later, Rhode Island was granted a second charter, which guaranteed it complete religious freedom and granted it the greatest degree of self-government of all of the thirteen colonies. By the time of Roger Williams's death in 1683, Rhode Island had become well known as a refuge for the oppressed.

Ann Hutchinson
Line drawing courtesy of Amy Pak

Thomas Hooker
Library of Congress, Prints and Photographs
Division [LC-USZ62-134559]

ESTABLISHMENT OF CONNECTICUT

A Puritan minister named Thomas Hooker had arrived in Massachusetts from England in 1633. He brought most of his congregation from England with him, and together they settled in a little town near Boston, the site of present-day Cambridge. A year later, Hooker sought authorization from the General Court to settle in Connecticut. At first the General Court denied his request because they did not want settlers drawn away from the colony. However, when people began to leave the colony anyway, the General Court reversed its decision and appointed an eight-man commission to govern the group for one year.

On May 31, 1636, Hooker led a group of thirty-five men with their wives, children, and servants (about one hundred people in all), along with 160 cattle, pigs, and goats west. They followed Native American trails and traveled by foot for nearly two weeks under difficult and hazardous conditions. Their hope was to find good farmland and religious freedom. At the end of their journey, they established a new settlement in the Connecticut River valley, which was first called Newton and later renamed Hartford. The location of their new home was wonderful. They had selected some of the best farmland in New England — rich, fertile soil in which almost any crop would grow. There were meadows good for grazing cattle, dense forests with valuable timber and animals for the fur trade, and waters with large schools of salmon and shad.

In May of 1637, the Massachusetts-appointed commission for Connecticut ended. By that time there were about eight hundred people scattered along the Connecticut River in what were known as the three river towns—Windsor, Wethersfield, and Hartford. These towns reorganized themselves into the self-governing colony of Connecticut. The following year, a new colony called New Haven was formed at the mouth of the Quinnipiac River. It was established by John Davenport, a nonconformist minister who had fled persecution in England. The government of New Haven was stricter than that of the other Puritan colonies. It functioned as a theocracy, meaning that this colony's religious leaders also served as its political leaders. Furthermore, its people could not vote and therefore had little say in the government. The Word of God was its only rule. Although New Haven battled to remain independent, it was ordered to unite with Connecticut in 1662.

From the beginning of the movement of English settlers into Connecticut, the Pequot tribe in the Mystic River valley was resentful of their presence. In 1637, after several Pequot attacks on the colonists, a combined force of several hundred settlers along with Mohegan and Narragansett tribesmen burned the Pequot fort in a surprise attack at dawn. All but five of the Pequot men, women, and children in the fort died. Over the next few weeks, the remaining members of the Pequot tribe were hunted down and killed or captured.

As a result of the Pequot Massacre, the New England Confederation was formed in 1643. Connecticut, Plymouth, Massachusetts Bay, and New Haven banded together for the purpose of defending their colonies against the Indians, as well as from possible outside invasion by the French and Dutch. The confederation also made it easier for the people of the region to do business with each other. This New England Confederation was one of the earliest examples of unity among the English colonies in America.

A milestone in the history of the Connecticut colony was the creation of the Fundamental Orders of Connecticut in 1639. Guided by Hooker, the colony developed a constitution with ideas that foreshadowed those in the U.S. Constitution and became part of other colonial and state constitutions. According to Hooker, the people must be careful to limit the power of their lawmakers; and lawmakers must be accountable to the people for their actions. In the Fundamental Orders of Connecticut, the foundation of all authority was said to lie in "the free consent of the people." There were to be no religious restrictions on voting, and the governor was to be elected by the people and prohibited from serving two terms in a row. With the Fundamental Orders, Connecticut became the first English colony in America with a written plan of government.

For as much as it hath pleased Almighty God by the wise disposition of his divine providence so to order and dispose of things that we the

John Davenport
Library of Congress, Prints and Photographs Division [LC-USZ62-38496]

Inhabitants and Residents of Windsor, Hartford and Wethersfield are now cohabiting and dwelling in and upon the River of Connectecotte and the lands thereunto adjoining; and well knowing where a people are gathered together the word of God requires that to maintain the peace and union of such a people there should be an orderly and decent Government established according to God, to order and dispose of the affairs of the people at all seasons as occasion shall require; do therefore associate and conjoin ourselves to be as one Public State or Commonwealth...

— from the Fundamental Orders of Connecticut

Because Connecticut had originated without a charter, its colonists had no legal claim to the land. In 1662, Charles II agreed to issue a liberal charter, based on the Fundamental Orders, which made Connecticut a royal colony. Connecticut was also allowed to take over the colony of New Haven, and it was given an additional large tract of land, which led to years of property disputes with Rhode Island. When the Dominion of New England was later formed, Connecticut refused to surrender its charter to Governor Andros. According to legend, the Connecticut charter was hidden in a large oak tree that later came to be known as the Charter Oak. The charter supposedly remained in the tree until James II died in 1701. When this oak tree finally fell in 1856, some of its wood was used to make the Connecticut governor's official chair.

IMPACT

- The Laconia Company, founded by Sir Fernando Gorges and John Mason, two English merchants, established the first English settlement in New Hampshire in 1622. This fishing and timbering community prospered modestly but never established the desired lucrative fur trade.

- About 1640, two Puritan towns were established in New Hampshire. John Wheelwright, banished by the Massachusetts

Bay Colony, played a key role in their development. In the years that followed, the New Hampshire colony needed help from Massachusetts to survive attacks from Native Americans and French Canadians.

- The first known European colonist in Rhode Island was a hermit minister named William Blackstone, who moved to Rhode Island in 1630 when the Puritans arrived in Massachusetts Bay. Eight years later, Roger Williams, banished from the Massachusetts Bay Colony, led a group to Rhode Island and established Providence Plantations.

- The Rhode Island Colony, under Williams's leadership, became known as a refuge for the oppressed. Williams supported the principle of separation of church and state and spoke out for religious liberty and freedom of conscience for all.

- Dutch fur traders, Pilgrims from Plymouth, and a Massachusetts fur trader named John Oldham all traveled to Connecticut in 1633. However, the first permanent community in Connecticut was established by Thomas Hooker, a Puritan minister, and his congregation in 1636.

- The Connecticut Colony, along with the two Massachusetts colonies and the colony of New Haven, formed the New England Confederation in 1634 to defend themselves against French and Dutch invasions and attacks by Native Americans. This confederation was one of the earliest examples of unity among the colonies. The Fundamental Orders of Connecticut (1639), developed under Hooker's leadership, contained ideas that foreshadowed those in the U.S. Constitution, and those ideas became part of other colonial and state constitutions.

PETER MINUIT AND WALTER VAN TWILLER
1626–1637

THE PURCHASE OF MANHATTAN ISLAND.

LESSON 12

ATMOSPHERE

NEW NETHERLANDS AND
THE DUTCH WEST INDIA COMPANY

As early as 1614, the Dutch had begun trading regularly with the Iroquois Confederacy in New York. The year before, the Dutch explorer Adriaen Block had traded for furs along the Hudson River and anchored off the island that is now Manhattan. Based upon the explorations of Block and Henry Hudson, the Netherlands claimed a large area in North America, which included parts of New York, New Jersey, Delaware, and Connecticut. They named this region New Netherlands.

By 1621, the Dutch West India Company had been formed by a group of wealthy businessmen and received trading rights to New Netherlands. Primarily interested in trading with the Iroquois for pelts, this company realized that American furs were as valuable as American gold. The demand for beaver, fox, sable, and other pelts was quite high in Europe in the early seventeenth century. The pelts were used to make luxurious coats, hats, and blankets. By 1624, the Dutch West India Company had established at least two outposts in New

Netherlands—one at Fort Orange (present-day Albany) and one near the area that is now New York City.

However, it was difficult for the company to find colonists willing to leave the Netherlands and sail to America. During this period, the Netherlands had the highest standard of living of any nation in the world as well as more religious tolerance than any other European nation. People wanted to come to the Netherlands, not leave it. Finally, in 1624, a small group of Dutch families agreed to be sent by the Dutch West India Company to settle in America. Some of this group settled on what is now Governor's Island in New York Harbor; the others went to various forts in New York or scattered into Delaware, Connecticut, and New Jersey.

NEW JERSEY

A small number of Dutch settlers began moving into New Jersey during the 1620s. However, the Dutch West India Company put most of its effort into building towns and forts in the region that became New York. During the 1630s and 1640s, a few Dutch farm families moved into the New Jersey portion of New Netherlands.

EVENT

ESTABLISHMENT OF NEW YORK

In 1626, three more Dutch ships (the *Cow*, the *Sheep*, and the *Horse*) landed on Manhattan Island, the site where the Hudson River widens to form a harbor as it flows into the ocean. On board one of these ships was Peter Minuit, whom the Dutch West India Company had appointed to be the director-general of the New Netherlands colony. Soon after his arrival, Minuit made perhaps the most famous real estate deal in history.

He bought Manhattan Island from some Native Americans for beads and trinkets worth about sixty guilders (twenty-four dollars). However, since Native Americans did not believe that land could be

Purchase of Manhattan
Library of Congress, Prints and Photographs Division [LC-USZ62-16252]

owned by people but belonged to everyone, their intent most certainly was not to transfer ownership of the island to the Dutch.

Minuit supervised the construction of a fort on Manhattan, as well as houses, public buildings, and streets. This city, which the Dutch named New Amsterdam, had enough food for its settlers from the very beginning. Business was also brisk, as the Dutch made many deals with the Native Americans. New Amsterdam quickly attracted merchants from all over Europe and became known as a sailor's town — an easygoing seaport with more taverns than churches. According to a French priest who visited New Amsterdam in the early 1640s, more than eighteen different languages could be heard spoken there.

The Dutch West India Company continued to have difficulty finding many Dutch families interested in settling in the area. In order to attract more colonists, the company decided to offer anyone willing to pay for fifty or more settlers to come to New Netherlands the right to buy huge pieces of land there. These landowners became known as patroons, Dutch for "lords of the manor." Patroons were given great power, acting as both judge and jury in cases on their land; they also had the authority to keep their workers from leaving the property without permission.

Old Silvernails

Dutch colonists began moving deeper and deeper into the Hudson River valley, establishing settlements on Staten Island, Long Island, Brooklyn, the Bronx, Harlem, and Yonkers. In 1646, Peter Stuyvesant was sent to New Netherlands to bring order to the colony after a massive uprising of Native Americans in the area, which had been precipitated by actions taken by the former governor. He became the last director-general of New Netherlands. Stuyvesant was known as Old Silvernails, because the stick of wood that replaced his right leg was decorated with silver nails. Stuyvesant had lost his leg in an unsuccessful Dutch attempt to capture St. Martin from the Spanish. A tough, determined man, Stuyvesant had no patience for laziness or disorder.

Peter Stuyvesant
Line drawing courtesy of Amy Pak

When Stuyvesant arrived in New Amsterdam, he found the houses there in poor condition, the fort in disrepair, and the streets narrow and crooked. Immediately he set to work with great energy to supervise the cleanup of the city. The fort was repaired, many fine brick and stone homes were built, roads were paved, garbage was carted away, and trade was reinvigorated. The colony's first police force was organized, a fire code was formulated and enforced, and stiff penalties were imposed on those caught in drunken brawls. Stuyvesant also ordered a wall built across the northern edge of New Amsterdam to protect the town from attack. This wall was removed in 1700, but the place where it stood became known as Wall Street.

Stuyvesant brought order to the government with his autocratic rule, and he negotiated treaties with several Native American tribes in the area. In 1655, Stuyvesant enlarged New Netherlands with the takeover of New Sweden, a colony on the Delaware Bay (including parts of present-day New Jersey, Delaware, and Pennsylvania). However, Stuyvesant's many projects and improvements required higher taxes, which the residents of New Amsterdam resented. He also frequently ignored the orders of the Dutch West India Company and persecuted Quakers and Jews who came to the area.

In August of 1664, a fleet of four English warships appeared in New Amsterdam harbor. These ships had been sent by James, the English Duke of York, to take over New Netherlands. The land had been given to him by his brother King Charles II. England and the Netherlands were already at war, and the presence of the Dutch in North America was disturbing to the English. By 1664, England had a long chain of colonies along the Atlantic seacoast, interrupted only by New Netherlands. When King Charles II was advised that the Dutch colony was interfering with English trade and that its people were unhappy under Stuyvesant's leadership, he made the decision to seize it.

On board one of the English ships in the New Amsterdam harbor was Governor John Winthrop, Jr., of Connecticut, son of the famous Massachusetts governor. Winthrop brought with him a summons to the Dutch government to surrender the colony. Stuyvesant was determined not to surrender, and he pleaded with his fellow

Wall Street c. 1859
Library of Congress, Prints and Photographs Division [LC-USZ62-20789]

Dutchmen to resist. However, they refused to fight alongside him, realizing that they were hopelessly outgunned and that their fort did not have enough food to hold out long against a siege.

Thus, with no shots fired, Dutch rule ended after only fifty years. In September of 1664, Stuyvesant signed the documents that officially handed New Netherlands over to England. The English treated the conquered Dutch people with humanity and kindness, giving them the choice to stay in America or return to Holland. Almost all of the Dutch chose to stay, even Stuyvesant.

New Amsterdam Becomes New York

In October of 1664, the colony was renamed New York in honor of the new owner of the land — James, Duke of York. New York's charter contained no provision for a representative assembly because the duke refused to allow one.

New Amsterdam
Library of Congress, Prints and Photographs Division [LC-USZ62-42805]

Between 1660 and 1684, King Charles II would create five new English colonies in North America. In addition to New York, he established New Jersey, Delaware, Pennsylvania, and the Carolinas. The king created these colonies partly as a way to repay people who had helped him to regain the throne and partly as a way to repay people to whom he owed money. Charles gave the largest amount of land to his brother James, who became sole proprietor of all land between the Connecticut and Delaware rivers. However, James, as Lord High Admiral, was too busy rebuilding the English navy to travel to America to see his proprietary lands. When Charles II died in 1685 and James became king, New York changed from a proprietary colony to a royal colony.

As king, James created the Dominion of New England, which included New York. The people of New York had countless complaints against the Dominion government, and the situation there became quite tense. When Andros, the Dominion's governor, was finally deposed in 1689, a number of New Yorkers wanted a bigger role in the government. They rallied around Jacob Leisler, a German-born soldier who had worked for the Dutch West India Company. Leisler led a revolt of middle-class people, who took control of New York

City and made him the new governor of the colony. However, two years later, the English monarchs William and Mary sent soldiers and a new royal governor to re-establish royal authority over New York. Leisler and several of his followers were arrested and tried on charges of treason. All of them were released except Leisler and his son-in-law, who were hanged.

ESTABLISHMENT OF NEW JERSEY

The New York and New Jersey colonies

After the English takeover of New Netherlands in 1664, the Duke of York organized the area to the west of New York and gave it to two of his friends—Sir George Carteret and Sir John Berkeley. Carteret supposedly named the area New Jersey after his home on the island of

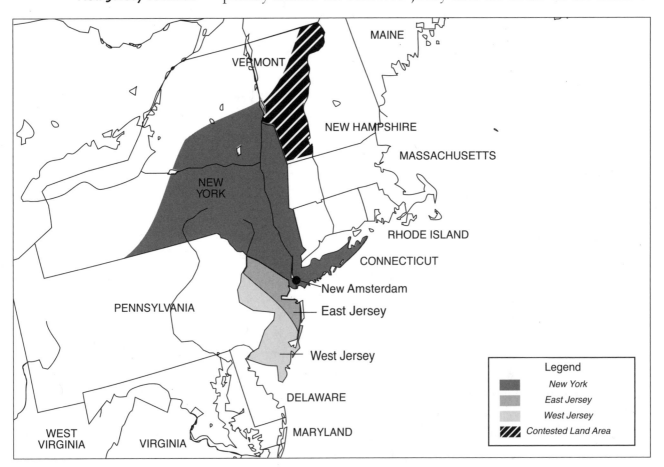

Legend

New York

East Jersey

West Jersey

Contested Land Area

Jersey in the English Channel. Carteret and Berkeley promised immigrants to New Jersey freedom of religion, a representative assembly, and the power to levy taxes. However, the immigrants were not allowed to purchase land in New Jersey outright. Rather, land was granted to them for their use, but they were required to pay an annual rental fee to the proprietors called a quit rent. This fee was waived for the first seven years. When this deferment ended in 1670, problems would arise.

Carteret and Berkeley never personally came to New Jersey. They sent Philip Carteret, a cousin of Sir George, to New Jersey to govern for them. In July 1665, Carteret and thirty immigrants arrived at Elizabethtown, New Jersey. Puritans from Long Island had recently established three other communities nearby. Population in New Jersey was scant in the beginning and confined to its eastern part.

Over time, immigrants began to pour into New Jersey. Quakers arrived from England, Scotland, Ireland, and Wales. Finns, Swedes, and Germans also came. In 1674, Lord Berkeley needed money to pay debts and sold his half of New Jersey to a group of Quakers. William Penn was involved in this transaction. Carteret and the new Quaker proprietors agreed to divide New Jersey into two parts: East New Jersey (owned by Carteret) and West New Jersey (the unsettled region owned by the Quakers). The Quakers made immediate plans to settle their region due to the increasingly harsh persecution in England. The population in western New Jersey increased rapidly.

When Carteret died in 1680, he left his proprietorship to his wife and trustees with instructions to sell the land to pay off his debts. Thus, the eastern portion of New Jersey was sold at a public auction in 1682 to twelve men, most of them Quakers. These men in turn sold smaller plots to others. Ultimately, twenty-four proprietors owned and governed eastern New Jersey. However, proprietary government was increasingly resented throughout New Jersey. When James II created the Dominion of New England in 1686, the New Jersey proprietors were forced to surrender all of their governing authority.

When the Dominion ended, the proprietors again assumed control of New Jersey and rioting against their rule occurred throughout the

Signatures of the Lords Proprietor, including Carteret and Berkeley
Courtesy of North Wind Picture Archives

colony. Once again, the proprietors were forced to relinquish their governmental powers. In 1702, East New Jersey and West New Jersey were united as the royal province of Jersey, and for the next thirty-six years the governor of New York also served as the governor of New Jersey. Of course, the people of New Jersey were resentful of this arrangement and were finally allowed to have their own governor in 1738.

IMPACT

- By 1624, the Dutch West India Company had established two outposts in New Netherlands—the North American land they had claimed based on the explorations of Adriaen Block and Henry Hudson. By 1628, the settlement of New Amsterdam was thriving under the leadership of Peter Minuet.

- Peter Stuyvesant, the last director-general of New Netherlands (1646 – 1664), brought order to the colony after a massive Native American uprising and enlarged the colony by taking over New Sweden (a colony located on the Delaware Bay). However, in 1664, Stuyvesant handed New Netherlands over to England with no resistance. The colony was renamed New York in honor of the new owner of the land, James, Duke of York.

- A small number of Dutch settlers began moving into New Jersey during the 1620s and continued to do so in small numbers in the decades that followed. After the English takeover of New Netherlands in 1664, the Duke of York gave this area west of New York to two of his friends—Sir George Carteret and Sir John Berkeley.

- In 1674, Lord Berkeley sold his half of New Jersey to a group of Quakers. Carteret and the new Quaker proprietors agreed to divide New Jersey into East New Jersey and West New Jersey.

The population in the Quaker-owned western New Jersey began to increase rapidly. When Carteret died, East New Jersey was sold at a public auction. In 1702, East New Jersey and West New Jersey were united as the royal province of Jersey.

LESSON 13

ATMOSPHERE

ZWAANENDAEL AND THE LENNI-LENAPE

In 1610, a sea captain from Virginia named Samuel Argall got caught in a storm and ended up in a bay, which he named the De La Warr Bay in honor of the Virginia governor, Lord De La Warr. A decade later, the Dutch began trading with the Lenni-Lenape tribe in the area around Delaware Bay. They also became interested in hunting for whales in the bay. By 1631, the Dutch had established a base for whaling and trade, which they called Zwaanendael ("valley of the swans"). About thirty colonists sailed from the Dutch town of Hoorn and settled just inside Cape Henlopen. They proceeded to build a fort, plant crops, hunt for whales, and build a friendly relationship with the Lenni-Lenape.

Lenni-Lenape longhouses
Courtesy of North Wind Picture Archives

However, a misunderstanding between the Dutch and the Lenni-Lenape soon doomed Zwaanendael. Problems apparently arose when the Dutch suspected nearby natives of stealing a tin Dutch coat of arms that was nailed to a tree. According to some sources, the Dutch demanded that the guilty party be punished, and the Lenni-Lenape killed the suspected thief and brought his scalp to the Dutch. Other stories accuse the Dutch of killing the brave suspected of removing the tin symbol. Regardless of the disagreement over who killed the brave, all agree that tensions between the Lenni-Lenape and the Dutch continued to escalate. Finally, a group of braves killed all of the colonists in a sneak attack and burned all their buildings to the ground.

WILLIAM PENN

The principal figure in the establishment of the English colony of Pennsylvania was the Quaker visionary William Penn. As a child, Penn was raised in the Church of England. He lived a life of privilege as the son of a wealthy British admiral, who was a friend of King Charles II. As a young adult, however, William abandoned the faith of his father to join the Society of Friends. This decision led to his expulsion from college, several confinements in jail, and a lifetime of persecution.

When Penn's father died, the English king owed him a large sum of money. William requested that Charles repay this debt by granting him land in America, and the king agreed to do so. In March of 1681, Charles II signed a charter that granted Penn an area in America as large as England itself. The new colony, to be named Penn's Wood (Pennsylvania), consisted of land west of the Delaware River between New York and Maryland. It was established as a proprietary colony, one in which ownership of the land and control of the colony was invested in Penn and his heirs. Other English proprietary colonies included New York, New Jersey, the Carolinas, and Georgia.

LORD BALTIMORE'S CHARTER

The early history of the colony of Maryland is intertwined with the history of the Calvert family. George Calvert, an important English politician in the 1620s, decided to leave the Church of England and convert to Catholicism. During this period in English history, Catholics were even more persecuted than Puritans. They were not allowed to attend mass openly, and they were heavily fined for not belonging to the Church of England. After his conversion Calvert had to relinquish his job as secretary of state. However, Calvert managed

William Penn
Library of Congress, Prints and Photographs Division [LC-USZ62-1949]

to remain a favorite of King James I, who made him a baron and gave him the title Lord Baltimore.

In 1632, King Charles I issued Lord Baltimore a charter to start a colony north of Virginia, granting him more than ten million acres of land north of the Potomac River. This area included all of present-day Maryland and Delaware and parts of Virginia, West Virginia, and Pennsylvania. It was described in the charter as Terra Marie (Maryland), probably named in honor of Queen Henrietta Marie. The Catholic wife of James I was thought to be the person responsible for Calvert's receiving the charter. In return for this generous land grant, Baltimore promised to give the crown one-fifth of all the gold and silver discovered in Maryland and to pay the crown the symbolic tribute of two Indian arrowheads a year.

According to the terms of the royal charter, Baltimore was appointed the lord proprietor of his colony with absolute control of its administration, upkeep, and defense. His powers included the right to collect taxes, wage war, set up courts, establish manors, and make all laws. The charter allowed for the existence of an assembly, but the assembly did not have the authority to initiate legislation. It could merely approve or disapprove laws submitted by the proprietor. Settlers were granted all the rights of Englishmen, and religion was not mentioned. However, Baltimore saw Maryland as a refuge for persecuted Catholics and dreamed of establishing a colony in which Catholics and Protestants would live together in peace.

George Calvert died the same year that he received his colonial charter from the English king. His twenty-six-year-old son, Cecil, inherited the title Lord Baltimore and the Maryland land grant. Cecil named his brother Leonard governor of the colony and planned that his colony would be based on the English feudal system. He instructed Leonard to grant six thousand acres of Maryland land to relatives of the Calvert family. Gentlemen who brought five other people with them to the colony would be given two thousand acres of land. These members of the English elite would then rent smaller plots of their manors to farmers and tenants called freeholders. Unfortunately, this

ARMS OF THE CALVERT FAMILY

Calvert family coat of arms
Line drawing courtesy of Amy Pak

Full-size working replica of the *Kalmar Nyckel*

Courtesy of the Kalmar Nyckel Foundation, Wilmington, Delaware, www.kalmarnyckel.org

Peter Minuit

Library of Congress, Prints and Photographs Division [LC-USZ62-33018]

plan set up an unequal system of land grants that created difficult social and class distinctions.

EVENT

ESTABLISHMENT OF DELAWARE

In March of 1638, fifty Swedes arrived in Delaware on two ships—the *Kalmar Nyckel* and the *Vogel Grip*. A Dutchmen named William Usselinx had obtained a charter from Sweden to organize a company headed by both Swedes and Dutch to establish a settlement in America. Peter Minuit, former governor of New Netherlands, was hired as director of the company's expedition to the New World. The *Kalmar Nyckel* and the *Vogel Grip* sailed up the Delaware River to the mouth of a smaller stream that flowed into it. The Swedes named this stream Christina Creek after their young Swedish queen. They landed a short distance up Christina Creek at a natural dock. This land, which today is the city of Wilmington, was bought from Native Americans in the area by Peter Minuit. According to legend, Minuit paid for it with a copper kettle.

The Swedish settlers built a square log fort with two log houses inside to store goods and provisions. Historians believe that these Swedes were the first in America to build log cabins, which they based on the houses in their homeland. After the fort was completed, they laid out a village, which they named Christina. This settlement came to be known as New Sweden, and it lasted only seventeen years.

When New Netherlands heard about the establishment of New Sweden, the Dutch governor sent an angry protest to Minuit. He insisted that Christina was located on land belonging to the Dutch and that the Swedes must leave. Minuit ignored this protest. A new governor for New Sweden was eventually appointed, and Minuit set sail for Holland. He was lost at sea and never heard from again.

In 1643, the new governor of New Sweden, Johan Printz, relocated its capital farther up the Delaware River — from Fort Christina to

Tinicum Island, not far from what today is the city of Philadelphia. The Swedes called this settlement New Gothenburg.

At first the Swedes had difficulty attracting many settlers to New Sweden. However, eventually word began to spread that the land along the Delaware River was rich and excellent for farming. From 1643 to 1653, New Sweden grew and prospered under the leadership of Governor Johan Printz. Called Big Tub by the Lenni-Lenape, he was seven feet tall and weighed over four hundred pounds. Printz was an autocratic and foulmouthed man, who liked to hang people who opposed him. However, he also was a great administrator and succeeded in holding New Sweden together for ten years with little help from the homeland.

Johan Printz (Big Tub)
Public Domain

Swedish to Dutch to English

By 1655, Stuyvesant with a fleet of seven ships and six hundred men was ready to seize New Sweden. In a ten-day campaign, the Dutch succeeded in conquering the Swedish colony. The Swedish colonists were allowed to remain in the area if they agreed to take an oath of allegiance to the Netherlands.

Only nine years passed before the Dutch/Swedish settlement in Delaware was taken over by the English in 1664 and placed under the rule of New York. The town of New Amstel, an important Delaware port, was renamed New Castle. Almost twenty years later, King Charles II granted William Penn this land on the west bank of the Delaware Bay and River. These three lower Delaware counties had not been a part of Penn's original land grant because they were considered part of New York. However, Penn saw these counties as a threat to Philadelphia. He feared that ships coming from the Atlantic would reach New Castle before Philadelphia and rob Philadelphia of the sea trade that would make it great. From 1682 until 1704, Delaware would be part of the colony of Pennsylvania, and from 1704 until 1776 the two colonies would share a governor. However, this separation was not a legal one because Delaware's right to exist was not legitimized by a charter from the crown.

New Castle on the Delaware
Public Domain

ESTABLISHMENT OF PENNSYLVANIA

In the fall of 1681, Penn sent an advance party of colonists to Pennsylvania to select a proper site for the new colony. He instructed them to choose the location with care — to look for a high, dry spot near the Delaware River. Penn also cautioned them to be careful not to offend the Lenni-Lenape in the area. The following spring, Penn sent a surveyor to lay out the city of Philadelphia. Because Penn expected its citizens to be peaceful, he planned no walls or fortifications for Philadelphia.

By the spring of 1682, Penn had finished drawing up his Charter of Liberties, a framework for the government of Pennsylvania. Penn's colony was to be established with a governor who had power to veto laws and appoint judges, a lieutenant governor, a Council, and an Assembly. The Assembly was to be elected by the colony's freemen, which included all male landowners. The Council's job was to propose all laws, which the Assembly could approve or reject. Both trial by jury and freedom of religion were guaranteed. William Penn saw his colony as a holy experiment, open to people of all faiths. Only Rhode Island would be able to match Pennsylvania for its religious tolerance and freedom. Penn's treatment of the Lenni-Lenape was also noteworthy, insisting that they be paid a fair price for their land and resolving to live peaceably with them.

On October 27, 1682, Penn and about one hundred colonists, mostly Quakers, sailed for America on board the *Welcome*. A smallpox epidemic killed almost a third of the passengers before they reached Pennsylvania. After a brief stop in New Castle, Delaware, Penn and his expedition arrived in Philadelphia. Penn found that the commissioners had laid out Philadelphia according to his instructions. The streets were broad and straight, and there were ten substantial brick and stone houses and a trading post/tavern already constructed. Penn was able to stay in Philadelphia for only two years before he was forced to return to England in order to settle a boundary dispute between Pennsylvania and Maryland.

Due to the generosity of Penn's land grants, the population of Pennsylvania grew quickly. In the southeastern region, in and around

Philadelphia, there were mostly English and Welsh Quakers, who were trained as lawyers, doctors, skilled craftsmen, and merchants. In the valleys west of Philadelphia, near the Delaware River, were German, Dutch, and Swiss farmers. Many of them were Amish or Mennonite. Because their own word for *German* was *Deutsch,* they eventually became known as the Pennsylvania Dutch. Beyond the

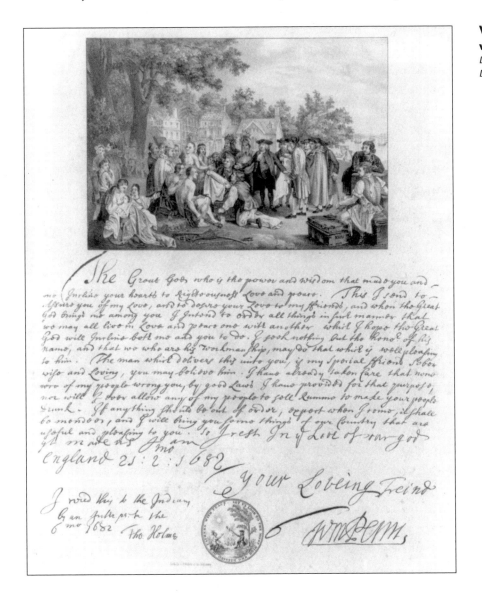

William Penn's treaty with the Indians
Library of Congress, Prints and Photographs Division [LC-USZ62-3933]

City of Philadelphia
Library of Congress, Prints and Photographs Division [LC-USZ62-22392]

Allegheny Mountains were Scotch-Irish settlers, who primarily worked as traders and trappers.

After Penn returned to England, friction between the Council and Assembly began to escalate as the Assembly sought more power. Penn wrote letters urging them to work together in harmony, but his letters went unanswered. While in England, Penn continued to advertise his colony by sending pamphlets describing its beauty to Wales, Scotland, Ireland, Holland, and Germany. As a result of Penn's promotion, colonists began flocking to Pennsylvania. By 1700, the population of Penn's colony had multiplied to twenty thousand people. Philadelphia had become the largest and most prosperous city in the colonies with a diverse population representing many languages and occupations.

While back in England, Penn was arrested twice and put on trial for treason; both times he was released due to insufficient evidence. When England went to war with France, the pacifist Quaker government of Pennsylvania refused to send men to help the upper regions of New York that were threatened by French Canadians and their Indian allies. Because the Pennsylvania colonists failed to help their fellow Englishmen, the crown suspended Penn's charter and made Pennsylvania a royal colony. In 1694, the English monarchy agreed to restore Penn's proprietary rights if he returned to Pennsylvania to straighten out its government and agreed to help defend New York.

Penn's Return to Pennsylvania

Thus in 1699, after a fifteen-year absence, Penn returned to his colony. Although Pennsylvania was economically prosperous, it was in political disarray. Penn wrote a new constitution for his colony, which guaranteed certain rights and gave more control of the government to the people. Unfortunately, the many stresses and misfortunes in Penn's life ruined his health and led to his suffering a stroke that paralyzed him for the remainder of his life. However, both of his sons later served as governor of Pennsylvania.

ESTABLISHMENT OF MARYLAND

Lord Baltimore outfitted two ships for his Maryland colonists—the *Ark* and the *Dove*. On board these ships were Lord Baltimore's brother Leonard, whom he had appointed governor, two Jesuit priests, seventeen Catholic gentlemen and their wives, and approximately two hundred other people (many were members of the Church of England). The ships set sail for America in November 1633 and arrived in the Chesapeake Bay at the end of February of 1634. The expedition soon purchased a Piscataway Indian village located on a high bluff near the mouth of the Potomac River and named it St. Mary's. These Native Americans had already planned to move because they felt threatened by the more powerful and

The Delaware, Pennsylvania, and Maryland colonies

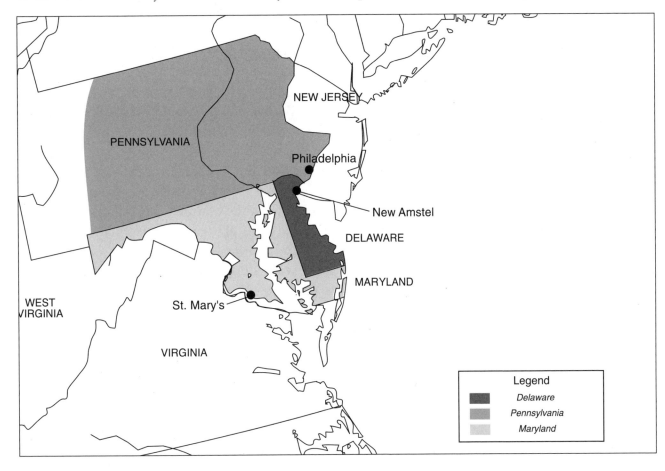

warlike Susquehannock tribe. Therefore, they were happy to sell the English their wigwams and fields in exchange for the axes, hatchets, hoes, and cloth they offered.

The colonists arrived in time for spring planting, and they used the cleared Piscataway field to raise corn. They also lived in the deserted Indian huts until they could build more substantial homes. Over time, they erected a church, guardhouse, storehouse, mill, and a number of houses. Leonard Calvert and the other gentlemen worked alongside their servants to construct these buildings. Eventually, manors would spring up along the Potomac, Patuxet, and St. Mary's rivers.

Baltimore's colony prospered from the very beginning. Since he kept his colonists well supplied, they were never forced to experience a starving time like others had. Because the Maryland settlers were able to establish good relations with the natives, they avoided many of the hardships that plagued Jamestown. New settlers flooded into the region, attracted by the promise of religious freedom. Maryland soon developed an agricultural economy similar to Virginia's; that is, tobacco became its most profitable export. African slavery would eventually become a dominant factor in the production of that tobacco.

Protestants, Catholics, and The Toleration Act

During the time of the English Civil War, Protestants in Maryland became more aggressive toward the Catholic-controlled government there. For several years, the political situation in Maryland was in turmoil. In 1649, Lord Baltimore decided to replace the Catholic government in his colony with a Protestant one. That same year the Toleration Act was passed by the assembly, which stated that no Christian (Catholic or Protestant) could be harmed for his beliefs. However, this promise of religious freedom did not apply to Jews or atheists, who could be hanged.

In 1652, after the Puritans had deposed the English king and taken control of the national government, commissioners were sent to Maryland to set up a Puritan government there. The Toleration Act was also repealed, which meant Catholics were no longer protected from persecution. Lord Baltimore was deprived of his colonial

Broadside on the Maryland Toleration Act
Public Domain

administrative powers but retained his property rights. Eventually, Lord Baltimore won the support of Cromwell, and by 1657 he had regained control of his colony and reinstated the Toleration Act.

After the Glorious Revolution of 1688, Lord Baltimore's enemies took advantage of Protestant fears that the deposed Catholic king (James II) would attempt to establish a foothold in Maryland. While Lord Baltimore was in England, Protestants took control of the Maryland government and sent a petition to the English crown, asking that Maryland be made a royal colony. In 1691, Lord Baltimore once again lost his proprietary rights over Maryland. When Maryland became a royal colony, its settlers were forbidden to hold Catholic or Quaker services. Many Catholics decided to flee the colony, and those who remained no longer exercised any power in the Assembly.

IMPACT

- An early Dutch settlement named Zwaanendael in Delaware (1631) was doomed by a misunderstanding between the Dutch and the Lenni-Lenape. In 1639, a Swedish settlement under the leadership of Peter Minuit (former governor of New Netherlands) was established where Wilmington is today.

- New Sweden prospered under the leadership of Governor Johan Printz. However, in 1655 New Sweden was seized by the Dutch under Peter Stuyvesant, and in 1664 the Dutch/Swedish settlement in Delaware was taken over by the English and placed under the rule of New York. Twenty years later, King Charles II granted William Penn the three Delaware "lower counties."

- The Quaker visionary William Penn was the principal figure in the establishment of the proprietary colony of Pennsylvania. Penn saw this colony as a holy experiment open to people of all faiths.

- Because of the generosity of Penn's land grants, the population of the Pennsylvania colony grew quickly. This colony became economically prosperous but often fell into political disarray.

- The colony of Maryland was established by the Calvert family (the Lords Baltimore) in 1634 on the basis of a royal charter granted by the English king for the establishment of a colony north of Virginia. Maryland was soon seen as a refuge for persecuted Catholics.

- Baltimore's colony prospered from the beginning and never experienced a starving time. It developed an agricultural economy similar to Virginia's; tobacco was its most profitable export.

LESSON 14

ATMOSPHERE

THE LORDS PROPRIETOR'S COLONY OF CAROLINA

In 1663, King Charles II granted eight prominent English nobles land in America that stretched from Virginia to Spanish Florida. These high-ranking Englishmen, who had helped Charles recover the throne after the Puritan Revolution, became known as the Lords Proprietor. They included Sir William Berkeley, Sir George Carteret, Sir John Colleton, Anthony Ashley Cooper (Earl of Shaftesbury), George Monck (Duke of Albemarle), Edward Hyde (Earl of Clarendon), William Lord Craven, and John Lord Berkeley.

More than thirty years earlier, King Charles I had awarded the same area to Sir Robert Heath. During the years that Heath held the charter to this region it was named Carolana. At the time that Charles II revoked Heath's charter and gave it to the eight Lords Proprietor, there were no good maps or descriptions available of Carolana (changed to Carolina).

The Lords Proprietor were not interested in living in Carolina. Their goal was to make money by having colonists use the land to produce wine, silk, and olive oil. At first the proprietors hoped to attract settlers to Carolina from Virginia and New England. In fact, a

Sir Ashley Cooper, the Earl of Shaftesbury
Library of Congress, Prints and Photographs Division [LC-D419-179 — some question exists as to whether this portrait is actually Cooper, but it is presumed so.]

**Signatures of the
Lords Proprietor**
Courtesy of North Wind Picture Archives

small number of Virginians had already settled around Albemarle Sound in the northern part of Carolina around 1653. However, the Lords Proprietor soon decided that the southern part of Carolina offered more economic potential than the north, and they began concentrating on settling South Carolina first.

THE GEORGIA CHARTER

The English colony of Georgia was established as a result of the efforts of James Oglethorpe. It was a unique colony founded for humanitarian and military reasons. Oglethorpe served in the English army as a young man and was later elected to Parliament, working on a committee that investigated conditions in the country's prisons.

Then in 1732, Oglethorpe and some influential friends obtained a charter for land in America in the region southwest of the Carolinas, between the Savannah and Altahama Rivers. They named the region Georgia in honor of King George II. They also asked permission to start a colony there for London's poor; the majority of the settlers would be debtors who had been imprisoned. The colony would be set up as a charity and administered by twenty trustees. A committee of over one hundred clergymen began to raise money and gifts of supplies and equipment for Georgia. Both preachers and poets predicted that this new English colony would become a Garden of Eden, where people would live together in harmony and prosperity.

EVENT

ESTABLISHMENT OF NORTH CAROLINA

Because North Carolina proved to be a tough land to tame, it grew more slowly than South Carolina. Its geography was much like Virginia's — with a tidewater (coastal) region, then a piedmont (plateau), and a mountainous region beyond. Although North Carolina had a number of rivers flowing into the ocean, its coastline did not have good harbors. For many years, North Carolina's only settlements were small settlements of tobacco farmers in the isolated northern Albemarle region, which was separated from Virginia by swamps. New Bern was the largest of these settlements. In addition to exporting tobacco, these colonists also shipped naval supplies to England.

Most of the Albemarle settlers were former indentured servants and other poor whites, who had been squeezed out of Virginia by the low price of tobacco. These tobacco farmers were dedicated to the principles of personal liberty. They managed to get rid of any governor sent to rule them—deposing one, imprisoning another, and banishing a third. However, they also struggled to survive economically, suffering through hurricanes, droughts, and the exorbitant fees charged by the Virginia ports that they depended upon to export their

The North Carolina, South Carolina, and Georgia colonies

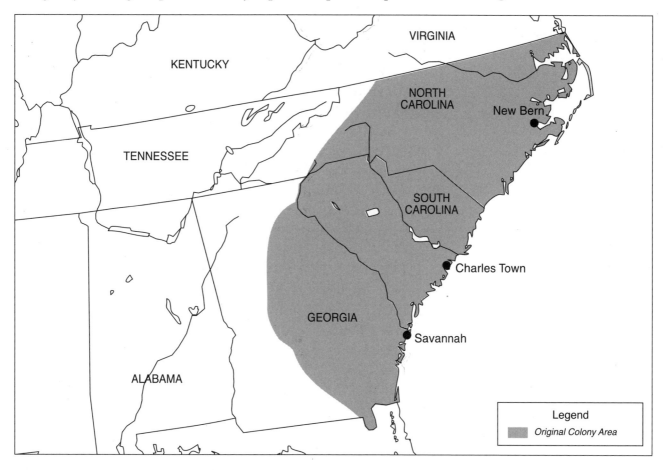

tobacco. Over time many religious outcasts and dissenters from Europe joined these independent-minded Albemarle tobacco farmers in North Carolina.

In 1677, a group of North Carolinians were involved in an attempt to overthrow English control of their colony. These colonists, led by John Culpeper, seized the governor of the colony and threw him in jail. Then they established their own government with Culpeper as governor. Eventually, the Lords Proprietor had this rebellion (which became known as Culpeper's Rebellion) put down. Culpeper went back to England to negotiate a compromise with the Lords Proprietor, but instead he was arrested and charged with treason. He was acquitted, his life was spared, and he returned to America.

Many North Carolina settlers were cruel and dishonest in their dealings with the Native Americans, cheating them of their land unmercifully. Finally in 1711, the Tuscarora tribe sought revenge by raiding several North Carolina settlements and burning, scalping, and murdering the colonists there. Because they had been sold guns by some of the settlers, the Tuscarora braves were actually much better armed than the colonists. Thousands were killed during two years of fighting. Settlers from South Carolina and Virginia eventually came to the rescue of their North Carolina neighbors, bringing men and money that enabled them to break up the power of the Tuscarora. However, the Lords Proprietor did little or nothing to help the North Carolina colonists during the Tuscarora attacks.

ESTABLISHMENT OF SOUTH CAROLINA

To recruit English settlers for South Carolina, Anthony Ashley Cooper talked the other proprietors into putting up money to print pamphlets telling of Carolina's wonders. The proprietors also decided to give one hundred acres of land to heads of families who settled there and to offer freedom of religion. Finally in August 1669, three ships—the *Carolina*, the *Port Royal*, and the *Albemarle*—set sail from England and headed to South Carolina. On board were approximately 140 people from many different religious backgrounds. Although the *Albemarle* and the *Port Royal* were wrecked in storms at sea, the

Carolina and a ship rented in Bermuda finally reached the coast of South Carolina in March 1670. When the Englishmen arrived on the Carolina coast, they chose a site for settlement. The area was briefly known as Albemarle Point, but its name was soon changed to Charles Town (even later changed to Charleston).

Because this original site was swampy and unhealthy, the settlement was eventually moved to a nearby peninsula, where the Ashley and Cooper rivers met and formed a nice sheltered harbor. Although the colonists at Charles Town never experienced a starving time, the first ten years of the settlement were difficult. Food was often in short supply, and the threat of an attack from the Spanish at St. Augustine always loomed.

Charleston c. 1780
Library of Congress, Prints and Photographs Division [LC-USZ62-46162]

During this first decade, a large number of English settlers came to South Carolina from Barbados, an English colony in the West Indies. These settlers, who became known as the Goose Creek Men, opposed the proprietary government of South Carolina and sought more local government control. They demanded and received a representative assembly, which constantly disagreed with the governor and the council appointed by the proprietors. A significant matter of dispute between the proprietors and many South Carolina settlers was the proprietors' practice of charging quit rents for use of the land.

From the beginning, the settlers at Charles Town were able to sell furs and naval supplies, such as tar and turpentine, to England. However, the proprietors soon became discouraged because they were receiving little profit from their colony. Rice, which grew well in the nearby swamps, eventually became the staple crop that ensured Charles Town's prosperity. The settlers at Charles Town also began to grow indigo, a plant used to dye cloth a rich purple color.

Indigo was an ideal second crop to grow with rice because it needed no attention in winter (the season when rice must be planted). But both rice and indigo required a cheap labor force, which the Carolina settlers found in African slaves. By 1708, South Carolina's economy was based on slave labor, and African slaves outnumbered whites in the colony. Some of these Africans would develop their own language called Gullah, a combination of English, French, and several African languages, which is still spoken by some in South Carolina today.

In the early 1680s, the proprietors began to concentrate on recruiting religious dissenters to South Carolina. From 1682 to 1684, five hundred English Presbyterians and Baptists arrived in the colony. Later, French Huguenots would come as well — with tastes and ideas that contributed to the creation of an aristocratic Charles Town society. As the city began to grow in both size and wealth, it emerged as the busiest seaport and largest city in the South. It developed into a sophisticated and cosmopolitan city with beautiful Georgian-style houses owned by wealthy planters and merchants. Younger sons of English nobility were especially attracted to this elegant city.

DIVISION OF SOUTH CAROLINA AND NORTH CAROLINA

For a long time, the people of North Carolina experienced many difficulties. However, the colony eventually succeeded because of its settlers' determination. By 1712, North Carolina was officially separated from South Carolina. Seventeen years later, King George I paid the Lords Proprietor a large sum of money for their land, and North Carolina and South Carolina became royal colonies. South Carolina remained quite prosperous, whereas North Carolina's economic growth continued more slowly.

ESTABLISHMENT OF GEORGIA

By the fall of 1732, more than one hundred colonists (thirty-five families) had been accepted by the trustees to go to Georgia. These colonists, along with James Oglethorpe, departed England on a ship named the *Ann* and arrived in Charles Town in January 1733. The South Carolina settlers were delighted by their arrival, because Georgia would serve as a buffer between them and the Spanish in Florida. A few Spanish priests and soldiers had settled in Georgia after the establishment of St. Augustine, but the Spanish had only a weak hold on the region.

Oglethorpe, along with Colonel William Bull from Charles Town, sailed south to look for a site to plant the Georgia colony. They chose a location eighteen miles inland from the mouth of the Savannah River. In February 1733, the Georgia colonists landed at Yamacraw Bluff and began establishing their new settlement, which they named Savannah after the river and the Savannah tribe. By fall, one out of nine of the Georgia settlers had died, primarily due to diseases such as dysentery and influenza. Food, however, was not a problem, because the colonists had supplies from England, South Carolina, and the Native Americans.

This first English settlement in Georgia was laid out by Oglethorpe with the help of Colonel Bull. Each family who was part of the new community was given a home and a garden plot totaling five acres, as well as another forty-five acres outside of Savannah for its main farming grounds. Oglethorpe designed the city with broad streets and squares at intervals to serve as marketplaces. Oglethorpe also made

James Oglethorpe
Line drawing courtesy of Amy Pak

Tomochichi
Courtesy of North Wind Picture Archives

signing a treaty of peace and friendship with the nearby Creek tribe a priority. In fact, Tomochichi, the Creek chief, became Oglethorpe's good friend. The local natives learned to trust and respect Oglethorpe and they were willing to fight alongside the English against the Spanish.

Georgia's trustees had decreed that only Protestants were to be allowed in the colony. However, when a group of Jews sailed into Savannah, Oglethorpe welcomed them. In the first years of the colony, many persecuted Protestants immigrated to Georgia from all over Europe. Most colonists were either English adventurers or those seeking religious freedom. In fact, few English debtors ever reached Georgia. Most of them decided that life in prison would be better than life in the Georgia wilderness and refused to leave England.

Overbearing Trustees

Georgia's colonial charter provided for a governor to be named by the trustees. However, the trustees never appointed one, and they ruled Georgia by their own regulations. Over time the settlers rebelled against their decisions, and the trustees began to relax some of their requirements. For instance, the trustees had decided that the chief occupation in Georgia should be raising silk and required every landholder to plant at least one hundred mulberry trees to feed silkworms. The colonists soon resisted this regulation because Georgia's climate was not suitable for raising silkworms. The trustees relented and allowed the colonists to grow rice and produce naval stores from the pine forests.

Another unpopular decision by Georgia's trustees was to limit the amount of land each settler could own. They did this to prevent land speculation. The most allowed was usually ten to fifty acres, although those who would pay passage to bring over ten servants were given five hundred acres. Settlers were not allowed to own their land for ten years and were charged quit rents for its use. The trustees eventually changed this policy. Although slavery was prohibited by the trustees, colonists soon began to sneak in slaves because they were not able to clear and farm enough of their land alone. In 1750, slavery was made legal in Georgia, and within fifteen years one half of the colony's population was African slaves. The trustees reversed themselves for the final time when they decided to no longer prohibit strong liquor in Georgia.

Dissatisfied with the trustees' overbearing rule of Georgia, Oglethorpe sailed back to England in 1743. He never returned to Georgia; he had lost his fortune trying to establish the colony. The trustees of Georgia surrendered their charter in 1752, and Georgia became a royal colony. By that time, Savannah had become an important seaport, and Augusta had become the largest fur-trading center in the South.

IMPACT

- In the 1630s, King Charles I awarded the coastal area from Virginia to Spanish Florida to Sir Robert Heath. During the period that Heath held the charter, the region was named Carolana. In 1663, King Charles II revoked Heath's charter and gave it to eight prominent English nobles who had helped him recover the throne after the Puritan Revolution. These eight men became known as the Lords Proprietor.

- Due to its geography, North Carolina grew more slowly than South Carolina. For many years, the only settlements in North Carolina were small groups of independent-minded tobacco farmers in the isolated northern Albemarle region. A group of them were involved in Culpeper's Rebellion, an attempt to overthrow proprietary control of the colony.

- The Lords Proprietor were interested in making money by having colonists use their land to produce wine, silk, and olive oil. They established a settlement at Charles Town in 1670, which brought them little profit at first. Rice and indigo (which depended upon slave labor) eventually became the staple crops that ensured Charles Town's economic survival.

- By 1712, North Carolina was officially separated from South Carolina. South Carolina continued to prosper, and North Carolina's economic growth remained slow.

- The colony of Georgia, established by James Oglethorpe in 1732, was founded for humanitarian and military reasons. Oglethorpe and some influential friends were given permission to establish a colony there for London's poor. It was also hoped that Georgia would serve as a buffer between the Spanish in Florida and the other English colonies.

- Oglethorpe was dissatisfied with the proprietors' overbearing rule of the Georgia Colony and returned to England in 1743, having lost his personal fortune. In 1752, the trustees of Georgia surrendered their charter, and Georgia became a royal colony. By this time, Savannah was an important seaport and Augusta was a large fur-trading center.

LESSON 15

Colonial Family Life . . . . 1600s — 1700s A.D.

ATMOSPHERE

A TYPICAL AMERICAN COLONIAL FAMILY

By 1750, the typical American colonial family consisted of a mother, a father, and about seven children. Although there were few divorces, there were many remarriages due to the death of a spouse. Almost one in four colonial children had lost at least one parent by the age of five, and one in two had lost one or both parents by age fourteen.

However, few widows or widowers stayed single for long because it was very difficult in colonial society for one person to support and raise a family. All the members of a colonial family relied upon one another for food, shelter, clothing, and a sense of belonging.

EVENT

COLONIAL MARRIAGE AND CHILDREN

Colonial men were recognized as head of their households; their word was considered law. When children disobeyed, their fathers were not reluctant to discipline them. Women in colonial society were also subject to the authority of their husbands, fathers, or older brothers.

American women during this period in history were not allowed to own property in their own name, to vote, or to run for public office.

Men and women in colonial America tended to marry at a slighter younger age than their European counterparts. Most colonial girls married by age sixteen or seventeen, and most boys went to work by age fourteen. Couples in the colonies often had babies every two years until they reached their late thirties. However, childbirth was quite a dangerous experience for both mother and child, and one out of four babies born in the American colonies died before reaching adulthood.

The colonial children who survived the early years of life and reached the age of three were expected to start helping the household with simple chores, such as feeding the farm animals or washing the dishes. There were few differences in the way colonial adults and children lived; both young and old worked hard and had little free time. In fact, most of childhood was spent learning skills needed for adult life. Colonial families spent almost all of their time together — eating three meals together daily and spending an hour or two together around the fireplace at night. In the evenings they enjoyed doing handicrafts, reading the Bible aloud, and discussing the day's events.

EDUCATION FOR COLONIAL CHILDREN

Schools varied greatly from region to region in the American colonies. In the New England colonies, Puritans were very concerned about education. They believed that it was important for children to learn to read in order to be able to read the Bible. The first school in New England was established in Boston in 1635, and the first American college (Harvard) was founded a year later.

By 1642, the Massachusetts Bay Colony had passed a law requiring parents to teach their children to read. Five years later, the Olde Deluder Satan Act required every town with more than fifty families to establish a grammar school. Shortly thereafter, the other New England colonies, except Rhode Island, enacted similar laws. Although girls were taught to read, they were not allowed to attend grammar schools or college. However, they could attend dame

Harvard
Line drawing courtesy of Amy Pak

schools for a few years, which were private elementary school classes taught by women in their homes.

In 1683, the first school in Pennsylvania was founded. After this date, every Quaker community provided for the elementary teaching of its children in some fashion. More advanced training was offered at the Friends Public School in Philadelphia, which still operates today as the William Penn Charter School. Although this school was free to the poor, parents who could afford the tuition were required to pay it. In Philadelphia there were also numerous private schools with no religious affiliation. Girls were not allowed to attend school unless they were Quakers, but the daughters of the wealthy were instructed by private tutors in music, dance, painting, French, grammar, and sometimes even bookkeeping.

Children in the Southern colonies were usually taught at home— either by their parents or by private tutors. Wealthy planters and merchants imported these private tutors from Scotland or Ireland. Thus, the upper classes in the Tidewater region had no interest in supporting public education. The fact that plantations were spread so far apart also made the formation of community schools difficult. When southern boys became teenagers, they were sent away to college or to Europe. The first southern college, William and Mary, was founded in 1693 near Jamestown. By the late colonial period, the Southern colonies had passed laws making it illegal to teach slaves how to read and write. Slaveholders and other southern whites had become frightened at the possibility of literate Africans planning and succeeding in an uprising.

Schools in all of the colonies were usually small. Most children learned to read using a thin, paddle-shaped, wooden board called a hornbook. This board had a paper sheet that was covered with a thin layer of bull's horn and listed the alphabet in both small and capital letters. It also often contained the benediction and the Lord's Prayer and usually hung on a string around the student's neck — ready for use at any time. The *New England Primer* was first published in 1690, and it was the first textbook used in the colonies. It combined the hornbook with the authorized catechism and taught the alphabet using two-line rhymes. Many of its poems had religious references.

A wise son maketh a glad father, but a foolish son is the heaviness of his mother.

Better is a little with the fear of the Lord, than great treasure and trouble therewith.

Come unto Christ all ye that labor and are heavy laden and he will give you rest.

Do not the abominable thing which I hate saith the Lord.

Except a man be born again, he cannot see the kingdom of God.

Foolishness is bound up in the heart of a child, but the rod of correction shall drive it far from him.

Godliness is profitable unto all things, having the promise of the life that now is, and that which is to come.

Holiness becomes God's house for ever.

It is good for me to draw near unto God.

—from the *New England Primer*

One-room schoolhouse
National Archives print [52-1034]

Generally, students of all ages attended class in one large room, and one teacher taught all of them. Most colonial teachers were men, and they were called schoolmasters. Many were retired soldiers in need of a job, although some of the best were clergymen with college degrees. Course work for colonial children generally consisted of the three Rs —reading, 'riting, and 'rithmetic. Sometimes, grammar, history, and geography were also taught. Penmanship was especially emphasized; legible handwriting was considered the sign of a cultured person. Generally, the teaching methodology used was rote learning.

Many colonial children only attended school when their parents did not need them to work at the family farm or shop. The school year was usually short — just a few months a year. The school day often started at eight in the morning, with a lunch break from eleven to one, and dismissal at four in the afternoon. Students sat on hard benches, and many did not have desks. Most classrooms had no pencils, paper, or blackboards, and they had few books. Most often, students wrote with goose-quill pens, which they dipped into home-made ink and used to write on pieces of birch bark. Colonial students were often punished for being tardy, falling asleep in class, answering questions incorrectly, or not learning their lessons quickly enough. For punishment a student might have memorized a long passage or written certain sentences over and over. Other methods of school discipline included placing the student in the corner wearing a dunce cap or a sign that said "fool" on his chest. There were also whippings with a hickory switch or birch rod. Some schoolmasters used the peg, which involved fastening the pupil's hair to a clip that was pegged to the wall at a height that kept him standing on tiptoes.

COLONIAL CLOTHING

During the colonial period, wealthy Americans were able to import silken and linen garments from Europe, whereas other settlers made their clothing from natural materials produced in the colonies.

Clothing Styles for Colonial Men

Colonial men in all levels of society wore breeches as their lower-body garments. Through the years, the length of the breeches and the materials used to make them varied. In the eighteenth century, upper-class men's breeches came to just beneath the knee. Leggings covered the leg from the knee to the top of the foot, and stockings were worn underneath the leggings.

In the eighteenth century, a gentleman's shirts were often made of linen, and his best shirts had wide cuffs and ruffles at the neck. Colonial upper-class men were hardly ever seen without a waistcoat, which was a vest that came down to the upper part of the thigh. They also wore some type of neckwear, usually a cravat draped about the throat and loosely tied in front. The uppermost layer of a gentleman's outfit was a coat worn over the waistcoat and breeches. As time went on, men's waistcoats and outer coats grew shorter, and their breeches became tighter and fancier.

Working-class men typically wore trousers that covered the leg. Men's shoes were made in a variety of styles, and black was by far the

Upper-class man
National Archives print [RG30NBox263]

Working-class men
Library of Congress, Prints and Photographs Division [LC-USZ62-57493]

most common color. Buckles were the primary means of fastening shoes, and upper-class men usually wore high heels. Boots were worn for riding, working, and sporting.

Eighteenth century men commonly wore wigs. By mid-century, wigs were available for most levels of society, and certain styles of wigs were associated with particular professionals. These wigs were constructed from human, horse, goat, or yak hair, and their styles changed constantly with fashion and personal preference. At home, men usually wore tri-corner hats instead of wigs.

Upper-class woman
National Archives print [RG30NBox263]

Clothing Styles for Colonial Women

Colonial upper-class women wore gowns that consisted of a bodice and a skirt joined together. The skirt opened in front to reveal a separate petticoat. For formal occasions these gowns were made of elaborate silk brocade and worn with formal gloves, lace-trimmed caps, pearl necklaces, and fans. Corsets, worn around the waist to minimize it, were an essential female foundation garment. As the years passed, women's skirts grew wider and wider and their corsets tighter and tighter.

Working-class women in the colonies usually wore dresses with straight skirts that came down to their ankles and bodices that laced up the back. Aprons covered their dresses as they took care of the day's work.

During the colonial period, American women kept their hair covered. They wore caps to dress their heads and to keep them from having to wash their hair as frequently. When going out, ladies almost always wore hats for fashion and for protection against the sun. Women also wore elbow-length, fingerless gloves (called mitts); heavy ones gave warmth in winter and light ones offered protection from the sun. Cloaks, covering the hair and dress, were worn for warmth as well. Women's shoes were made of leathers, worsteds, and silk fabrics and typically had high heels.

Clothing Styles for Colonial Children

Very young colonial children of both sexes wore dresses with close-fitting bodices. These bodices were usually fastened at the back and often had leading strings with bands attached to the shoulders to help parents guide their children as they learned to walk.

At age five or six years, colonial boys were breeched — put into their first pair of pants. Both boys and girls wore slippers in the winter and shoes of soft leather in the summer. Wealthy children might have store-bought shoes with hard soles from Europe. Colonial girls and boys, as well as their parents, typically wore bright-colored clothing — blues, reds, purples, and yellows.

Clothing Styles for Puritans and Quakers

For over one hundred years the Puritans of New England were known for their distinctively plain style of clothing. In fact, laws were passed in the early years of Massachusetts Bay regarding clothing requirements; but these laws grew less strict as time went on.

Puritan men wore dark plain coats and breeches, wool stockings, and black hats with wide brims and high crowns. They kept their hair short and rarely wore wigs. Puritan women dressed in long-sleeved dark gowns and stiff undergarments. Their clothing had no lace trim or bright ribbons, and they wore no gold or silver jewelry or makeup. American Quakers were similarly known for their plain clothing and lack of ornamentation.

COLONIAL HEALTH AND HYGIENE

The average life expectancy for an American during the colonial period was less than twenty-five years. Many children and adults died from diseases like malaria, cholera, pneumonia, smallpox, scarlet fever, tuberculosis, and rickets. Many illnesses were also caused by contaminated drinking water and spoiled food. Most colonists who became sick were treated at home by the housekeeper or mistress of the house, who used a supply of medicinal herbs and other simple remedies. Local barber-surgeons were only consulted after all other treatments failed.

By the time of the American Revolution, there were only a few American doctors trained in a medical school. Most physicians were either self-trained or trained by another doctor, and they usually

Working-class women
National Archives print [208-LU-25J-5]

Puritan dress
Library of Congress, Prints and Photographs Division [LC-USZ62-74739]

limited their treatments to rich people who were chronically ill. Colonial doctors had little knowledge of the real causes and cures of most diseases, and they had few effective painkillers and medicines to give to their patients. Two common treatments for illness were to bleed patients using leeches and to purge their digestive systems to remove harmful "humors" — imaginary fluids blamed for causing illness.

Colonial homes had no running water, bathrooms, or septic systems. There were outdoor toilets of wood or brick called privies, as well as chamber pots that would be used inside and then dumped outside. Most colonists did not believe in bathing every day or even every week because they considered a layer of dirt to be protection against germs. Usually a bath consisted of washing with a cloth dipped in a cold basin of water.

COLONIAL NUTRITION, EATING, AND COOKING HABITS

The American colonists originally wanted to eat the same foods that they had eaten in England and in other parts of Europe. However, many of those foods did not grow well in America, so the colonists learned to eat and cook new foods like corn, beans, squash, and pumpkins. They also learned to farm, hunt, and fish like the Native Americans.

Colonial homes usually contained no stoves or ovens, and, of course, colonial families had no freezers or refrigerators. Food was cooked in a big kettle over an open hearth. Most meals were stews — meat, corn, turnips, and other vegetables cooked together. Heavy brown bread was cooked in the steam that rose from the stew. Meat was preserved with smoking, and vegetables were preserved with pickling in vinegar. On Sundays, many colonial families ate baked beans, which were slow cooked with molasses and a piece of salt pork in the fireplace kettle all night.

Because most colonists believed that water made them sick, they drank very little of it. They also drank little milk because cows were not plentiful. Colonists did drink fruit juices, such as peach juice and apple cider, as well as beer and rum. It was not uncommon for colonial children to drink whiskey.

For many years there were no cookbooks published in the American colonies. Any cookbooks used by the colonists were brought over from England, and mothers passed on their favorite recipes by teaching them to their daughters. In 1742, a Williamsburg printer named William Parks was responsible for publishing what appears to be the first cookbook published in the colonies — *The Compleat Housewife: Accomplish'd Gentlewoman's Companion*. This 228-page volume was originally compiled in London by Eliza Smith, and by 1742 was in its fifth London edition. On the eve of the American Revolution, this cookbook was still popular in the Virginia Colony. There are six known copies of the Williamsburg edition still in existence today.

By the mid-eighteenth century, the English had realized that there was a market for their cookbooks in the colonies and began issuing American editions of their original publications. Susannah Carter's cookbook, *The Frugal Housewife*, was first printed in England in 1742. In 1772, she reissued the book with accommodations for American cooks. The Boston printer Paul Revere was responsible for producing the printing plates for the American edition. This particular cookbook could be found in the homes of many of the wives and mothers of the men who signed the Declaration of Independence and the United States Constitution.

Colonial children
National Archives print [RG30NBox263]

There are indeed already in the world various books that treat on this subject, and which bear great names, as cooks to kings, princes and noblemen, and from which one might justly expect something more than many, if not most of those I have read, perform; but found myself deceived by my expectations; for many of them to us are impractiable, others whimsical, others unpalatable, unless to depraved palates; some unwholesome; many things copies from old authors, and recommended without (as I am persuaded) the copiers ever having had any experience of the palatableness, or had any regard to the wholesomeness of them; which two things ought to

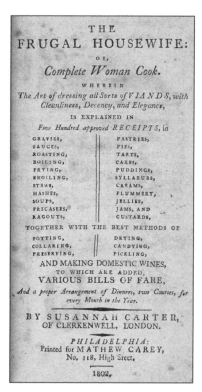

Title page of an 1802 edition of *The Frugal Housewife*

Public Domain

be the standing rules, that no pretenders to cookery ought to deviate from. These receipts are all suitable to English constitutions, and English palates, wholesome, toothsome, all practicable and easy to be performed.

—from *The Compleat Housewife*

In New England the growing season was short, so it was difficult for settlers in that region to grow enough fruits and vegetables to feed their families. These colonists rarely ate fresh vegetables. Instead, they consumed a lot of meat and fish and cooked the vegetables that they ate in sauces. When boats brought goats and cows from England, the colonists were able to have fresh milk, butter, and cheeses. Sugar was quite expensive and had to be shipped from England. Most people cooked with molasses, also brought over from England but cheaper than sugar, or with maple syrup (made from sap drained from maple trees). Two typical New England dishes included flapjacks (like pancakes) and hasty pudding, made from cornmeal, salt, and water and served with maple syrup and milk.

In the Middle colonies there was a longer growing season and better soil. The Dutch and Germans who settled there brought their own culinary traditions with them. The Dutch enjoyed cheeses, cookies, cakes, and pastries. The Germans ate a lot of cabbage and rye bread and had many different ways to cook pork. Colonists in the Middle colonies often built brick ovens into the inside wall of their fireplaces. Later, they moved these ovens outside of the fireplace, and eventually cast iron stoves became popular. Women baked cookies, cakes, breads, and pies about once a week.

The South had a good climate for crops and a long growing season. Many different types of food could be grown there, and Southerners also ate a lot of meat. Because of the warm weather, food spoiled quickly in the Southern colonies. The bad flavor of spoiled food was often hidden by adding spices like black pepper or chili pepper. Southerners often enjoyed eating hominy with their meats and vegetables. Hominy is corn with the hulls removed from the kernels (Indian style). Another popular southern dish was succotash—lima

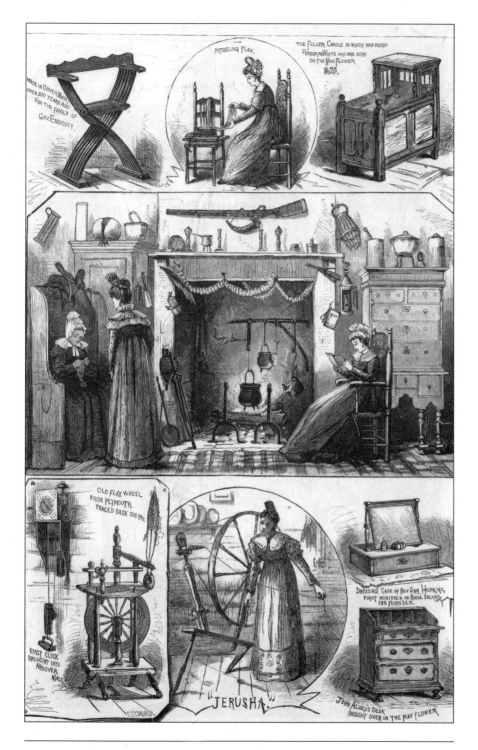

Depiction of a colonial New England farmhouse
Library of Congress, Prints and Photographs Division [LC-USZ62-102852]

beans and hominy or white corn cooked with butter, sugar, salt, pepper, and cream. African Americans in the South ate spicier foods than the European colonists. Some of their favorites included black-eyed peas, okra, and peanuts. An African specialty was hoppin' John, which consisted of black-eyed peas, onion, seasoning, and bacon served with rice.

Few colonial homes had separate dining rooms or even dinner tables. In order to eat, a family might lay boards across a packing case brought from Europe or on top of a workbench. Most food was served in bowls and eaten on wooden boards called trenchers. Forks were considered to be an unnecessary luxury when they were first brought over from Europe, but spoons were used. At meals children were generally expected to be quiet; "speak not" was the rule.

IMPACT

- Colonial men were recognized as head of their households, with both children and women subject to the authority of their fathers, husbands, or older brothers. There were few differences in the way colonial adults and children lived; everyone worked hard. Colonial families spent almost all of their time together.

- Schools varied from region to region in the colonies. In New England, Puritans were very concerned about education and quickly established public schools and colleges. In the mid-Atlantic colonies, such as Pennsylvania, there were numerous private schools with no religious affiliation. Children in the Southern colonies were usually taught at home by their parents or private tutors.

- Clothing styles varied for upper-class and lower-class colonial men and women. In the eighteenth century, many men wore wigs, and women usually kept their hair covered with caps or hats. Very young colonial children of both sexes wore dresses with close-fitting bodices, but at age five or six boys were breeched.

- The average life expectancy for colonial Americans was less than twenty-five years. There were only a few American doctors trained in medical schools, and they had little knowledge of the real causes and cures of most disease.

- American colonists wanted to eat the same foods that they had eaten in Europe. However, many of those foods did not grow well in America. So the colonists learned to grow and eat new foods like corn, beans, squash, and pumpkin and to hunt and fish like the Native Americans.

LESSON 16

Colonial Culture . . . . 1600s — 1700s A.D.

ATMOSPHERE

THE VARIOUS ASPECTS OF COLONIAL CULTURE

The people of colonial America developed a culture that was distinctly based upon their European roots. American society, government, economic activities, transportation, communication, religion, and entertainment all showed the influence of primarily English customs and accomplishments. Nevertheless, in America less aristocratic and more democratic traditions began to emerge. The colonists became more and more at home in a new land, where an individual's destiny was more closely tied to his accomplishments and less to his family background.

EVENT

COLONIAL SOCIETY

Early English settlers who immigrated to America came from a society of rigid class divisions. At first these American colonists attempted to follow the Old World social patterns. However, over time a uniquely American social structure developed, with less rigid class distinctions.

Just as it was in the homeland, wealth became the primary measure of status in colonial America. However, this wealth was usually acquired wealth, not inherited wealth. In the colonies ambition and intelligence meant more than who a person's parents were. There was no American nobility. Rather, America's aristocracy consisted of a select upper class of wealthy planters, merchants, lawyers, politicians, physicians, and clergymen. These members of America's elite copied the fashions of English gentlemen and lived in houses resembling the mansions of European nobility with fine furnishings and expensive artwork.

The vast majority of European settlers in American were yeoman farmers, trades people, shopkeepers, and skilled artisans. They lived on farms or in country villages. This colonial middle class was three times the size of the English middle class, and opportunities for its members to move up were plentiful. Colonial farmers, laborers, and craftsmen usually lived in small houses of wood with two to four rooms and a lean-to kitchen in the back. Their homes generally had little furniture or inside decoration. Of course, there were no inside bathrooms, only outhouses. Although these middle-class colonists did not have great wealth or much education, they did own property and the men had the right to vote.

Beneath the colonial middle class was a lower class, consisting of unskilled workers, landless farmhands, and indentured servants. Often their homes were just one-room huts or shacks with hard-packed dirt for floors and no real windows. On the bottom rung of American colonial society were African slaves and Native Americans. In fact, neither slaves nor natives were even considered to be a part of colonial society. Rather, they were seen as inferior groups to be subjugated and used.

The 1740 census counted 150,024 African slaves in America, and the vast majority of those lived in the Southern colonies. Thousands of new slaves arrived from West Africa each year. Slave traders made such huge profits that they referred to the Africans as "black gold." Most of these African slaves worked as field hands or domestic servants on southern plantations under conditions of extreme hardship.

Slave transport in Africa
Public Domain

For the most part, Native Americans identified with their own tribe or nation and did not feel linked to other tribes. Each tribe spoke its own language. Historians have estimated that more than two thousand native languages were spoken in the Americas in the early 1600s. Native American tribes were often in conflict with each other because of their need to control territory to ensure that they had enough to eat. Throughout the colonial period, more and more Native Americans were stripped of their land by European settlers and pushed farther and farther inland.

COLONIAL GOVERNMENT

All of the thirteen English colonies, except for Georgia, developed from companies of shareholders or from proprietorships, which were granted charters by the English crown. Many of these colonies eventually became royal colonies. However, almost from the beginning, it was generally accepted that the colonists had a right to legislative representation in their government. By the mid-eighteenth century most colonial governments had a governor, a council appointed by the governor, and an elected assembly. Most white male landowners were given the right to vote. In all of the colonies except Rhode Island and Connecticut, the king appointed the governor. In those two colonies, the governor was elected by the assemblies.

For much of the seventeenth century, the English were distracted by political events in the homeland. Therefore, they did not take the time to develop a coherent plan for governing their growing colonies. The natural conditions of America promoted a tough individualism in its settlers, which made them resistant to strong measures of control from the English government. With an ocean separating the colonies from the homeland, the colonies were largely self-governing. Royal governors could not depend on instructions from home because letters took at least eight weeks to reach London.

In 1686, the English crown made a move to tighten its control over the New England colonies, which had resisted an English attempt to regulate their commerce. That year, King James II approved the creation of the Dominion of New England, uniting the colonies from

New England south through New Jersey under its jurisdiction. A royal governor, Edmund Andros, was appointed to head this dominion. Andros was given authority to levy taxes by executive order and to implement several other harsh measures; he jailed those colonists who failed to comply. However, the dominion lasted only a few years. By 1689, Bostonians had imprisoned Governor Andros, and the colonies of the Dominion of New England quickly reinstated their previous governments.

During the early 1700s, colonial governors, appointed by the crown, attempted to exercise power over the colonies. However, at the same time, colonial assemblies sought to assert their rights. These assemblies were successful in solidifying two important powers: the right to vote on taxes and expenditures and the right to initiate legislation rather than merely respond to proposals made by the governor. Using these powers to limit the control of royal governors enabled assemblies to continue to establish the right of self-government in the colonies.

The American colonists believed they had inherited the hard-won rights and freedoms of Englishmen. They thought that they should enjoy the benefits of the Magna Carta, the English Bill of Rights, and English common law. They also were influenced by John Locke's *Second Treatise on Government* (1690), which stated that the people were endowed with natural rights of life, liberty, and property as well as the right to rebel if their government violates those natural rights. Nevertheless, even as late as 1750, the American colonies saw themselves as extensions of the realm of the English monarchy and did not aspire to political independence.

To understand political power right, and derive it from its original, we must consider, what state all men are naturally in, and that is, a state of perfect freedom to order their actions, and dispose of their possessions and persons, as they think fit, within the bounds of the law of nature, without asking leave, or depending upon the will of any other man. A state also of equality, wherein all the power and jurisdiction is reciprocal, no one having more than another; there being nothing more evident, than that creatures of the same species and rank, promiscuously born to all the same advantages of nature, and the use of the same faculties, should also be equal one amongst another without subordination or subjection, unless the lord and master of them all should, by any manifest declaration of his will, set one above another, and confer on him, by an evident and clear appointment, an undoubted right to dominion and sovereignty.

—from *Second Treatise on Government*

COLONIAL ECONOMICS

New England Colonies: Shipbuilding, Commerce, Fishing, and Whaling

Because of the thin, rocky soil and long winters of the New England colonies, settlers found it difficult to make a living from farming. So, the people in this region found other ways to survive economically. Using the plentiful timber available from New England forests, shipmasters in the region constructed vessels that sailed to ports all over the world. By the end of the colonial period, a third of all British ships were built in New England.

Whale fishery
Library of Congress, Prints and Photographs Division [LC-USZC2-1759]

The region's excellent harbors also promoted trade, and the cod industry provided a profitable export. The busiest and most prosperous port in the region was Boston. New England shippers eventually became involved in a lucrative triangular trade. They used New England rum to purchase African slaves, sold the slaves in the West Indies for molasses, and returned to New England to sell the molasses to the local rum producers.

Whaling was another important industry in New England. Whale oil was valuable for use in lamps, and the whale's waxy material made good candles. New Englanders also profited from the area's plentiful water power, harnessing it to establish saw mills and grain mills. As time went on, many settlers in New England began developing craft and cottage industries, which would continue to grow in significance.

Almost 95 percent of the people in the New England colonies were English immigrants, who came over in groups for religious reasons.

Many of them settled in villages surrounding the area's harbors and engaged in some kind of trade or business. Over time, shops were established in these villages, selling goods that could not be made at home and offering the services of blacksmiths, cabinetmakers, cobblers, wheelwrights, coopers, bakers, tailors, barbers, clockmakers, printers, and others. To produce the food necessary for their survival, some New Englanders worked small farms and used common pasturelands. Villages served as markets for this farm produce.

Middle or Mid-Atlantic Colonies: Agriculture and Manufacturing

Life in the Middle colonies was more diverse and cosmopolitan than life in New England. This region was settled by immigrants from a number of countries—England, Holland, Sweden, Scotland, Ireland, Germany, Poland, France, Norway, Portugal, Italy, and Denmark. From the earliest years of their existence, most of the Mid-Atlantic colonies were established as profit-making enterprises rather than as religious communities. Initially, fur trading provided the region with a lucrative export to Europe. When the demand for furs diminished, agriculture and manufacturing provided a strong economic base for the Middle colonies.

Large farms in New York and Pennsylvania prospered, producing wheat, barley, and other grains for export. Pennsylvania factories manufactured textiles and paper. Cabinetmaking, weaving, and shoe-making developed as important cottage industries in these colonies. Trade in agricultural and manufactured goods flourished along the Hudson, Delaware, and Susquehanna rivers. By 1760, the population of New York City had exceeded that of Boston, but it had not overtaken that of the largest city in the Middle colonies—Philadelphia.

Southern Colonies: Agriculture

From the beginning, the South was almost entirely agricultural, with a small group of white plantation owners becoming enormously wealthy and powerful. These planters, who lived in the tidewater or coastal region of the South, were predominantly English immigrants. The principal crop grown on Southern plantations was tobacco; rice and indigo were also cultivated in the Carolinas and Georgia. These crops, harvested primarily by African slaves, were exported to England and to the other colonies. Naval stores (tar, turpentine) were another southern export. These products came from the forests of North Carolina and Georgia. The city of Charleston became the largest port and trading center in the South.

In addition to the small group of planters in the South, there was a large group of yeoman or subsistence farmers who worked smaller tracts of land in the backcountry. These settlers, primarily German and Scotch-Irish immigrants, were forced by necessity to be self-sufficient; they were also quite vocal in speaking out for the rights of the common man.

During the colonial period, factories in Maryland began producing iron. By the mid-1700s there was growth in large industries throughout the colonies, including construction, ironworks, mining, and finished products made in city workshops. However, few large population centers developed in the South before the American Revolution. Annapolis, the capital of Maryland, and Williamsburg, the capital of Virginia, were only small towns; and North Carolina had no cities.

Colonial Williamsburg
National Archives print
[Virginia State Chamber]

COLONIAL TRANSPORTATION AND COMMUNICATION

During the colonial period, horse-pulled wagons and sleighs were essential to land transportation. However, land travel was slow and time consuming because most roads were narrow, bumpy, and full of holes and became muddy and icy in bad weather. Before the mid-1800s, most roads in the colonies were dirt. A few were surfaced with gravel or oyster shells; some others were made with rough logs and they were known as corduroy roads. The first stagecoach run from New York to Boston was in 1772. The trip took six days with eighteen hours of travel per day. Boats were the other primary means of transportation in the colonies.

The first regular mail service in the colonies was begun in 1672. Men carrying mail on horseback became known as post riders. Mail

Stage wagon
Library of Congress, Prints and Photographs Division [LC-USZ62-1800]

Benjamin Franklin
Library of Congress, Prints and Photographs Division [LC-USZ62-90398]

was later delivered by stage wagon. When Benjamin Franklin became postmaster-general of the colonies, he had many of the post roads improved. In many villages, town criers reported the news. By 1750, every major American city had a newspaper, and the first subscription library had been established by Franklin in Philadelphia.

COLONIAL RELIGION

The thirteen American colonies were populated primarily by Protestants. In New England the predominant religious group was the Puritans, whereas in the South, Anglicans and Baptists predominated. In the Middle colonies there were a number of religious groups — Quakers, Dutch Reformed, Presbyterians, and Lutherans. Maryland, of course, was founded as a refuge for English Catholics.

For the Puritans in New England, church was a central part of life. Most Puritan church services were held in the meetinghouse, a large building in the center of town. Inside the meetinghouse were hard wooden benches, where the people often sat for two to three hours every Sunday listening to the sermon. Tickling rods were used to awaken those in the congregation who fell asleep, and those who made noise or wiggled during the service could be locked up in the stocks. Puritan worship services were known for their unadorned simplicity — no statues or ornamentation, no stained glass windows, and no vestments or altar cloths. Psalm singing was an important part of Puritan worship. The first book ever issued from a press in the American colonies was the *Bay Psalm Book*, published in Cambridge, Massachusetts, in 1640.

There have been three questions especially stirring concerning singing. First, what psalms are to be sung in churches? Whether David's and other scripture psalms, or the psalms invented by the gifts of godly men in every age of the church. Secondly, if scripture psalms, whether in their own words, or in such metre as English poetry is wont to run in? Thirdly, by whom are they to be sung? Whether by the whole churches together with their voices? Or by one man singing alone and the rest joining in silence, and in the close saying amen.

—from the *Bay Psalm Book*

Every part of life in New England Puritan communities was governed by strict rules of behavior issued by the church. Sundays were completely devoted to worship, and holidays or birthdays were not celebrated. Puritans were known for their "blue laws," rules banning work and play on the Sabbath that were written in books bound in blue paper. Fines and punishments could be imposed upon those who cooked, made a bed, shaved, ran, or performed many other activities on the Sabbath. A Puritan minister who exerted tremendous power for many years during the colonial period was the Reverend John Cotton. Cotton's pronouncements from the pulpit were often enacted into law. Even so, by 1750 religious life in New England had become less intense, and many of the tight social controls had been loosened.

Most of the people in the Middle and Southern colonies attended worship services in more familiar-looking church buildings. However, like the Puritans, worship occupied a large part of their Sundays. In the Southern and Middle colonies there was no one religious group that exerted control over life in the same way that the Puritans in New England did. Probably the most unique of the religious groups in the Middle colonies was the Society of Friends (Quakers). Quaker services, which they called meetings, were not led by ministers. Instead, everyone meditated in silence; and if someone felt God communicating directly to him, that individual felt free to stand and speak about his "inward light" or to shake and tremble. There were fewer churches in the Southern and Middle colonies than in New England, because people there generally lived farther apart. In some areas churches were supplied by preachers called circuit riders, who regularly traveled the same circuit (circle) of towns to fill pulpits.

From approximately 1730 until 1760, the American colonies were swept by a religious revival, which came to be known as the Great Awakening. Seen by some as a reaction to the cold rationalism of the Puritans and Anglicans, the Great Awakening placed an emphasis

Gilbert Tennant
Public Domain

Jonathan Edwards
Line drawing courtesy of Amy Pak

George Whitefield
Library of Congress, Prints and Photographs Division [LC-USZ62-120395]

upon religious experience and emotional manifestations (such as fainting, weeping, and physical movement). As a result of the Great Awakening, many thousands of Americans were introduced to the reality of the Gospel of Jesus Christ. People throughout the colonies were bound together more closely than before through the bonds of a shared experiential faith, leading to a loosening of denominational ties.

Two of the most important colonial revival preachers were Jonathan Edwards and Gilbert Tennant. Edwards, a New England preacher of great intellect, became known for his powerfully convicting sermons, such as "Sinners in the Hands of an Angry God." Gilbert Tennant, a Presbyterian preacher in the Middle colonies, founded an institution known as the Log Cabin to prepare young men for the ministry and to spread the message of the Awakening. During the period of the Great Awakening, famous English preachers, such as George Whitefield and John Wesley, also made trips to the colonies to preach to thousands of colonists.

God has laid himself under no obligation, by any promise to keep any natural man out of hell one moment. God certainly has made no promises either of eternal life, or of any deliverance or preservation from eternal death, but what are contained in the covenant of grace, the promises that are given in Christ, in whom all the promises are yea and amen. But surely they have no interest in the promises of the covenant of grace who are not the children of the covenant, who do not believe in any of the promises, and have no interest in the Mediator of the covenant.

—from "Sinners in the Hands of an Angry God"

COLONIAL RECREATION AND THE ARTS

In colonial America most New England villages had an area called the Common in the center of town, where people would gather before and after meetings and where cattle were allowed to graze. In the common areas of villages in the Southern and Middle colonies, families would also gather to discuss news; and children would fly kites and play hopscotch, tag, jacks, marbles, and hide-and-seek.

Other colonial children's games included rolling barrel hoops, blind man's bluff, leapfrog, tops, skittles (a forerunner of bowling), quoits (like horseshoes), and cat's cradle (a string game). Wealthy parents also bought imported English dolls, tea sets, dollhouses, miniature soldiers, and games for their children.

American tastes in music and art closely paralleled English tastes. However, there were far fewer high-brow cultural diversions in America than in England or other European countries. Plays, concerts, and museums were rare, even in major American cities such as Boston, Philadelphia, and Charleston. American entertainment was found in books, conversation, folk music, and dance. Although books were expensive, most colonial families owned at least a Bible.

Other popular books during the colonial period included *Pilgrim's Progress, Mother Goose, Aesop's Fables, Robinson Crusoe,* and *Gulliver's Travels.* Many families in the evening would gather in the main room of the house; someone would read aloud, while others sewed, knitted, or whittled. Frontier families also enjoyed gathering together for quilting bees as well as house- and barn-raisings.

Some favorite colonial songs included "Hush Little Baby," "London Bridge," "Here We Go Round the Mulberry Bush," and "Lazy John." Although Puritans did not approve of music outside the church, other colonists enjoyed listening to or playing the fiddle, spinet, or harpsichord. Dances and balls were also popular among Southern landowners. Many colonial men enjoyed sports and games and evenings spent in the local tavern—playing cards, billiards, backgammon, and gambling at dice. Women, however, were excluded from time spent in games and sports and at the tavern because they were expected to stay home and take care of the children and household responsibilities.

John Wesley
Line drawing courtesy of Amy Pak

A quilting bee
Library of Congress, Prints and Photographs Division [LC-USZ61-193]

IMPACT

- Over time American class divisions became less sharply drawn than those in Europe. Wealth was still the primary measure of social status, but it was acquired wealth — not inherited. The colonial middle class was three times the size of the English middle class, and opportunities to move up were plentiful.

- Almost from the beginning it was accepted that the American colonists had a right to legislative representation in their government. These colonists saw themselves as inheriting the hard-won rights and freedoms of Englishmen. However, even as late as 1750, they saw themselves as an extension of the realm of the English monarchy and did not aspire to political independence.

- Each of the three regions supported different economic enterprises. The New England colonies were known for their commerce, shipbuilding, fishing, and whaling. The economic base of the Mid-Atlantic colonies was provided by agriculture and manufacturing. The South was almost entirely agricultural, relying upon the export of rice, indigo, and tobacco and the slave labor needed to grow those crops.

- The thirteen English colonies in America were populated primarily by Protestants — predominantly Puritans in New England and Anglicans and Baptists in the South. The Mid-Atlantic colonies contained a mixture of religions — Quaker, Dutch Reformed, Lutheran, and Presbyterian. Maryland was, of course, a haven for Catholics.

- Horse-pulled wagons and sleighs were essential to land transportation in the colonial period. Boats were the other primary means of transportation. The first regular mail service in the colonies began in 1672, and by 1735, every major American city had a newspaper.

- American taste in music and art loosely paralleled English tastes, but there were fewer highbrow cultural diversions in the colonies. American entertainment was found primarily in books, folk music, dance, sports, and games.

UNIT THREE
THE PERIOD OF REVOLUTION

Lessons 17 – 24

There are few topics in American history that have aroused more controversy than the discussion of the causes of the American Revolution. However, historians have generally pointed to three primary factors leading to the outbreak of war:

- A growing sense of American identity
- The imposition of parliamentary policies upon the colonies, despite the fact that the Americans had no representation in Parliament
- Efforts of colonial leaders to inflame anger against the British

Discontent of some kind is at the root of every revolution in history, and the American Revolution is no exception. For many years prior to the outbreak of war, forces were at work that eventually led the colonists to declare their independence from Great Britain. The English institutions that had been transplanted to the American continent in the early seventeenth century were shaped over time by the political, economic, and social conditions peculiar to the New World. Eventually, the colonists recognized that their population was growing faster than that of the homeland and that they experienced greater religious freedom than the British. They also came to prefer American simplicity and self-reliance to the more aristocratic British society. Many in the colonies began to feel that life in the New World was better than life in the mother country.

Despite the growing sense of American identity, for more than fifty years prior to the French and Indian War, there was still a strong attachment between the American colonies and the mother country. The colonists never seriously considered the thought of forming an independent American nation. However, between 1763 and 1775, many Americans grew increasingly discontent with British rule, and they rebelled against it more and more. During the years following the French and Indian War, the British Parliament passed laws taxing the colonies, regulating their trade, denying them the right to extend westward. Furthermore, England stationed troops in the colonists' midst. Many colonists believed these policies were an attempt to strip them of their liberties as Englishmen.

The enactment of each new parliamentary regulation brought increasing indignation and resentment on the part of the American colonists. Encouraged by the writings and speeches of colonial leaders (such as Thomas Paine, Samuel Adams, and Patrick Henry), more and more colonists protested and rebelled against what they considered to be unjust and immoral British legislation. The cry of "no taxation without representation" became a rallying point for their anger. Eventually, the colonists reached a point of no return in their defiance of the British government, and war became inevitable.

All American History

CAPTURE OF FORT DU QUESNE, 1758.

LESSON 17

The French and Indian War . . . . 1754 — 1763 A.D.

ATMOSPHERE

A COLONIAL EXTENSION OF THE SEVEN YEARS' WAR

What became known as the French and Indian War was actually a colonial extension of the Seven Years' War in Europe, in which the British fought the French, Austrians, and Spanish. Although fighting began in 1754, the French and Indian War did not officially begin until May of 1756. This seven-year conflict pitted England against France, and most Native Americans allied themselves with the French. This was an imperial struggle over colonial wealth, trade, and territory that would decide which European power would control North America. The bloodiest American war in the eighteenth century, the French and Indian War cost more American lives than the American Revolution and involved people on three continents.

By 1750, British territory in the New World consisted of much of the east coast of North America, whereas the French held eastern Canada and the Louisiana territory. Tensions between the British and French in North America had been rising for a number of years, and each side wanted to increase its land holdings there. The French had founded a string of forts, missions, and fur-trading posts in the region bounded by the four major cities of Quebec, Montreal, Detroit, and

Capture of Fort Duquesne
Library of Congress, Prints and Photographs Division [LC-USZ62-57648]

Colonel George Washington
Library of Congress, Prints and Photographs Division [LC-USZ62-112547]

New Orleans. As the British began to move west, clearing land and hunting game, the French and Indian trappers became angry at losing their hunting grounds. The result was that bands of Native Americans, encouraged by the French, began raiding British frontier settlements.

In an effort to keep the British from expanding into the Ohio River valley, the French began to build a chain of new forts from the St. Lawrence River to the Mississippi River in the early 1750s. But the British crown had already claimed this region. One of these French forts, Fort Duquesne, was built near Pittsburgh — an area that the British said belonged to their Virginia colony. In late 1753, the British governor of Virginia sent a twenty-one-year-old surveyor named George Washington to Fort Duquesne to tell the French to leave the area.

When the French refused to go, the governor sent Washington back with a small militia force of about 150 men. Washington and his men fired on the French patrol unsuccessfully. The Virginians were forced to retreat, but they received authorization to build a fort nearby—a crude fortress they named Fort Necessity. A large French force soon surrounded Fort Necessity, trapping Washington and his soldiers inside. A third of the Virginians were killed, and Washington was forced to surrender and return to Virginia with the message that the Ohio Territory belonged to the French. This clash marked the beginning of the French and Indian War.

EVENT

FIRST PHASE OF THE FIGHTING (1754 – 1755)

During 1754 the American colonists managed on their own against the French. Virtually all of the American native tribes decided to ally themselves with the French; only the Iroquois sided with the British. The Iroquois had been enemies of the French since Champlain had sided against the Iroquois in their war with the Huron. Their Indian allies provided a great advantage, but the French in America did suffer from two major disadvantages: they had to rely on soldiers hired by the French fur-trading companies and they had to rely on food from the homeland. The British American colonies were protected by their own militias and they were able to produce their own food.

On the other hand, the British colonies each had their own government, and they did not always work well together. The French forces had the advantage of being controlled by a single government. Furthermore, French settlements were close together, making them easier to defend.

In 1755, the British sent Major General Edward Braddock to oversee the British colonial forces. Accompanied by George Washington, Braddock and his force of over fourteen hundred men headed to Fort Duquesne in another attempt to oust the French. On their way, Braddock and his men were surprised by a French and Indian ambush and were badly routed. British regiments, trained in the linear European way of combat, found it difficult to win in the forests of America against the French and Indians, who used guerrilla tactics. General Braddock himself was mortally wounded near Fort Duquesne, leaving Washington to extricate the British and colonial forces from the wilderness. Once again the French had maintained their control of the Ohio River valley. In the North, however, they were successful in winning a battle on Lake George and establishing Fort Edward on the Hudson River and Fort William Henry on Lake George in upstate New York.

**Major General
Edward Braddock**
Line drawing courtesy of Amy Pak

SECOND PHASE OF THE FIGHTING (1756 – 1757)

By 1756 the British and French governments had formally declared war, and the conflict spread from America to the West Indies, India, and Europe. Although the fighting in America became part of a global conflict known as the Seven Years' War, the British were especially determined not to allow the French to become victorious on the battlefield in the New World. The new British commander-in-chief, Lord Loudoun, managed the war effort closely, demanding exact counts of soldiers and money from the colonies. American colonial assemblies began to refuse to cooperate with the British.

General Louis Montcalm
Library of Congress, Prints and Photographs Division [LC-USZ61-239]

General Jeffrey Amherst
Library of Congress, Prints and Photographs Division [LC-USZ62-57636]

General James Wolfe
Library of Congress, Prints and Photographs Division [LC-USZ62-48404]

Although the French were outnumbered almost two to one by the British and the colonials, they dominated the battlefield during this phase of the war. In 1756, the British were soundly defeated by the French under General Louis Montcalm at Fort Oswego on Lake Ontario in upstate New York. Following the battle, Montcalm was horrified to discover that their Indian allies had killed many wounded British soldiers, taken scalps, and made slaves of other captives. In 1757, the British soldiers at Fort William Henry surrendered to Montcalm and his men, who promised them safe passage back to England. Again, the Native Americans fighting with the French massacred more than 180 British soldiers and took over 300 captive. This battle and the massacre that followed were portrayed by James Fenimore Cooper in *The Last of the Mohicans*.

THIRD PHASE OF THE FIGHTING (1758 – 1763)

The tide began to turn in favor of England in 1758 when Lord William Pitt came out of retirement to direct the British war effort. Under Pitt's guidance, the British began adapting their war strategies to the landscape and terrain of the American frontier. Pitt eventually began to give the American colonists greater independence in pursuing the war effort, which increased their cooperation and enthusiasm. He promised payment to them in proportion to their support of the war and gave colonial assemblies control over recruitment. Thousands more British soldiers were sent to America to fight, and British generals Jeffrey Amherst and James Wolfe began to score victories in battles. Meanwhile, the French were beginning to be abandoned by many of their Native American allies.

In July 1758, the French fortress of Louisbourg on Cape Breton Island was captured by Amherst and Wolfe and their forces. This victory gave the British control of the Bay of St. Lawrence. Then British and American forces burned Fort Duquesne before retreating north. In the same year, British troops captured Fort Frontenac on Lake Ontario, which was the main supply center for French forces in the Great Lakes region. With this victory, the British were able to completely cut off the French troops from reinforcements of men, food, and weapons.

During the next year of fighting, the British captured Fort Niagara, which completed their domination of the Great Lakes area. A British expedition led by General Amherst also seized Fort Ticonderoga and Crown Point, opening British passage to Montreal. Another British group, commanded by General Wolfe, sailed up the St. Lawrence River. Just outside the French city of Quebec, the British met the French in battle on the rainy morning of September 13, 1759. The French suffered a massive defeat in a dramatic uphill attack by the British. General Wolfe and the French general Montcalm were both killed. Quebec, the strongest French fortress in Canada and the lynchpin of French power in North America, fell into England's dominion.

By September of 1760, the British controlled the American frontier. The French army had formally surrendered to General Amherst in Montreal and to Major Robert Rogers at Fort Detroit, the last two French strongholds in America. Although scattered fighting would continue for the next few years in Canada, basically the war in America was over. The Seven Years' War continued elsewhere for several more years, with Spain becoming involved against the British early in 1762. However, strong British sea power completely destroyed any hopes of a French victory.

The Plains of Abraham
Library of Congress, Prints and Photographs Division [LC-USZC4-6879]

TREATY OF PARIS

The treaty ending the French and Indian War was signed in Paris on February 10, 1763. The Treaty of Paris, which also ended the European Seven Years' War, gave all of North America east of the Mississippi River, except for New Orleans, to England. The French turned over their claim to New Orleans and the lands west of the Mississippi to Spain as compensation for Spain's surrender of Florida to the British.

Although the war with the French was over, the British continued to fight with Native Americans over land claims. Shortly after the Treaty of Paris was signed, Pontiac's Rebellion flared up. Many of the battlefields were the same as those in the French and Indian War (Forts Pitt, Niagara, Detroit). The Indians, however, were already exhausted by years of fighting, and they capitulated to the British in

1765. Although conflict ceased for a time, enmity between Native Americans and the British in America would be an ongoing problem for many years to come.

RESULTS OF THE WAR

The French and Indian War effectively ended French political and cultural influence in most of North America. The British gained massive amounts of land, greatly strengthening their hold on the continent, and established their commercial and naval supremacy. However, war expenses and increased military costs following the war led the British Parliament to levy the first direct taxes it had ever imposed on the American colonies (they had levied a limited number of external

Significant French and Indian War battlesites

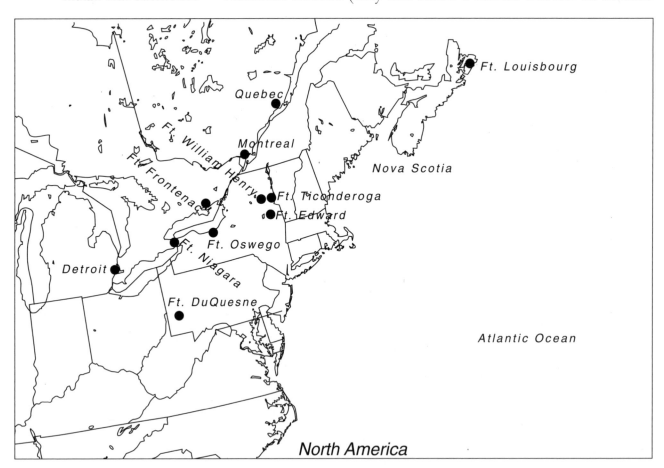

North America

taxes or trade duties in the past). This action, along with other restrictive measures, played a major role in the worsening relationship between England and her colonies, which would eventually lead to the Revolutionary War.

For the first time, American colonists had united together against a common enemy. This unifying experience established George Washington as the first American war hero. The colonial militiamen fighting in the war had seen themselves as volunteers in a "people's army," in contrast to the British army, which they considered to be coercive and authoritarian. The battle experience that these American fighting men gained would prove beneficial when the time came for them to fight England for their independence.

IMPACT

- The French and Indian War, a colonial extension of the Seven Years' War, pitted the British against the French, who were allied with most Native Americans tribes, in a struggle that decided which European power would control North America.

- Although the French dominated the fighting during the early years of the war, England became victorious when they adapted their war strategies to the terrain of the American frontier and succeeded in gaining the cooperation and support of the colonial assemblies.

- The Treaty of Paris of 1763 (ending the French and Indian War) established England's supremacy in North America. However, expenses from the war greatly increased England's debt, leading to the levying of taxes on the American colonists—a move that contributed to the deterioration of England's relationship with her colonies and eventually to the outbreak of the American Revolution.

- The French and Indian War united the American colonies for the first time against a common enemy. George Washington was established as the first American hero, and the battle experience gained in this war would prove helpful to the colonists when they fought England for their independence.

LESSON 18

A Time of Crisis in Colonial Relations . . . . . 1764 – 1767 A.D.

ATMOSPHERE

PRELUDE TO WAR

For over 150 years, the thirteen colonies in America were largely left alone by the mother country. One reason for this was the great distance between Britain and her colonies. A voyage across the Atlantic from Boston to London required at least three months. Thus, communication between England and the thirteen colonies was never current.

Another reason for England's "salutary neglect" of its colonies was its frequent involvement in European conflicts. England's priority was to gain military victories, not administrate its colonies. Therefore, the American colonists learned to manage on their own. They grew self-reliant and independent, and they developed a large measure of self-government.

However, the thirteen colonies were certainly not united as a single body. In fact, they usually acted like individual nations. Each colony had its own government and religious and cultural identity. The strongest link unifying the colonies was their allegiance to the British crown. The American colonists thought of themselves as English citizens, living in the colonies, with the same rights as other

King George III
Line drawing courtesy of Amy Pak

Englishmen. In 1763, the thirteen colonies were not interested in declaring their independence from England.

When England won the French and Indian War, it became the dominant European power in North America. With an enormous amount of new territory to govern, the British were faced with many new responsibilities and problems. Probably the most pressing need was money to cover all the new expenses associated with their enlarged empire and to deal with their enormous war debt (136 million pounds).

EARLY STEPS TO WAR

Throughout 1763 and the decade that followed, King George III and the British Parliament became determined that the thirteen colonies should help pay off England's war debt and pay for the British army kept in America to protect them. British leadership also decided that their rule over the colonies had been too lenient and should be stiffened to bring greater profit to the mother country.

During the French and Indian War, the British had been appalled that some colonists had continued to trade at Spanish and French (enemy) ports and that colonial assemblies had been reluctant to provide money and men for the war. With this change in the mindset of England's leaders, the period of time from the end of the French and Indian War to the beginning of the American Revolutionary War (1764 – 1776) developed into a time of crisis in British/American relations.

EVENT

PROCLAMATION OF 1763 — FIRST STEP TO WAR

After England's victory in the French and Indian War, land west of the Appalachian Mountains looked very appealing to American land speculators and to American settlers eager for land of their own. However, British leadership moved quickly to prohibit the colonists from settling land west of the Appalachians, and they sent ten thousand British troops to enforce this Proclamation of 1763.

The proclamation was designed to give the British government time to gain control of the vast territory won from France and to prevent more colonial conflicts with the Native Americans in the region. However, the American colonists considered this proclamation to be unjust and illegal and openly disobeyed it. American pioneers continued to move west in the years following the French and Indian War.

ENFORCEMENT OF THE NAVIGATION ACTS (1763) — SECOND STEP TO WAR

For more than 150 years, England had operated on the basis of the theory of mercantilism. According to this theory, the colonies existed for the economic benefit of the mother country. Beginning in 1660,

Proclamation of 1763 boundary line

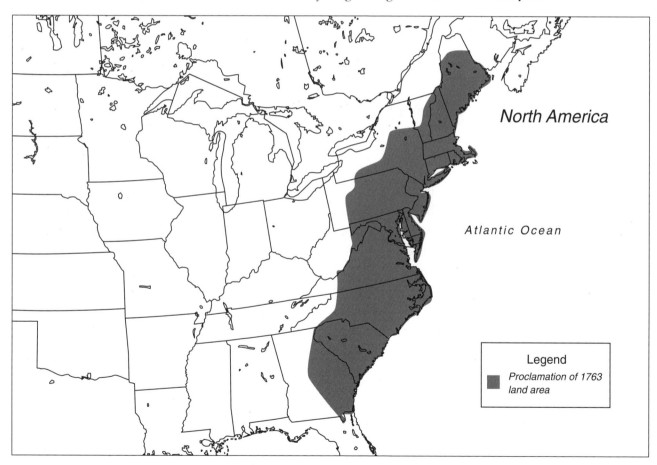

North America

Atlantic Ocean

Legend

Proclamation of 1763 land area

Colonists confronting British soldiers
Library of Congress, Prints and Photographs Division [LC-USZC4-4971]

England fleshed out this theory by imposing a series of regulations known as the Navigation Acts.

These acts basically stipulated that colonial exports and imports had to be carried on British or colonial ships and that all cargo was subject to tariffs or duties. However, the Navigation Acts were not rigorously enforced for many years, and evasion was easy due to the distance between England and America. In fact, smuggling became an accepted colonial profession. Only after the end of the French and Indian War did the British king and Parliament call for their nation's warships to stop all American vessels and search them for contraband cargo. Also, British officers of the crown were authorized to break into colonial homes and look for smuggled goods without search warrants. American colonists, ordered to pay tariffs on an increasing number of imports, became suspicious that British troops had been sent across the Atlantic to ensure that these tariffs were collected.

SUGAR ACT (1764) — THIRD STEP TO WAR

The Sugar Act of 1764, which replaced the Molasses Act of 1733, required the American colonists to pay a three-penny tax on each gallon of molasses entering the colonies from ports outside the British Empire. This tax hurt the New England colonies especially because these colonies imported molasses from the French and the Spanish West Indies for their rum industries.

To the British government, the Sugar Act was an entirely reasonable piece of legislation. However, the American colonists maintained that the Sugar Act violated their rights as British citizens. The cry of "no taxation without representation" echoed throughout the thirteen colonies because the Americans believed that it was unfair to be taxed by a parliament that had no representatives for whom they had voted. Two years later, the duty on molasses was reduced to one penny a gallon because the American colonies had often been successful in smuggling molasses from outside the British Empire.

QUARTERING ACT (1765) — FOURTH STEP TO WAR

Under the terms of the Quartering Act of 1765, American colonists were required to provide living quarters, fuel, candles, cider or beer, and transportation for British troops stationed in the colonies. Many Americans believed that this was an illegal way for Great Britain to take money from them without their consent. Although most colonists half-heartedly obeyed this law, they often provided fewer supplies than requested by the British. Most Americans complained about the frequently arrogant behavior of the British troops stationed in the colonies and resented the presence of these soldiers during peacetime.

Samuel Adams by Copley
National Archives print [148-CD-4-20]

STAMP ACT (1765) — FIFTH STEP TO WAR

In 1765, the British Parliament made its first attempt to tax the internal business of the colonies — by passing the Stamp Act. This law required colonists to buy British tax stamps and place them on many documents and forms — newspapers, bonds, insurance policies, bills of sale, diplomas, almanacs, and even packs of playing cards. British agents who attempted to enforce the Stamp Act faced resistance in all thirteen colonies. Some agents were even tarred and feathered or had their effigies burned in protest.

A citizens' group called the Sons of Liberty sprang up in Boston under the leadership of Samuel Adams to lead the resistance against the stamp tax. Soon there were Sons of Liberty groups in other colonies as well. Throughout all thirteen colonies, church bells rang in protest and crowds gathered under "liberty trees" to sing protest songs and hold rallies. Colonial merchants also agreed to stop importing British goods until the Stamp Act was repealed.

In the House of Burgesses in Virginia, Patrick Henry gave a rousing speech in which he called the stamp tax a threat to liberty. By October of 1765, nine of the thirteen colonies had sent delegates to a Stamp Act Congress held in New York. The four colonial assemblies that were not represented sent word that they would agree to whatever was decided at the meeting. At this congress a Declaration of Rights and Grievances was written, suggesting to the king that the colonies

Patrick Henry before the House of Burgesses
Library of Congress, Prints and Photographs Division [LC-USZ62-3775]

Stamp Act seal
Line drawing courtesy of Amy Pak

General Thomas Gage
Library of Congress, Prints and Photographs Division [LC-USZ62-40243]

should do their own taxing since they had no representation in the British Parliament and asking for a repeal of the Sugar and Stamp acts. The Stamp Act was repealed after a year because it was not enforceable. However, at the same time the Stamp Act was repealed, Parliament passed the Declaratory Act, which stated that it had the right to tax British colonies.

TOWNSHEND ACTS (1767) — SIXTH STEP TO WAR

The Townshend Acts (named for the British Chancellor of the Exchequer) required the American colonists to pay a duty on many products brought into the colonies from England — particularly lead, paint, glass, paper, wine, and tea. These acts also gave any royal officer the right to search colonial homes for taxable goods. With the passage of the Townshend Acts, the British government hoped to be able to collect enough money to pay the salaries of the royal governors and judges, making them independent of the colonial assemblies. Furious with these new laws, the American colonists quickly began a boycott of British imports, which was crippling to British merchants. By October 1768, George III was so annoyed with the widespread colonial disobedience to these acts that he ordered four thousand British troops under General Thomas Gage to be sent to Boston along with a flotilla of warships. Parliament did repeal all the Townshend taxes — except for the tax on tea — by 1770.

IMPACT

- For over 150 years, England's leaders largely ignored the American colonies due to the great distance between them and due to England's frequent involvement in European conflicts.

- Although the American colonies grew self-reliant and developed a large measure of self-government, they were not united as a single body and usually acted as individual nations. Their strongest link was their allegiance to the British crown.

- After their victory in the French and Indian War, the British were faced with many new problems and responsibilities. They decided that their rule over the American colonies had been too lenient and that the colonies should bring them greater profits to help cover new expenses associated with their enlarged empire.

- Actions taken by the British government and supported by British troops led to colonial cries of injustice and colonial disobedience. With each action, tensions between the mother country and her colonies escalated.

LESSON 19

Colonial Tensions Mount . . . . 1768 — 1774 A.D.

ATMOSPHERE

NEXT STEPS TO WAR

In the years following the French and Indian War, British officials obviously believed that the British government (and Parliament in particular) had the power to govern and tax the American colonies. The colonists, on the other hand, had developed a very different perspective on how they should be governed. These differing beliefs led to mounting tensions between the British and their American colonies—and eventually to the outbreak of war.

By the first decades of the eighteenth century, all but two of the colonies had an elected assembly and an appointed governor. Most of these governors were appointed by the British king and were given the power to make appointments. However, the colonial assemblies held the "power of the purse" because only the assemblies could pass revenue bills. They often used this power to gain control over appointments and sometimes even to gain influence over the governor himself. The American colonists came to view their elected assemblies as their defenders against the British king, the British Parliament, and the colonial governors.

Massacre on King Street
*Library of Congress, Prints and Photographs
Division [LC-USZ62-45554]*

In the years following 1763, the British Parliament took steps to regulate the colonies more strongly and eventually to levy taxes upon them, something that it had never done before. The British were acting upon their assumption that their Parliament was empowered to legislate for the entire British Empire. The Americans, on the other hand, assumed that those in the empire shared the British king and British rights and freedoms but could only be taxed by their own elected representatives. They protested that taxation without representation was tyranny.

Repeal of the Townshend Acts in 1770 did nothing more than temporarily ease the anger of the American colonists. A series of events that came in quick succession—the Boston Massacre, the burning of the *Gaspee*, the Tea Act, and the Boston Tea Party—added fuel to the fire of colonial indignation against the mother country and parliamentary resolve to punish colonial rebellion. Parliament's passage of the Intolerable Acts led to prompt resistance from the colonists. Nevertheless, when the first Continental Congress met in 1774, its goal was not to consider independence but to attempt to persuade the British government to recognize the colonists' rights as Englishmen.

EVENT

Paul Revere by Copley
Public Domain

THE BOSTON MASSACRE (1770) — SEVENTH STEP TO WAR
By 1768, the British troops ordered to Boston by the king had arrived, and the Bostonians felt like a conquered people. Serious tension developed between the British soldiers and the people of Boston. There was brawling on the streets and in the taverns, and schoolchildren hurled insults at the troops (calling them names such as lobster scoundrels and bloody-backs, in reference to their red coats). The British soldiers took over a number of public buildings in the city for their barracks and used the Boston Commons as a campground.

About eighteen months after the arrival of the British troops, an incident occurred that became known as the Boston Massacre. On March 5, 1770, scattered fights between British soldiers and local

Bostonians occurred throughout the day. Then a rumor began to spread throughout the city that two local boys had been beaten up by some soldiers. That evening a small contingent of British soldiers commanded by Captain Thomas Preston was stationed on duty at the Customs House on King Street. A group of city boys began taunting and throwing snowballs at the British sentry there, and eventually a crowd of local toughs joined the boys. When the sentry called for help, he was joined by a squad of British soldiers with bayonets on their loaded muskets. After the soldiers' arrival, the unruly mob continued to throw snowballs and other things at the British troops. Suddenly, a British musket went off and three Bostonians lay dead in the snow. Several other colonists were wounded; two of them died later from their wounds.

The Sons of Liberty were quick to label this event the Boston Massacre, saying those killed were martyrs for the cause of American liberty. Adams encouraged Boston silversmith Paul Revere to produce an engraving that depicted the massacre as British soldiers firing upon the peaceful people of Boston. Entitled *The Bloody Massacre Perpetrated in King Street*, Revere's engraving popularized this tragic event, stirring up more anti-British sentiment. Captain Preston and seven British soldiers were arrested and tried for murder. Defended by Patriot lawyers John Adams and Joshua Quincy, Preston and most of the soldiers were acquitted. Two soldiers were convicted of manslaughter but were allowed to go free after having their thumbs branded with the letter *M*.

Josiah Quincy, Jr.
Library of Congress, Prints and Photographs Division [LC-USZ61-1528]

BURNING OF THE GASPEE (1772) — EIGHTH STEP TO WAR
On June 9, 1772, the *Gaspee*, a British royal revenue ship, ran aground in Narragansett Bay (near Providence, Rhode Island) while chasing an American merchant ship suspected of smuggling. The crew of the *Gaspee* had been harassing colonial farmers and fishermen, often disregarding the colonists' rights in their zeal to stop the smuggling.

Eight boatloads of men from Providence rowed out to the *Gaspee* and set it on fire. The British government threatened to take the

John Adams
National Archives print [148-CD-4-11]

The burning of the *Gaspee*
*Library of Congress, Prints and Photographs
Division [LC-USZ62-36926]*

Governor Thomas Hutchinson
Public Domain

**The city of Boston
from Breed's Hill**
*Library of Congress, Prints and Photographs
Division [LC-USZ62-55120]*

guilty American colonists back to England for trial. However, no one would identify the guilty men, even though there were many eyewitnesses. No colonists were ever punished for the incident. The burning of the *Gaspee* caused further strain in the relationship between England and the American colonies.

COMMITTEES OF CORRESPONDENCE (1772) — NINTH STEP TO WAR

At the suggestion of Sam Adams, committees were organized in 1772 to relay messages, articles, and letters throughout the thirteen colonies. This correspondence detailed the way the British government was violating the colonists' rights. Adams reached the height of his political influence while using these committees of correspondence to spread his opposition to the actions of the British government. In addition to Samuel Adams, two other "radical" American leaders were instrumental in establishing these committees of correspondence—Sam's cousin, John Adams, and one of Boston's wealthiest merchants, John Hancock. By 1773, all of the colonies, except for Pennsylvania, had joined this committee network.

TEA ACT AND THE BOSTON TEA PARTY (1773) — TENTH STEP TO WAR

The British Parliament passed a law in 1773 that allowed the British East India Company to sell its tea below the price of the tea that colonial merchants had been smuggling in from the Dutch (to avoid paying the Townshend tax on tea). Colonial boycotts of British tea had taken a toll, and the British East India Company faced bankruptcy with a huge backlog of tea in its warehouses. A fleet of ships carrying cargoes of tea sailed into various colonial ports in 1773. Maryland colonists set fire to one of these ships and destroyed it. In New York City and Philadelphia, angry crowds of colonists kept tea crates from being unloaded.

The most infamous event protesting Parliament's tea law occurred in Boston, where three tea-laden British cargo ships sat anchored in the harbor. The governor of Massachusetts, Thomas Hutchinson, had refused to allow these ships to leave without unloading their cargo.

On the evening of December 16, 1773, local men, urged on by Samuel Adams and the Sons of Liberty, decided to prevent the British tea from being unloaded. Dressed as Mohawk Indians, they raided the British ships and dumped their 342 cases of tea into the water.

THE INTOLERABLE OR COERCIVE ACTS (1774) — ELEVENTH STEP TO WAR

The British Parliament immediately took steps to punish Boston for its tea party, seeking to make it an example to the other colonies. Parliament passed the following four laws, which became known as the Intolerable or Coercive Acts of 1774:

The Boston Tea Party
Line drawing courtesy of Amy Pak

- The Boston Port Bill closed Boston harbor to all shipping until the colonists compensated the British East India Company for all the tea that had been destroyed and Parliament for the tax due on the tea. This act put half of Boston out of work.

- The Massachusetts Government Act significantly changed the provisions of the colony's charter. It declared that the members of the Massachusetts Council would be appointed by the governor and not elected by the popularly elected assembly. Also, town meetings could only take place with the permission of the governor; juries would be appointed by the sheriffs, not elected; and the governor received full authority to appoint local officials and judges.

- The Administration of Justice Act said that the trial of British colonial officials accused of a capital offense could not take place in the colonies. These officials would be extradited to Britain and tried there. This effectively gave these officials free reign to do whatever they wished in the colonies.

- The Quartering Act was expanded to require American colonists to house and feed British officers and troops in their private homes.

The Quebec Act, tacked on to the Intolerable Acts, gave the French vast territories west of the Appalachians. It also guaranteed religious tolerance for Canadian Catholics.

The people of Boston refused to pay for any of the tea, despite the British attempt to destroy them economically. The Bostonians, who were totally dependent on their port to make a living through commerce and fishing, were not even allowed to receive food by sea.

Political cartoon
National Archives print [148-GW-436]

Word of Boston's situation was soon communicated to the other colonies through the committees of correspondence, and the Massachusetts colony was praised as a martyr, standing in defense of colonial rights. Other cities soon rushed donations of food and money to Boston by land.

As the months passed, the situation in Boston became quite volatile. Tea drinkers were assaulted, and tax collectors and other royal officials were tarred and feathered. In defiance of General Gage's martial law, the colonists set up the Massachusetts Committee of Public Safety, which was headed by John Hancock. This group urged communities to begin training local militia to resist the British rule. Many prominent pro-British Americans feared for their lives and fled to England.

John Hancock
Library of Congress, Prints and Photographs Division [LC-D416-255]

FIRST CONTINENTAL CONGRESS (1774) —
TWELFTH STEP TO WAR

On September 5, 1774, the First Continental Congress convened at Carpenter's Hall in Philadelphia with delegates from every colony but Georgia. Approximately fifty delegates were present, and they were not united in their goals. The conservatives (Tories) wanted restraint and compromise in their dealings with the British, whereas the radicals (Whigs) supported action or united resistance against what they considered to be Parliament's unlawful acts. Seeking independence from the mother country was not promoted as the goal of the meeting.

As the delegates discussed the Intolerable Acts, they decided that they would compose a statement of colonial rights and then identify the parliamentary violation of those rights. Thus, on October 14, the congress adopted the Declaration and Resolves, a list of American rights and grievances to be sent to King George III and Parliament. This document conceded that Parliament could regulate colonial commerce but not raise revenue without the colonists' consent. It affirmed that the Americans enjoyed the rights of British citizens to life, liberty, and property, and it petitioned the British government to correct the wrongs being done to its colonies.

Political cartoon entitled, "Poor old England endeavoring to reclaim his wicked American children"
Library of Congress, Prints and Photographs Division [LC-USZ62-34862]

Before adjourning, the First Continental Congress established the Continental Association, which called for a pledge from all American heads of household to neither export nor import goods to or from England. Every city and town was urged to choose inspection committees to enforce this boycott. The congress also approved resolutions advising the colonies to begin training and arming its militia for war. The delegates agreed to meet again in May if the British government did not change its policies. They adjourned on October 26, 1774. As the months passed, the British Parliament and king ignored the colonies' Declaration and Resolves and offered little hope that they would back down on the tea tax. Meanwhile, trade was at a standstill in the once prosperous city of Boston and ships were rotting at anchor in the harbor.

Whereas, since the close of the last war, the British parliament, claiming a power of right to bind the people of America by statute in all cases whatsoever, hath, in some acts expressly imposed taxes on them, and in others, under various pretenses, but in fact for the purpose of raising a revenue, hath imposed rates and duties payable in these colonies, established a board of commissioners with unconstitutional powers, and extended the jurisdiction of courts of Admiralty not only for collecting the said duties, but for the trial of causes merely arising within the body of a county…

And whereas, Assemblies have been frequently dissolved, contrary to the rights of the people, when they attempted to deliberate on grievances; and their dutiful, humble, loyal, & reasonable petitions to the crown for redress, have been repeatedly treated with contempt, by His Majesty's ministers of state:

The good people of the several Colonies of New Hampshire, Massachusetts bay, Rhode Island and Providence plantations, Connecticut, New York, New Jersey, Pennsylvania, Newcastle Kent and Sussex on Delaware, Maryland, Virginia, North Carolina, and South Carolina, justly alarmed at these arbitrary proceedings of parliament and administration, have severally elected, constituted, and appointed deputies to meet, and sit in general Congress, in the city of Philadelphia, in order to obtain such establishment, as that their religion, laws, and liberties, may not be subverted…

That the foundation of English liberty, and of all free government, is a right in the people to participate in their legislative council: and as the English colonists are not represented, and from their local and other circumstances, cannot properly be represented in the British parliament, they are entitled to a free and exclusive power of legislation in their several provincial legislatures, where their right of representation can alone be preserved, in all cases of taxation and internal polity, subject only to the negative of their sovereign, in such manner as has been heretofore used and accustomed…

In the course of our inquiry, we find many infringements and violations of the foregoing rights, which, from an ardent desire that harmony and mutual intercourse of affection and interest may be restored, we pass over for the present, and proceed to state such acts and measures as have been adopted since the last war, which demonstrate a system formed to enslave America.

Resolved, That the following acts of Parliament are infringements and violations of the rights of the colonists; and that the repeal of them is essentially necessary, in order to restore harmony between Great Britain and the American colonies, viz. …

To these grievous acts and measures Americans cannot submit, but in hopes that their fellow subjects in Great Britain will, on a revision of them, restore us to that state in which both countries found happiness and prosperity, we have for the present only resolved to pursue the following peaceable measures: 1st. To enter into a non-importation, non-consumption, and non-exportation agreement or association. 2. To prepare an address to the people of Great Britain, and a memorial to the inhabitants of British America, & 3. To prepare a loyal address to his Majesty, agreeable to resolutions already entered into.

—from the Declaration and Resolves

Prime Minister Pitt
Library of Congress, Prints and Photographs Division [LC-USZ62-28073]

**Patrick Henry addressing the
First Continental Congress**
*Library of Congress, Prints and Photographs
Division [LC-USZ62-17110]*

THE DIE WAS CAST!

By 1775, there were approximately 2.5 million people living in the American colonies. In 1700, there had been twenty people in England for every one person in America. Seventy-five years later, there were only three people in England for every American colonist. Resistance against the homeland had begun to unify these colonists, as they faced a common enemy together. More and more of the American colonists agreed with James Otis, who wrote, "The very act of taxing, except over those who are represented, appears to me to be depriving them of one of their most essential rights as freemen..."[4] Ben Franklin insisted that "we (the colonies) have an old mother that peevish is grown. She snubs us like children that scarce walk alone. She forgets we've grown up and have sense of our own."[5]

Meanwhile, London newspapers were referring to the American colonists as a "mongrel breed." According to King George III, "The dye is now cast, the Colonies must either submit or triumph...There is no inclination for the present to lay fresh taxes on them, but I am clear there must always be one tax to keep up the right."[6] William Pitt, the former prime minister, proclaimed in the House of Lords, "I maintain that the Parliament has the right to restrain America. Our power over the colonies is sovereign and supreme. This is the mother country; they are the children. They must obey."[7]

Thus, the American Revolution evolved as a confrontation between a parent and a child. What obedience did the colonies owe their mother country, and what freedoms did the mother country owe her colonies? King George III and the British Parliament saw the colonists as rowdy children who had no respect for the rules. Many of the American colonists saw Britain as a stern, unfair parent whose laws, taxes, and troops threatened their freedoms. In the years from 1763 until 1775, England and the thirteen colonies moved farther and farther down the road to open, bloody conflict between a cranky mother and a disobedient child.

IMPACT

- A series of events, coming in quick succession, added fuel to the fire of the American colonists' anger against Great Britain. The first, known as the Boston Massacre, came as a result of escalating tensions between the people of Boston and the British soldiers sent to their city.

- Relations between the mother country and her colonies were strained further when colonists from Providence, Rhode Island, burned the *Gaspee,* a British revenue ship.

- Under the leadership of Samuel Adams, John Adams, and John Hancock, the Americans organized committees of correspondence to relay messages throughout the colonies.

- The British Parliament punished Boston for its infamous tea party by closing the city's harbor and changing the colony's charter. As the months passed, the situation in Boston became volatile.

- At the First Continental Congress in 1774, delegates adopted the Declaration and Resolves, a list of colonial rights and grievances sent to the British king and Parliament. They also approved resolutions calling for the training and arming of colonial militia for war.

LESSON 20

The War for Independence Begins . . . . 1775 — 1776 A.D.

ATMOSPHERE

TENSIONS REACH A BOILING POINT

In the fall of 1774, local militia units throughout the colonies had begun drilling. They also started stockpiling arms and ammunition. By 1775, tensions had been building between Great Britain and her American colonies for more than ten years, and the militiamen had become known as minutemen, because their goal was to be prepared to fight the British on a minute's notice. However, General Gage and his British officers did not consider these local "bumpkins, peasants, and illiterate plowboys" to be a serious threat. They believed that the colonists would soon be humbled into submission. Recruits continued to swell the ranks of the Sons of Liberty, especially in Massachusetts, which Parliament had declared to be in a state of rebellion. The Massachusetts Committee of Public Safety had succeeded in establishing a network of spies, which was prepared to alert the local militia to any military threats from the British.

The minutemen
Library of Congress, Prints and Photographs Division [LC-USZC4-7646]

EVENT

DAVID AND GOLIATH

Any military conflict between Great Britain and its American colonies would be like the giant Goliath fighting the shepherd boy David. Great Britain had many advantages over its colonies: three times the population of the colonies; the support of some of the colonists who sided with the homeland; a large, well-trained, and experienced army; the largest navy in the world; and money to buy arms, purchase supplies, and pay for foreign mercenaries (soldiers from other countries paid to fight for Great Britain).

However, the American colonists had a few advantages of their own: fighting to defend their homeland and their freedoms; knowledge of the terrain and of the "wilderness strategy" (guerilla tactics learned from fighting the Native Americans); bolder and more capable military leaders; and the possibility of receiving aid from Britain's enemies (France and Spain).

THE BATTLES OF LEXINGTON AND CONCORD (APRIL 19, 1775)

In April 1775, General Thomas Gage received secret orders from the British government to take military action against the rebels in Massachusetts to destroy their collection of military supplies and to capture their leaders, John Hancock and Sam Adams. Dr. Joseph Warren, one of the Patriot leaders, learned about Gage's orders and on April 16 sent Paul Revere to alert Adams and Hancock. Revere promised that he would warn them when the British forces started to march. Because Revere was not certain that he would be able to leave Boston with the message, he planned to light one lantern in the Old North Church steeple if the British were coming by land and two lanterns if the British were coming by sea.

On the evening of April 18, Gage ordered seven hundred British troops to the town of Concord, which is about twenty miles northwest of Boston. Concord, which had the largest supply of colonial weapons in the area, was also close to Lexington, where John Hancock

Dr. Joseph Warren
Library of Congress, Prints and Photographs Division [LC-USZ62-9036]

Old North Church
Library of Congress, Prints and Photographs Division [LC-USZ62-46025]

and Sam Adams were hiding. When Boston Patriots became aware that the British soldiers were being ferried across Boston Harbor, Paul Revere had two lanterns hung in the church steeple. Then Dr. Warren sent both Revere and William Dawes to warn the people of Lexington and Concord that the British were on their way.

Revere and Dawes succeeded in arousing most of the countryside as they cried out their warning at the homes of militia leaders all along the way to Lexington. They also were successful in reaching Adams and Hancock, who escaped in time. However, before Revere and Dawes could reach Concord, they were stopped by a British patrol. By this time, a third Patriot, Dr. Samuel Prescott, was riding with Revere and Dawes. Although the British captured all three men, Dawes and Prescott escaped. In the process of escaping, Dawes was thrown from his horse and was forced to walk back to Lexington because his horse ran away. Prescott, however, rode on to Concord to warn the colonists there.

British forces reached the town of Lexington near dawn on April 19, 1775. The horsemen's warnings had alerted the minutemen, who had dressed quickly, grabbed their muskets, and headed out to their prearranged meeting places. About seventy-five armed minutemen under Captain John Parker waited for the British as they approached the Lexington town green. These minutemen were greatly outnumbered by the advancing British troops. What Parker supposedly said that day is now carved in stone near the spot where he probably stood: "Stand your ground. Don't fire unless fired upon. But if they mean to have a war, let it begin here!" Eight minutemen were killed and ten wounded in the clash at Lexington. One British soldier was also killed.

Battle of Lexington
Library of Congress, Prints and Photographs Division [LC-USZ62-103793]

While the British troops continued on to Concord, the men and women of Concord were busily moving the arms and ammunition stored there to new hiding places in nearby towns. Just outside of Concord, British soldiers were met by three or four hundred minutemen at North Bridge. In the resulting skirmish, three British soldiers and two minutemen were killed. Finally, the minutemen retreated. Moving on into Concord, the British forces set fire to the town courthouse, cut down the Liberty Pole, and destroyed any

**Ethan Allen
at Fort Ticonderoga**
*Library of Congress, Prints and Photographs
Division [LC-USZ62-96539]*

Benedict Arnold
Line drawing courtesy of Amy Pak

remaining military supplies. As they headed back to Boston, the British soldiers were fired on by minutemen hiding behind trees and stone fences. British losses for the day numbered about 250 (killed, wounded, or missing), and American losses numbered about 90. A small company of American farmers had stood up against one of the most powerful armies in the world.

THE SURPRISE ATTACK AT FORT TICONDEROGA (MAY 10, 1775)

Less than a month after the skirmishes at Lexington and Concord, colonial forces succeeded in capturing Fort Ticonderoga in New York. Located on the western shore of Lake Champlain, Ticonderoga was originally a French fort, but it was seized by the British in the French and Indian War. It still held a stockpile of cannon, artillery, and tons of lead shot.

In ten bloodless minutes about two hundred Americans surprised the British garrison and captured it. These victorious Americans consisted of a rowdy group of frontiersmen called the Vermont Green Mountain Boys, led by Ethan Allen, as well as some men from Connecticut led by Benedict Arnold. This American victory stalled a planned British invasion of the colonies from Canada and enabled American forces to plan an invasion of Canada.

SECOND CONTINENTAL CONGRESS (1775)

The Second Continental Congress convened in Philadelphia on May 10, 1775, the day that Fort Ticonderoga fell. The delegates included Patrick Henry, Thomas Jefferson, John Hancock, Benjamin Franklin, John Adams, Sam Adams, and Richard Henry Lee. In mid-June, this congress voted to create the Continental army and soon unanimously selected George Washington to be its commander. Washington set off for Boston within a week, learning of the Battle of Bunker Hill along the way. Congress was then left with the responsibility of deciding how to recruit more soldiers, supply the army, and pay for the war.

In July 1775, the Continental Congress made a final effort to settle the colonists' differences with the mother country peacefully. Because some of the delegates were still not prepared to agree to a declaration of independence, they voted to present a petition to King George III. This petition, which became known as the Olive Branch Petition, protested the harsh actions of the British toward the colonists and called for greater moderation on the part of the mother country. However, the petition did not call for an end to the union between Britain and her colonies, and its language reflected deep loyalty to the king.

Thomas Jefferson
National Archives print

July 8, 1775, To the King's Most Excellent Majesty.
Most Gracious Sovereign: We, your Majesty's faithful subjects of the Colonies of New-Hampshire, Massachusetts-Bay, Rhode-Island, New-Jersey, Pennsylvania, the Counties of Newcastle, Kent, and Sussex, on Delaware, Maryland, Virginia, North Carolina, and South Carolina, in behalf of ourselves and the inhabitants of these Colonies, who have deputed us to represent them in General Congress, entreat your Majesty's gracious attention to this our humble petition....

We shall decline the ungrateful task of describing the irksome variety of artifices practised by many of your Majesty's Ministers, the delusive pretences, fruitless terrours, and unavailing severities, that have, from time to time, been dealt out by them, in their attempts to execute this impolitick plan, or of tracing through a series of years past the progress of the unhappy differences between Great Britain and these Colonies, that have flowed from this fatal source.

Benjamin Franklin
Library of Congress, Prints and Photographs Division [LC-USZ62-90398]

Your Majesty's Ministers, persevering in their measures, and proceeding to open hostilities for enforcing them, have compelled us to arm in our own defence, and have engaged us in a controversy so peculiarly abhorrent to the affections of your still faithful Colonists, that when we consider whom we must oppose in this contest, and if it continues, what may be the consequences, our own particular misfortunes are accounted by us only as parts of our distress.

**Washington taking command
of the Continental army**
National Archives print [148-GW-178]

General William Howe
Public Domain

Knowing to what violent resentments and incurable animosities civil discords are apt to exasperate and inflame the contending parties, we think ourselves required by indispensable obligations to Almighty God, to your Majesty, to our fellow-subjects, and to ourselves, immediately to use all the means in our power, not incompatible with our safety, for stopping the further effusion of blood, and for averting the impending calamities that threaten the British Empire....

We beg further leave to assure your Majesty, that notwithstanding the sufferings of your loyal Colonists during the course of this present controversy, our breasts retain too tender a regard for the kingdom from which we derive our origin, to request such a reconciliation as might, in any manner, be inconsistent with her dignity or welfare. These, related as we are to her, honour and duty, as well as inclination, induce us to support and advance; and the apprehensions that now oppress our hearts with unspeakable grief, being once removed, your Majesty will find our faithful subject on this Continent ready and willing at all times, as they have ever been with their lives and fortunes, to assert and maintain the rights and interests of your Majesty, and of our Mother Country....

That your Majesty may enjoy long and prosperous reign, and that your descendants may govern your Dominions with honour to themselves and happiness to their subjects, is our sincere prayer.

—from the Olive Branch Petition

When the Olive Branch Petition was presented to George III, he refused to even consider it. Then on August 23, the king issued a proclamation stating that the colonists were in "open and avowed rebellion." Thus, the door closed on any further efforts toward reconciliation between Britain and her colonies.

Meanwhile, lines of division were being drawn among the American colonists. The consensus among most historical scholars is that as many as 20 to 25 percent of the colonists (500,000 – 625,000) would decide to support the British cause during the Revolution. These Americans were known as Loyalists or Tories. Historians have also generally believed that between 40 and 50 percent of the colonists were Patriots or rebels. The remaining Americans did not claim allegiance to either side.

BATTLE OF BREED'S HILL AND BUNKER HILL (JUNE 17, 1775)

After the battles of Lexington and Concord, American militiamen moved to fortify the roads and hills around the edge of Boston, hemming the British troops inside the city. In May 1775, troop reinforcements arrived from Britain, along with three more British generals— William Howe, Henry Clinton, and John Burgoyne. These generals persuaded Gage that he needed to control the hills on the nearby Charlestown peninsula in order to keep the colonists from setting up guns there to bombard Boston. Thus, the British made plans to move north across the Charles River and fortify Charlestown.

Colonel William Prescott
Library of Congress, Prints and Photographs Division [LC-D4-16124]

When the Americans learned of the British plan, they decided to beat the British to Charlestown and establish a defensive position on Breed's Hill and Bunker Hill before the British could move in. On the evening of June 16, Patriot forces under the leadership of Colonel William Prescott stole away to the Charlestown peninsula and worked all night digging trenches and building breastworks. The main fortifications were built on Breed's Hill rather than Bunker Hill, because it was smaller, more vulnerable, and closer to Boston.

Early the next morning, the British were astonished to see American fortifications on the hill. Soon, British warships began bombarding the Charlestown hillside with cannonballs. However, this inflicted little damage on the Americans, and the British subsequently decided to send General Howe with troops by land to take the hills. Howe led two bloody and ineffective charges up Breed's Hill. In order to conserve their ammunition, Colonel Prescott supposedly instructed his American forces not to "fire until you see the whites of their eyes."

Finally, after obtaining reinforcements and badly needed ammunition, General Howe ordered a bayonet charge to seize the hill. By this time, the Patriots had run out of ammunition. When the British made their third run up Breed's Hill, the Americans could not return their fire. British forces succeeded in making their way into the trenches on the hill, where they began killing Americans. Some of the colonists fought with their hands, feet, and teeth to ward off the British attack. The Patriots retreated to nearby Bunker Hill, but they were soon flushed out of that area as well.

Technically, the Battle of Breed's Hill was a British victory. The British did succeed in driving the Americans off the Charlestown peninsula, but the victory was a costly one. The British lost almost eleven hundred soldiers (dead and wounded), whereas the American losses were less than half of that (about four hundred). Unfortunately, the Patriot leader Dr. Joseph Warren was killed during this battle. At

First battles of the American Revolution

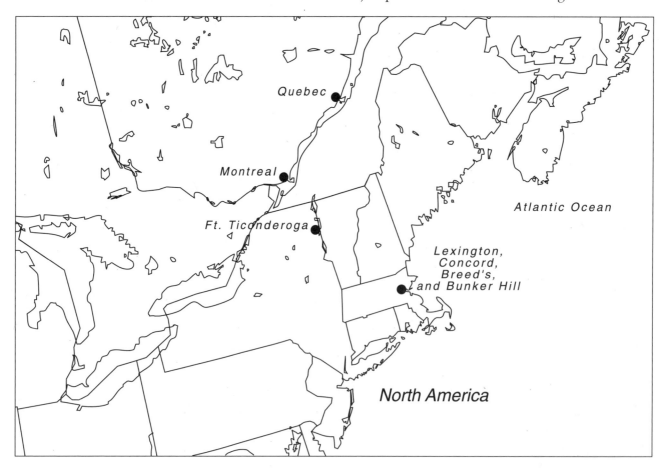

Breed's Hill, the colonists learned that the British army was not invincible, and this battle became a rallying point of resistance against British rule. Interestingly, even though this battle was fought primarily on Breed's Hill, it was remembered for many years in American history as the Battle of Bunker Hill.

A CANADIAN INVASION AND FAILURE IN QUEBEC (DECEMBER 30 – 31, 1775)

In the summer of 1775, the Second Continental Congress authorized an American invasion of Canada. The Americans hoped to deprive Britain of a northern gateway through which to attack the colonies. Patriot forces under Brigadier-General Richard Montgomery set out

Battle of Bunker Hill and the death of Dr. Joseph Warren
National Archives print [148-GW-454]

Daniel Morgan
Library of Congress, Prints and Photographs
Division [LC-USZ62-49177]

for Canada in August 1775. He established a base of operations and succeeded in capturing Montreal in November.

Meanwhile, Benedict Arnold had set out from Massachusetts in September with one thousand volunteers, including Captain Dan Morgan. Arnold planned to march up to Canada through Maine, but his route turned out to be difficult for his poorly supplied troops. By the time Arnold's men reached Canada, they were exhausted and starving, having eaten their leather moccasins to stay alive.

In early December, Montgomery and Arnold joined forces near Quebec. The Americans chose to attack Quebec under cover of a storm on December 30 and suffered a disastrous defeat. Montgomery was killed within minutes and Arnold was wounded. Captain Morgan took over for Arnold and led his men into the city, where they waited for Montgomery and his forces. As the Americans waited, the British regrouped and succeeded in driving the colonial forces back out of the city. Morgan and his men surrendered to the British, ending Patriot dreams of conquering Canada.

By the end of December 1775, the British Parliament had closed all American ports to trade, meaning American ships and cargos could be seized by the British navy as "open enemies." King George had hired thousands of Hessians to send to the colonies to fight, shocking the colonists who thought of the rebellion as a family fight. These Hessians were mercenaries — that is, they fought for pay for other countries— and they had the reputation of being brutal fighters. By early 1776, ten of the thirteen colonies had moved to establish their own independent governments. One by one, British-appointed colonial governors had been thrown out and provincial congresses had taken control of colonial governments.

IMPACT

- Although the British appeared to have the advantage of greater resources, the American colonists had advantages too, including a fervent desire to defend their homeland.

- The first shots of the American Revolution were fired at Lexington and Concord (Massachusetts) in April 1775, where a small company of American militiamen stood up against a powerful British military force. Even though the colonists lost at the Battle of Bunker Hill and Breed's Hill in June 1775, the British losses were heavy. This showed the colonists that the British were not invincible, and it became a rallying point against British rule.

- The Green Mountain Boys, led by Ethan Allen, and some Connecticut miliatiamen under Benedict Arnold captured Fort Ticonderoga in New York, where the British had stock-piled artillery. This victory stalled a planned British invasion from Canada.

- The Second Continental Congress met in May 1775 and voted to create a Continental army and unanimously selected George Washington to be its commander. In a final attempt to prevent war, the delegates sent the Olive Branch Petition to King George III, who refused to consider it and declared the colonies to be in open rebellion.

- American forces under Richard Montgomery, Benedict Arnold, and Dan Morgan were ultimately unsuccessful in their invasion of Canada.

LESSON 21

War in the Northeast . . . . 1776 — 1777 A.D.
The Declaration of Independence . . . . 1776 A.D.

ATMOSPHERE

COMMON SENSE

Thomas Paine emigrated to America from England in November 1774. Paine had caught the attention of Benjamin Franklin while he was overseas. When Paine arrived in America, he settled in Philadelphia, where he established himself as a writer and editor. (In England Paine had worked as a preacher, teacher, and grocer. He had also gone bankrupt as a corset maker.) As tensions mounted over the next year between America and Britain, Paine began recording his thoughts about their hostility. This record was published in a fifty-page pamphlet, *Common Sense*, on January 10, 1776. This booklet sold over 120,000 copies in ninety days. A half-million copies were eventually sold, which is remarkable in a country of perhaps two million literate adults.

In *Common Sense* Paine denounced British tyranny and called for American independence, something hardly anyone had openly written about. He declared that Britain's hold on the colonies, particularly its trade restrictions and taxes, was exploitative and harmful to the American economy. According to Paine, a tiny island three thousand miles away should not be running a great continent. Independence

Thomas Paine
Line drawing courtesy of Amy Pak

for the colonists was just *common sense*. In fact, the Americans had a moral obligation to free themselves from the tyranny of the English monarchy and an absolute right to independence and freedom.

Paine's pamphlet won many Americans over to the idea of independence from Britain. Colonists read the booklet and passed it on to their friends. People argued about its fiery ideas. Written in language that common people could understand, *Common Sense* served to propel the colonies toward the Declaration of Independence six months later.

Meanwhile, Paine continued writing pamphlets about the war. George Washington read one of Paine's essays to his men on Christmas Day of 1776, inspiring them to win a much-needed victory against the British at Trenton. One of Paine's essays, "The Crisis," began with these words: "These are the times that try men's souls. The summer soldier and the sunshine patriot will, in this crisis, shrink from the service of their country; but he that stands it now, deserves the love and thanks of man and woman"[8] In another of Paine's essays he coined the term: *United States of America.*

Thomas Paine was a man of deep beliefs, and *Common Sense* was perhaps the single most influential political pamphlet ever published. John Adams said, "I know not whether any man in the world has had more influence on its inhabitants or affairs for the last thirty years than Tom Paine."[9] Although Paine was not a wealthy man, he gave a third of his earnings to help Washington's army and he refused to take any money for his patriotic writings. By giving the printing rights to that literature to the government, he donated nearly one million dollars to America's struggle for independence.

General Henry Knox
Library of Congress, Prints and Photographs Division [LC-USZ62-12273]

Train of artillery from Fort Ticonderoga
National Archives print [111-SC-100815]

EVENT

BRITISH EVACUATION OF BOSTON (MARCH 17, 1776)

After the American victory at Fort Ticonderoga, General Henry Knox was commissioned to remove the cannon and artillery from the fort and transport them to Boston. Using eighty yokes of oxen and forty-two strong sleds, Knox succeeded in moving the cargo to the top of Dorchester Heights in Boston. General Howe, who had taken command of the British army several months before, realized that the British could no longer hold Boston with American cannons pointed at them. Thus, he decided to evacuate his army to Canada, freeing Boston of British troops. On March 17, 1776, General Howe, his seven hundred soldiers, and one thousand Loyalists sailed to Halifax, Nova Scotia.

After the departure of the British, Patriot troops marched into Boston and took possession of the city. The people of Boston rejoiced, and the Continental Congress had a gold medal struck and presented to General Washington with the thanks of the United Colonies. However, even as the British left Boston, General Washington realized that their ultimate destination was most certainly New York, which had a superb port and numerous Loyalists. Enemy control of the Hudson River would cut off the New England colonies from those in the South, enabling the British to turn on either region and crush it bit by bit. Therefore, Washington decided to move his headquarters from Boston to New York. In April 1776, he marched his troops southward and positioned them on the western end of Long Island in anticipation of the British arrival. Three months later, Howe and his troops landed at New York City.

Richard Henry Lee
Library of Congress, Prints and Photographs Division [LC-USZ62-21298]

THE DECLARATION OF INDEPENDENCE (JULY 4, 1776)

On June 7, 1776, Richard Henry Lee, a delegate from Virginia, stood at the Continental Congress and resolved that "these United Colonies are, and of right ought to be, free and independent states, that they are absolved from allegiance to the British crown…"[10] For many days the delegates debated Lee's call for independence. In anticipation of a vote for independence, on June 11, the Continental Congress appointed a committee to draft a formal resolution declaring American independence. The five members selected to serve on this committee were Thomas Jefferson, John Adams, Benjamin Franklin, Robert Livingston, and Roger Sherman. The committee in

An original copy of the Declaration of Independence
National Archives

---

turn delegated Jefferson, another delegate from Virginia, to write the first draft of the resolution.

Although Jefferson was only thirty-three years old, he was well known as a brilliant writer, inventor, and lawyer. For two weeks Jefferson worked diligently in private to compose a document, writing behind a veil of secrecy imposed by the congress. Jefferson's original draft was first revised by Adams, then by Franklin, and finally by the full committee. In all, forty-seven alterations were made on the text before it was presented to the Continental Congress. The committee's final draft of the Declaration of Independence consisted of two parts: justification of the colonists' right to overthrow a government that denied them their natural rights and a list of colonial

The Declaration of Independence by John Trumbull
National Archives print [148-GW-662]

grievances against the British king (unjust taxation, curtailment of colonial trade, and development of a military dictatorship in the colonies).

On July 1, 1776, the delegates at the Continental Congress listened to Jefferson's document. Then they discussed, debated, and revised it. Jefferson was not happy with some of the changes. Sitting next to Jefferson was Benjamin Franklin, who, at seventy, was the oldest and perhaps the most famous delegate. Franklin was known throughout the colonies and Europe as a printer, writer, statesman, and scientist. As the debate continued, Franklin supposedly told Jefferson, "I have made it a rule... to avoid becoming the draftsman of papers to be reviewed by a public body."[11]

A majority vote was needed to pass the resolution, and each colony had one vote. If the vote was not unanimous, the colonies would no longer be unified in the war effort. According to John Adams, getting all thirteen colonies to agree to pass the resolution would be as difficult as getting thirteen clocks to strike at the same time. Finally, John Hancock, president of the Continental Congress, urged everyone to go along with the Declaration. "We must all hang together," Hancock urged. Benjamin Franklin added, "Yes, we must indeed all hang together, or most assuredly we shall all hang separately."[12]

On July 2, the delegates at the Continental Congress voted to accept Richard Henry Lee's resolution calling for American independence. The vote was twelve to zero, with New York abstaining. Caesar Rodney, a delegate from Delaware who was suffering from cancer, rode all night long in the rain from his home in Dover to Philadelphia to cast his vote. Rodney's vote was needed for Delaware to vote in favor of independence since that colony's other two delegates were split (one for and one against). John Dickinson and Robert Adams from the Pennsylvania delegation were opposed to the adoption of the resolution. Apparently, Benjamin Franklin worked hard to persuade them to stay away from the vote. With their absence a majority of the Pennsylvania delegation voted in favor of adopting the resolution.

Franklin, Adams, and Jefferson drafting the Declaration of Independence
Library of Congress, Prints and Photographs Division [LC-USZ62-96219]

Caesar Rodney's ride
Library of Congress, Prints and Photographs Division [LC-USZ62-43963]

Then on July 4, the Continental Congress voted to approve the Declaration of Independence. Late that afternoon, the original document was signed by John Hancock, president of the Continental Congress. Hancock's signature was big and bold. He supposedly remarked that he wrote so large so that the king wouldn't "have to put on his glasses." Fifty-six delegates signed their names to the bottom of the page, risking their fortunes and even their lives to make America free.

The Declaration of Independence made all-out war certain. Congress had copies of the Declaration printed as handbills and delivered and read to the colonial armies. When the Declaration was read to Washington's troops in New York, they turned into a mob and tore down a statue of King George III. Within days, copies of the Declaration had been read far and wide throughout America.

IN CONGRESS, July 4, 1776.
The unanimous Declaration of the thirteen united States of America,

When in the Course of human events, it becomes necessary for one people to dissolve the political bands which have connected them with another, and to assume among the powers of the earth, the separate and equal station to which the Laws of Nature and of Nature's God entitle them, a decent respect to the opinions of mankind requires that they should declare the causes which impel them to the separation.

We hold these truths to be self-evident, that all men are created equal, that they are endowed by their Creator with certain unalienable Rights, that among these are Life, Liberty and the pursuit of Happiness. That to secure these rights, Governments are instituted among Men, deriving their just powers from the consent of the governed, That whenever any Form of Government becomes destructive of these ends, it is the Right of the People to alter or to abolish it, and to institute new Government, laying its foundation on such principles and organizing its powers in such form, as to them shall seem most likely to effect their Safety and Happiness. Prudence, indeed, will dictate that Governments long established should not be changed for light and transient causes; and accordingly all experience hath shewn, that mankind are more disposed to suffer, while evils are sufferable, than to right themselves by abolishing the forms to which they are accustomed. But when a long train of abuses and usurpations, pursuing invariably the same Object evinces a design to reduce them under absolute Despotism, it is their right, it is their duty, to throw off such Government, and to provide new Guards for their future security. Such has been the patient sufferance of these Colonies; and such is now the necessity which constrains them to alter their former Systems of Government. The history of the present King of Great Britain is a history of repeated injuries and usurpations, all having in direct object the establishment of an absolute Tyranny over these States. To prove this, let Facts be submitted to a candid world.

—from the Declaration of Independence

Mob tearing down statue of King George III in New York
Library of Congress, Prints and Photographs Division [LC-USZC4-1476]

THE FIGHT FOR NEW YORK (AUGUST – OCTOBER, 1776)

In June and July of 1776, British troops under the command of General Howe arrived in New York Harbor. They had sailed from Nova Scotia and Britain. Landing on Staten Island, they were joined by American Loyalists and Canadian volunteers. British troops under General Henry Clinton and General Charles Cornwallis, who had failed in an attempt to conquer the South, also headed to New York. By mid-August there were thirty-two thousand British troops in the area, greatly outnumbering Washington and his twenty thousand men who were waiting for them on a fortified area on the western end of Long Island. Although Washington did not expect to be able to hold New York City, he wanted to make the British fight for it.

The British drove the outnumbered Americans from one defensive position to another. A succession of battles in Brooklyn, Manhattan, Long Island, Kips Bay, Harlem Heights, New York City, and White Plains all ended in American defeat. By mid-November the British had captured some three thousand of Washington's best troops and tons of vital supplies at Fort Washington on northern Manhattan

General Henry Clinton
Public Domain

Island. Washington and his troops had retreated from New York, crossing the Hudson River and beginning a long, grueling march through New Jersey.

On November 20, in a surprise attack across the Hudson River, General Cornwallis and his forces overran Fort Lee and began the British invasion of New Jersey. Patriot troops dwindled in number as enlistments ran out, desertions took their toll, and the necessary reinforcements failed to arrive. In early December, Washington and his exhausted men crossed the Delaware River at Trenton into Pennsylvania. They were safe for the moment because Washington had brought all the available boats over with him to prevent the British from following.

Fighting continues in the Northeast

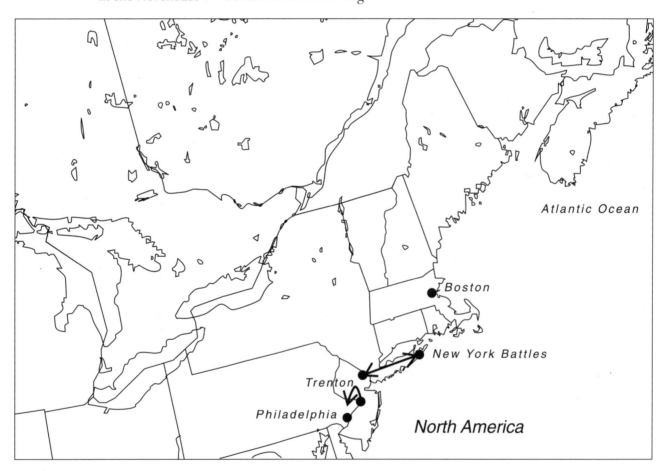

However, Washington's forces were near collapse. They were poorly armed, thinly clothed, hungry, and disheartened. Never had the Patriot cause been at such a low ebb. Convinced that cold weather and desertions would finish off the rebels, General Howe saw no reason to press the campaign through the winter. Thus, on December 13, Howe made the decision to go into winter quarters, keeping the main British garrison in New York and establishing a strip of outposts across central New Jersey. By failing to press after the Americans, the British provided the Patriots with an opportunity to heal and regroup.

General Charles Cornwallis
Public Domain

IMPACT

- *Common Sense*, a fifty-page pamphlet written by Thomas Paine and first published in January 1776, won many Americans over to the idea of independence from Britain and propelled the colonies toward the adoption of the Declaration of Independence six months later.

- After the American victory at Fort Ticonderoga, General Henry Knox moved the fort's cannon and artillery to Boston. Realizing that they would no longer be able to hold Boston, the British evacuated the city and a large number of Loyalists to Canada in March 1776.

- Realizing that the British troops were ultimately headed to New York, General Washington marched his troops southward in April 1776 and positioned them on the western end of Long Island.

- On July 4, 1776, the Continental Congress adopted the Declaration of Independence, which contained a justification of the colonists' right to overthrow a government that denied them their natural rights. The Declaration included a list of grievances against the British king.

- In June and July of 1776, British troops arrived in New York Harbor, where they were joined by American Loyalists and Canadian volunteers. British forces succeeded in driving the greatly outnumbered Americans from one defensive position to another, and the Americans suffered defeat in a succession of battles.

- By mid-November of 1776, Washington and his troops had retreated from New York. They marched through New Jersey and crossed into Pennsylvania in early December. Although Patriot forces were near collapse, the British chose not to press the campaign and made the decision to go into winter quarters in New York.

LESSON 22

ATMOSPHERE

THE BRITISH ARMY

British forces fighting in America during the Revolutionary War included British regulars or redcoats, Hessian mercenaries, Loyalists, and Native Americans. At its peak, these forces numbered about fifty thousand. There were also about 460 ships serving in the British navy at the time of the American Revolution.

The uniform of a British redcoat was made of heavy wool, which was hot in the summer and itchy in the winter. The top garment was a tight-fitting red overcoat decorated with piping, lace, and buttons of pewter or brass. An x was made across the soldier's chest by two belts, which held a bayonet and a cartridge box. Under the red overcoat was a vest of red or white, as well as a pair of white breeches. The breeches fit so tightly that the soldier would have to put them on wet.

British regulars also wore knee-length boots and a large clumsy hat with no brim. They usually carried a knapsack and gear, weighing about 125 pounds. The knapsack contained extra clothing, a blanket, a tent, and food. Their other gear included a 14-pound musket, a bayonet, several pounds of musket balls, and a shovel.

Typical British uniform
Library of Congress, Prints and Photographs Division [LC-USZ62-45201

261

Typical Continental uniform
*Library of Congress, Prints and Photographs
Division [LC-USZ62-26725]*

To wash his white pants, powder his hair, and clean his belts and buttons might take a British redcoat three or more hours. The British dress for battle proved to be a major liability in the type of guerilla warfare that was waged in America. Their red coats made British regulars perfect targets. However, British troops were generally better equipped and supplied than American forces and rarely forced to go without food, clothing, or arms.

THE AMERICAN ARMY

General Washington did not believe that part-time militias could defeat the British army in a long war. Therefore, he worked to build an American army of professional soldiers (called Continentals or regulars), who enlisted to serve for several years. However, most colonists preferred to serve in a local militia and to support the army whenever a major battle threatened nearby. Because recruitment was a constant problem for the American military, there were rarely more than fifteen thousand soldiers under Washington's command at any given time. The American navy, consisting of fifty ships and two thousand privateers, often succeeded in damaging British trade during the Revolution and capturing supplies intended for the British army.

American soldiers often went without pay, food, and proper clothing. The Continental Congress had little money to fight the war. Transportation was also poor. Many soldiers stayed in the army only because they were promised free land after the war was over. In the first years of the conflict, American forces fought bravely but lacked training and discipline. As the war progressed, colonial soldiers gained experience and skills.

The colonists generally went into battle in the only clothing they had, which was drab homemade clothes made of buckskin. Most men wore a homemade hunting shirt, gray or brown breeches, and a three-cornered hat. This type of outfit provided them with superb protective coloration. A few state regiments, however, were well equipped and wore official uniforms. The Americans had to provide their own muskets and knives, make their own musket balls, and bring whatever else they needed from home.

EVENT

TRENTON (DECEMBER 26, 1776)

After Washington and his men crossed the Delaware River into Pennsylvania, the Patriot general began looking for an opportunity for an American counterattack against the British. Washington believed that even a small success would raise the spirits of his demoralized troops and buy him the time needed to build a proper army. Trenton was the logical target for this attack because the other British outposts in New Jersey were too far away to catch by surprise. The garrison at Trenton had fewer than eighteen hundred soldiers, mostly Hessians. Washington knew that the German troops would celebrate the Christmas holiday, possibly leading to a security lapse. Thus, he set the date for the attack on Trenton for Christmas night.

On the bitterly cold Christmas night of 1776, about twenty-four hundred American troops crossed the ice-choked Delaware River during a sleet storm. At daybreak the Americans charged into Trenton, completely surprising the Hessians. By nine thirty in the morning the fighting was over. Not one American was killed and only a handful were wounded. Washington and his troops took more than nine hundred prisoners, along with much-needed arms and supplies. This American victory at Trenton gave a tremendous boost to the sagging morale of the Patriots.

PRINCETON (JANUARY 3, 1777)

On January 2, 1777, General Cornwallis reached Trenton with about six thousand British soldiers, leaving three regiments in Princeton as a rear guard. The British found that the colonial soldiers had created entrenched positions in Trenton and seemed prepared to fight. Cornwallis decided to quit the field, allowing his men to rest for a full-fledged attack against the Americans the next morning.

General Washington decided to retreat from Trenton in the middle of the night. He and his men stole around Cornwallis's army so quietly and deviously that the British never suspected what had happened. Taking back roads around the British, the Americans swung toward Princeton.

At dawn, a group of Patriot soldiers ran into British soldiers commanded by Colonel Charles Mawhood. These British troops were headed toward Trenton from Princeton to support Cornwallis's attack. General Hugh Mercer, who was leading the American soldiers, attacked the British soldiers immediately. After a few exchanges of fire, Mawhood's regiment charged into the Americans with their bayonets. At this point, Washington took personal command of the field.

Demonstrating great personal courage, Washington galloped across the battlefield ahead of the American troops and rode within

Washington crossing the Delaware
National Archives print [66-G-15D-25]

thirty yards of the British before ordering his men to fire. When the smoke cleared, the British were in retreat, and Washington was unharmed. Meanwhile, in Princeton, the British rear guard retreated to the grounds of Princeton College, where they soon surrendered after the Americans brought in cannon.

Back in Trenton, Cornwallis found the American camp deserted. A short while later, he began receiving reports of the American attack on Princeton. Cornwallis marched on Princeton, but his advance was slowed by a small American militia force, which destroyed the bridge over the creek. These Patriots then joined Washington, whose men had gathered what supplies they could find in Princeton and fled.

At the Battle of Princeton, eighty-six British soldiers were killed or wounded, and two hundred were captured. Following this second consecutive British defeat, Howe ordered British troops to withdraw from most of New Jersey. About forty Americans were killed or wounded at Princeton, and they moved into winter camp in Morristown, New Jersey. Morristown was a difficult target to assault because it was surrounded by thickly wooded hills. Somehow the Patriot army managed to survive the grueling winter there.

The American victories at Trenton and Princeton provided a great morale boost for the Americans and encouraged the French to release supplies to the American war effort. By spring, the Continental Congress had been able to purchase guns, muskets, gunpowder, shoes, and clothing to be distributed among the Patriot troops.

Green Mountain Boys flag
Public Domain

THE AMBUSH AT BENNINGTON, VERMONT (AUGUST 16, 1777)

In early 1777, the British planned to retake control of New York in the hope of dividing the rebellious colonies in half. There were three British armies that were to be a part of the invasion forces:

- the troops under General John Burgoyne, who planned to drive the colonists from Lake Champlain and march south into the Hudson River valley;

General John Burgoyne
Public Domain

- the troops under General Howe, who planned to thrust up the Hudson River from New York City; and

- the troops under Lieutenant Colonel Barry St. Leger, who planned to strike out from Canada west of Burgoyne's forces and then advance eastward through the Mohawk valley.

These three forces intended to meet in Albany and trap the American army there.

In June Burgoyne left Montreal and moved down Lake Champlain to Fort Ticonderoga, recapturing that garrison for the British on July 5. As Burgoyne and his men continued their march southward, General

Much military action

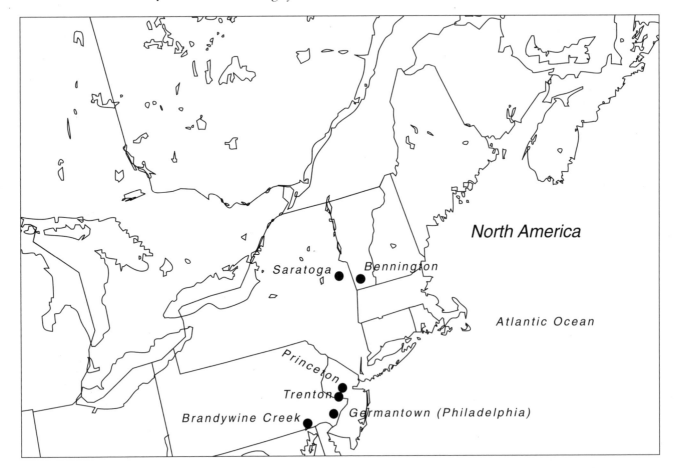

Philip Schuyler sent one thousand men with axes to fell trees across their path. The Americans also dammed streams and flooded lowlands, further slowing the advance of the British forces. The result was that Burgoyne's troops began to run short of supplies, especially food.

Therefore, Burgoyne decided to send a regiment of about eight hundred soldiers, including British, Hessians, Tories, and Indians, on an expedition to capture American supplies at Bennington, Vermont. As the British regiment neared Bennington, they were ambushed by about sixteen hundred New England militiamen and the Green Mountain Boys. Over two hundred of the British forces were killed, and seven hundred were taken prisoner. By contrast, only thirty Americans were killed and forty wounded. Not only had Burgoyne failed to gain his needed supplies, his army was weakened, leading to its defeat by the Americans at Saratoga.

General Philip Schuyler
Library of Congress, Prints and Photographs Division [LC-USZ62-56166]

THE BATTLE AT BRANDYWINE CREEK (SEPTEMBER 11, 1777)

By the summer of 1777, General Howe had decided to move his troops first into Pennsylvania, rather than marching immediately to meet Burgoyne's and St. Leger's forces at Albany. Howe believed the British needed to capture Philadelphia, the capital of the newly formed American nation and a major supply center, to demoralize the Patriots and ensure a final British victory. Furthermore, Howe had been embarrassed by Washington's successful maneuvering at Trenton and Princeton and hoped to lure Washington into battle and destroy his army. In July, Howe and his forces sailed south from their encampment in New Jersey, landing at the top of the Chesapeake Bay about fifty miles southwest of Philadelphia.

When Washington learned of Howe's movement southward, he marched his own force of eleven thousand soldiers south to Wilmington, Delaware. On September 3, the majority of Howe's army began marching toward Philadelphia. For the next five days, the two armies positioned themselves along the White Clay Creek, but neither Howe nor Washington engaged. Although Washington expected Howe to march toward him in Wilmington, Howe preferred

Brandywine Creek
Library of Congress, Prints and Photographs Division [LC-USZ62-113211]

to meet the Americans elsewhere. The British general feinted north, forcing Washington to change his defensive ground to the Brandywine River in Chadds Ford, Pennsylvania.

Finally, on September 11, the opposing troops clashed at Brandywine Creek. One wing of the British army swung around the Americans and attacked them from behind. The surprised Patriots were finally forced to retreat, but casualties were heavy on both sides. Fifteen days later, the British marched into Philadelphia, forcing the Continental Congress to flee first to Lancaster and then to York, Pennsylvania.

Several weeks later, on October 4, Washington struck back at British forces camping north of Philadelphia at Germantown. However, Washington's complicated battle plan created confusion, and in the heavy fog and smoke the Americans fired on one another. Again, the Patriots were forced to retreat. Nevertheless, the Americans had fought well, and their near victory prevented Howe from joining Burgoyne in New York. Howe and his forces occupied the city of Philadelphia throughout the winter. Some in the Continental Congress urged Washington to attack the British in Philadelphia, but Washington realized that his men were too worn-out and ill equipped. Therefore, he decided to take his troops to nearby Valley Forge to camp for the winter.

THE BATTLES OF SARATOGA
(SEPTEMBER 19 – OCTOBER 17, 1777)

By September, General Burgoyne, with about 7,700 troops, was approaching Albany. The advance of St. Leger's forces along the Mohawk River had been thwarted by American troops under the command of Major General Benedict Arnold. On September 19, at the Battle of Freeman's Farm — the first Battle of Saratoga — an American army under General Gates lost ground to the British forces under General Burgoyne. However, the British suffered heavy losses.

As General Burgoyne and his men entrenched around Freeman's Farm, they awaited forces under General Henry Clinton, which had supposedly left New York City to march north to Albany. After waiting several weeks, Burgoyne was low on supplies and facing an American army that was growing in numbers. On October 7, Burgoyne sent fifteen hundred British soldiers to test the American left flank. The Patriots, under the leadership of Benedict Arnold and Daniel Morgan, responded and attacked. The British withdrew to Saratoga, where they were surrounded by the Americans. From October 10 – 17, Burgoyne continued to resist the Americans until he finally decided that further fighting was useless.

The surrender of Burgoyne and his five thousand soldiers to General Gates on October 17 proved to be the turning point of the American Revolution. The Patriot victory at Saratoga provided a tremendous morale boost for the Americans, who had demonstrated that they could defeat a large British army in the field. After Saratoga, King George III sent peace commissioners to America because he feared an open alliance between France and the colonies. Also, the British Parliament offered to repeal all acts passed since 1763, respect the Americans' right to tax themselves, and withdraw all British troops. The Americans refused the British offer, preferring complete independence.

The American victory at Saratoga did indeed persuade the French to offer an alliance to the Americans, an alliance founded on France's desire for revenge against the British and the patient diplomacy of Benjamin Franklin, American ambassador to France. The French had been secretly supplying the Americans with gunpowder and arms since 1776. In December of 1777, France recognized American independence; and in early 1778, the French offered to enter into military and commercial treaties of alliance with the colonies. In the months that followed, France provided the Americans with two million dollars in aid, as well as French troops and a fleet of French warships. By 1779, the Spanish had also entered the war—as an ally of France, not the colonies.

THE ARTICLES OF CONFEDERATION (1777 – 1781)

On November 15, 1777, the Continental Congress adopted the Articles of Confederation. These articles, written by a committee headed by

Burgoyne's surrender at Saratoga
Library of Congress, Prints and Photographs Division [LC-USZC4-2912]

General Horatio Gates
Library of Congress, Prints and Photographs Division [LC-USZ62-45258]

John Dickinson
*Library of Congress, Prints and Photographs
Division [LC-USZ62-48883]*

John Dickinson, were an attempt to establish a national government for the united colonies. However, they were not ratified by all of the colonies and put into effect until 1781. Thus, the colonies fought almost the entire war without a national government.

> To all to whom these Presents shall come, we the undersigned Delegates of the States affixed to our Names send greeting.
>
> Articles of Confederation and perpetual Union between the states of New Hampshire, Massachusetts-bay Rhode Island and Providence Plantations, Connecticut, New York, New Jersey, Pennsylvania, Delaware, Maryland, Virginia, North Carolina, South Carolina and Georgia.
>
> The Stile of this Confederacy shall be "The United States of America."
>
> Each state retains its sovereignty, freedom, and independence, and every power, jurisdiction, and right, which is not by this Confederation expressly delegated to the United States, in Congress assembled.
>
> The said States hereby severally enter into a firm league of friendship with each other, for their common defense, the security of their liberties, and their mutual and general welfare, binding themselves to assist each other, against all force offered to, or attacks made upon them, or any of them, on account of religion, sovereignty, trade, or any other pretense whatever.
>
> —from the Articles of Confederation

**First page of the
Articles of Confederation**
National Archives

The Articles of Confederation created a nation that was a "league of friendship and perpetual union." Under the Articles, the newly formed state governments retained most of the power. Because the Americans were reluctant to establish a powerful central government, they created a loosely structured unicameral national legislature that protected the sovereignty of the individual states. Each state had only one vote in this legislature, regardless of its population; and nine out of thirteen states had to approve a bill for it to become law.

Under the Articles of Confederation, the American national government had no power to levy taxes, raise an army, or regulate interstate commerce. Rather, each state had the power to collect its own taxes, issue its own currency, and provide for its own militia. There was no federal court system to interpret laws, and there was no federal executive to enforce them. Any amendments to the Articles of Confederation required the agreement of all thirteen states.

IMPACT

- Forces fighting for the British during the American Revolution included British regulars (redcoats), Hessian mercenaries, Loyalists, and Native Americans. Although British troops were generally better equipped and supplied than American forces, the uniform of a British regular proved to be a major liability in the guerilla warfare waged in America.

- General Washington worked to build an American army of professional soldiers, called Continentals or regulars. However, because most colonists preferred to serve in a local militia, there were rarely more than fifteen thousand soldiers under Washington's command at any given time. American Patriots generally went into battle in the only clothing they had (drab buckskin), which provided them with superb protective coloration.

- American victories under Washington at Trenton and Princeton (December 25, 1776 – January 3, 1777) provided a great morale boost for the Patriots and encouraged the French to release supplies to the American war effort.

- Embarrassed by American victories at Trenton and Princeton, the British commander General Howe was determined to capture the American capital at Philadelphia and destroy Washington's army. British victories at Brandywine Creek and Germantown enabled the British to take over Philadelphia in September 1777, but the Americans had fought well and prevented Howe from returning to New York.

- The American victory at Saratoga in October 1777 proved to be the turning point of the American Revolution. As a result of this British defeat, the French recognized the colonies' independence and offered to enter into military and commercial treaties of alliance with them.

- In November 1777, the Continental Congress adopted the Articles of Confederation, establishing a national government for the united colonies. Under the Articles, the newly formed state governments retained most of their power. The national government had no power to levy taxes, raise an army, or regulate interstate commerce.

LESSON 23

ATMOSPHERE

THE BACKBONE OF THE PATRIOT CAUSE

Men and women of all social classes, races, and ages contributed to the Patriot cause in the American Revolution. Although many of the colonial upper class were reluctant revolutionaries, a number of America's lawyers, merchants, and planters did join the Sons of Liberty and serve in the Continental Congress. However, colonial artisans, shopkeepers, and small farmers were the backbone of the Revolution.

Most colonial women stayed home during the war. While the men were away fighting, women were required to do the work of husband *and* wife. Patriot women ran farms and businesses, sewed clothes for soldiers, and helped to make gunpowder and cannonballs. When battles were fought near their homes, many of these women fed and cared for the wounded. Some colonial women followed the army, acting as cooks and laundresses, and a few actually fought in battles. A woman named Deborah Sampson fought for three years disguised as a man named Robert Shirtliffe. When she came down with a fever and ended up in a field hospital, an amazed doctor learned the truth. It had not been too difficult to keep her

Deborah Sampson presenting a letter to Washington
Library of Congress, Prints and Photographs Division [LC-USZ62-76274]

275

Martha Washington
*Library of Congress, Prints and Photographs
Division [LC-USZ62-113386]*

Abigail Adams
*Library of Congress, Prints and Photographs
Division [LC-USZC4-5767]*

gender a secret since soldiers slept in their uniforms and rarely bathed.

Perhaps two of the best-known women from this era are Martha Washington and Abigail Adams. During the years that her husband George served as the commander of the Continental army, Martha managed their Mt. Vernon plantation. However, when the army stayed in winter quarters in Cambridge, Morristown, and Valley Forge, Martha traveled to the camp and stayed with her husband—seeking to encourage and support him. She also sewed, rolled bandages, and comforted the troops.

Long separations also kept Abigail from her husband John as he served in the Continental Congress and as an American ambassador abroad. Abigail was one of her husband's trusted advisors. She wrote him hundreds of witty, colorful letters that boldly expressed her opinions and recounted her experiences as a woman seeking to run a farm with little help in a time of wartime shortages and dangers.

Colonial children helped the war efforts by making cartridges, baking biscuits, canning food, and making soldiers' bags that were known as wallets. Children and women also acted as spies because they were not as likely to be suspected as men. Women whose husbands had gone off to fight were often alone with their children when an invading army looted and destroyed their homes.

Approximately five thousand African American men and boys are said to have fought on the side of the Patriots. Following the Boston Massacre, African Americans fought at the battles of Concord, Lexington, and Bunker Hill. However, when Washington assumed command of the Continental army, he banned the further recruitment of blacks for the army. After the difficult winter at Valley Forge and a large number of desertions from the Continental army, Washington reversed this ban. Because the British promised freedom to any slaves leaving their Patriot masters, a number of African Americans fought on the side of the British. Many white Americans, especially in parts of the South where blacks outnumbered whites, did not want blacks to have guns because they feared a slave uprising.

EVENT

THE WINTER AT VALLEY FORGE
(DECEMBER 19, 1777 – JUNE 19, 1778)

Washington and his troops arrived at Valley Forge, Pennsylvania, on December 19, 1777. Valley Forge, three thousand acres of farmlands and woods, was named for a nearby iron foundry that the British destroyed. Howe's troops were quartered in Philadelphia, twenty-five miles to the east. Valley Forge was elevated and close enough to Philadelphia for the Americans to keep watch on Howe's troops but not so close that Howe might try a surprise raid.

At the beginning of their stay at Valley Forge, the American forces consisted of about twelve thousand soldiers and 350 officers. Most of the men were dressed in torn clothing, and over twenty-five hundred of them had no shoes. They kept their feet wrapped in canvas or cowhide. They were hungry, tired, and cold. Washington wrote to the Continental Congress, "You might have tracked the army from White Marsh to Valley Forge by the blood of their feet."[13] According to the Marquis de Lafayette, "They had neither coats nor hats nor shirts nor shoes. Their feet and their legs froze until they were black, and it was often necessary to amputate them."[14]

Because there were no buildings at Valley Forge to use as barracks, about twelve hundred very crude huts (sixteen-by-fourteen feet) were quickly erected to provide shelter for the men. These huts, each housing an average of twelve men, were smoky, damp, and drafty. Feeding the troops was a daunting challenge, primarily because of transportation difficulties. At Christmas the troops had only a few spoonfuls of rice and fire cake (fried flour and water) and two ounces of liquor to celebrate. Smallpox, typhoid fever, and dysentery were rampant; much of the sickness was traceable to poor personal hygiene and unhealthy sanitation. The death toll at Valley Forge has been estimated as high as three thousand.

At first the American officers at Valley Forge feared that the troops there might mutiny. Over the weeks there were some desertions. However, Washington set a strong example by sharing in the hardships

Winter at Valley Forge
Line drawing courtesy of Amy Pak

Marquis de Lafayette
Library of Congress, Prints and Photographs Division [LC-USC4-572]

Baron Von Steuben
Library of Congress, Prints and Photographs
Division [LC-USZ62-45483]

General Henry Clinton
Public Domain

and sufferings of his soldiers. His wife Martha joined him for the winter and sought to encourage the soldiers. By spring, General Nathanael Greene had taken over as quartermaster. He worked with great determination and energy to find adequate food and supplies for the Patriots. After the first three months of shortages, there followed three months of relative abundance for the troops at Valley Forge.

On February 23, 1778, Baron Von Steuben arrived at Valley Forge from Prussia, where he had served under Frederick the Great. Von Steuben was a tough German professional soldier, who spoke little English but excelled in teaching tactics and in coordinating maneuvers. After a short trial period, Von Steuben was appointed inspector general in charge of a training program of drill formations. Day after day, Von Steuben worked drilling the American soldiers. His good humor, hands-on-style of demonstration, and cursing in broken English made the Prussian's intense training regimen more palatable to the Patriot soldiers. He turned a disorderly group of recruits into a strong, confident, and unified fighting unit, able to fight on equal terms with the British regulars.

By June 1778, General William Howe had resigned, and General Henry Clinton had been appointed to replace him as the new commander-in-chief of the British forces in America. On June 18, General Clinton made the decision to pull the ten thousand British troops out of Philadelphia and bring them to New York. Now that France had entered the war, the British were concerned that a French fleet might bottle their forces up in Philadelphia. An estimated three thousand Tories also left the city with the British troops.

Within hours of their departure, the American cavalry entered Philadelphia. Ready to move against the retreating British, Washington abandoned Valley Forge and waited for the British to make their move north through New Jersey. Soon the growing American army of twelve thousand men began pursuing Clinton and his forces toward New York. Meanwhile, a French naval squadron with one hundred warships and transports with four thousand French troops had sailed from France in May, headed to America. This French fleet was far superior to any that the British could concentrate in American waters and represented a strategic advantage to the Americans upon which Washington hoped to capitalize.

THE BATTLE OF MONMOUTH COURTHOUSE (JUNE 28, 1778)

After crossing the Delaware River at Lambertville, Washington sent several strong Patriot detachments ahead to harass and slow down the British. When Washington learned of the enemy's march to the village of Monmouth Courthouse, New Jersey, he ordered his main army in full pursuit. By the morning of June 28, the two armies were within striking distance of each other. General Charles Lee, Washington's second-in-command, was ordered to attack the British as they left Monmouth Courthouse.

Fighting shifts from the North

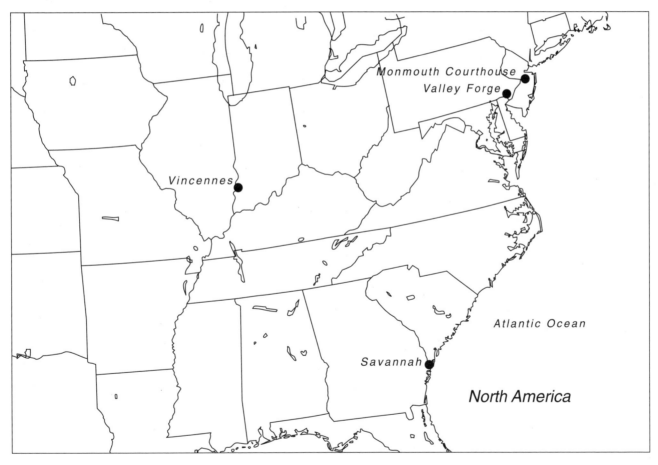

**Molly Pitcher at the
Battle of Monmouth**
*Library of Congress, Prints and Photographs
Division [LC-USZC4-4969]*

General Lee launched the assault but then led his men into a confused retreat. The British under Clinton immediately counterattacked and enveloped the American right flank. Only the arrival of General Washington and Baron Von Steuben prevented an American rout. Von Steuben re-formed Lee's troops and led them back into battle. The battle continued until nightfall, and both sides held their original positions.

A woman named Mary Hays McCauly apparently served with her husband, an artilleryman, at the Battle of Monmouth. Because Mary's story was retold so many times, some of the details conflict in the different versions of her story. According to oral tradition, Mary carried water in a pitcher back and forth from a well to her husband and his fellow artillery gunners during the fighting at Monmouth. Because of her actions, Mary was given the nickname, Molly Pitcher.

Some authorities believe that there were many "Molly Pitchers" during the Revolution—that the term was generally used by soldiers in battle calling for the water boy, who was usually a woman. The oral tradition surrounding Hays McCauley also maintains that she took over the rammer staff of her husband's gun when he was hit and that General Washington recognized her efforts publicly and called her Sergeant Molly. A flagstaff and a cannon stand at McCauly's gravesite in Carlisle, Pennsylvania, and her actions have been commemorated with a sculpture on the battle monument.

The Battle of Monmouth Courthouse was the longest and hottest of the American Revolution. Clinton and his forces escaped at nightfall, and Washington's tired army could not pursue them. However, fighting the British to a draw was considered to be somewhat of a victory for the Patriots. Monmouth Courthouse would be the last major battle in the North. Clinton moved on to New York City, and Washington crossed the Hudson River and established his headquarters in White Plains, New York, where he would remain until 1781.

THE BATTLE FOR SAVANNAH (DECEMBER 29, 1778)

Meanwhile, the British had decided to shift the focus of the war to the South, where they felt it would be easier to be victorious because of

Count Pulaski
*Library of Congress, Prints and Photographs
Division [LC-USZ62-56684]*

the large number of Loyalists living there. In December 1778, the British seized Savannah, Georgia. This was the first stage of Britain's southern strategy, which called for the capture of a major southern port to use as a base to rally southern Loyalists and launch further military campaigns. Within a few months, the British controlled all of Georgia. Joint American-French forces, under the command of General Benjamin Lincoln, tried to take Savannah back on October 9, 1779. However, the Americans and French suffered enormous casualties, among them the Polish count Casmir Pulaski. Pulaski, considered the father of the American cavalry, had his horse shot from underneath him and died of wounds he received in the fall.

George Rogers Clark
Line drawing courtesy of Amy Pak

WAR ALONG THE WESTERN FRONTIER

The area west of the Appalachian Mountains and north of the Ohio River was the scene of bitter fighting during the American Revolution. On the western frontier, American settlers were being terrorized by Native Americans allied with the British.

Under the leadership of George Rogers Clark, an expedition of forces from Virginia set out to take the Ohio River valley from the British and their Indian allies. Known as the Washington of the West, Clark was a brave and intelligent frontiersmen and surveyor. He and his men moved across the flat prairies and thickly wooded country, capturing the British governor of the region and succeeding in weakening the British hold on the frontier. An important British fortified post in the region, which fell to the Americans, was Vincennes, Indiana.

I HAVE NOT YET BEGUN TO FIGHT!

Although the small American navy was no match for the huge British fleet, it did succeed in capturing many British merchant ships and seriously disrupting British trade. Approximately a thousand privately owned American ships augmented the strength of the American navy, prowling the Atlantic and attacking and plundering British ships.

John Paul Jones
Library of Congress, Prints and Photographs Division [LC-USZ62-56171]

Probably the most famous of America's naval heroes was John Paul Jones, the captain of the *Bonhomme Richard*, which was a merchant ship converted to a warship. On September 23, 1779, Jones attacked a British convoy in the North Sea, which was escorted by the *Serapis*, a fifty-gun British man-of-war. The *Serapis* promptly engaged the *Bonhomme Richard*, and in the furious battle that followed the American ship was severely damaged. However, the *Bonhomme Richard* still managed to stay afloat. When the captain of the *Serapis* called on the Americans to surrender, Jones supposedly replied, "I have not yet begun to fight!" Eventually, the *Serapis* was forced to surrender.

The fight between the *Serapis* and the *Bonhomme Richard*
National Archives print [148-GW-444]

IMPACT

- Men and women of all races, social classes, and ages contributed to the Patriot cause. Women and children served as spies, took care of responsibilities on the home front, and cared for the wounded. About five hundred African Americans fought on the side of the Patriots.

- While Washington and his troops spent the winter of 1777 – 1778 at Valley Forge, Pennsylvania, Baron Von Steuben from Prussia took charge of a training program of drill formations and movements, turning a disorderly group of recruits into a confident and unified fighting unit.

- In June 1778, the British abandoned Philadelphia and moved north through New Jersey back to New York. At Monmouth Courthouse, New Jersey, the American forces fought the British to a draw in the longest and hottest battle of the American Revolution. This was the last major battle in the North.

- By the end of 1778, the British had decided to shift the focus of the war to the South, where a large number of Loyalists lived. In December, the British seized Savannah, Georgia, successfully executing their strategy to capture a major southern port. Within a few months, the British controlled all of Georgia.

- An expedition of Virginia forces, under the leadership of George Rogers Clark, succeeded in weakening the British hold on the Ohio River valley (the western frontier), where American settlers were being terrorized by Native Americans allied with the British.

- Although the small American navy was no match for the British fleet, it captured many British merchant ships and disrupted British trade. Perhaps the most famous American naval hero during the war was John Paul Jones.

LESSON 24

ATMOSPHERE

UNCONVENTIONAL BUT EFFECTIVE PATRIOT STRATEGIES

Late in 1778, the British began to shift their main military efforts from the North to the South. After three years of fighting in the North, neither the British nor the American forces, now both positioned in the colony of New York, were strong enough to continue major operations. However, the advantage in the North had shifted to the Americans. General Washington had accomplished his primary objective—keeping the British forces off balance until a Continental army could be trained and organized to support the militia. By the beginning of 1779, the Americans were no longer fighting alone against the British. Spain had joined France in an alliance with the Americans, and Great Britain now faced the very real possibility of a major European war. A quick end to the American Revolution seemed doubtful.

Facing mounting Parliamentary opposition to the war, the king's ministers rekindled an earlier plan for defeating the colonists—the conquest of the Southern colonies, one by one, beginning with Georgia. Central to this strategy was the active participation of southern Loyalists, who the British believed would rise up in large numbers

General Francis Marion, the "Swamp Fox"
Library of Congress, Prints and Photographs Division [LC-USZ61-71]

General Thomas Sumter, the "Gamecock"

Library of Congress, Prints and Photographs Division [LC-USZ61-72]

General Andrew Pickens, the "Wizard Owl"

Library of Congress, Prints and Photographs Division [LC-USZ61-70]

to help defeat the Patriots. Once the South was conquered, the king's ministers hoped to establish bases there and sweep northward to final victory. This southern campaign appealed to the British because it permitted them to continue military operations with a minimal increase in manpower.

At first, the British southern strategy seemed to work as planned. Savannah and Charleston fell quickly to the British. Following these victories, Lord Cornwallis, the British commander in the South, moved his forces through the Carolina backcountry and enlisted the support of Loyalist militia units there. By the summer of 1780, British control of South Carolina seemed assured, especially after the disastrous defeat at Camden. Thus, Cornwallis prepared to begin a northward march with his troops.

However, just months later, the success of the British southern campaign seemed less certain. In October, a militia force defeated British and Loyalist units at Kings Mountain. At the same time, Francis Marion (the "Swamp Fox"), Thomas Sumter (the "Gamecock"), and Andrew Pickens (the "Wizard Owl") were busy harassing British troops and Loyalist forces in South Carolina. These three men had organized and trained small forces of poorly equipped Patriots in guerrilla tactics. Living off the land, these bands of Patriots staged small surprise attacks in which they captured British soldiers, rescued American prisoners, and sabotaged supply lines and communications. Their guerilla activities kept the war alive in South Carolina until the re-establishment of a standing American army there.

EVENT

THE BATTLE FOR CHARLESTON AND SOUTH CAROLINA (APRIL 2 – MAY 12, 1780)

In December 1779, General Clinton sailed from New York with General Cornwallis and approximately eighty-seven hundred redcoats and Hessians. They headed south and landed on an island near Charleston, South Carolina, on February 11, 1780. Charleston (known at the time as Charles Town) was a strategic colonial port and the center for the southern Continental army. The British forces immediately began a month-long approach to the mainland and slowly closed in on the city, seeking to cut it off from reinforcements and lines of communication.

On May 8, General Clinton demanded surrender from the Patriots. However, the leader of the colonial forces at Charleston, General Benjamin Lincoln, wanted to negotiate better terms. A day later, the British began bombarding the city, leading to Lincoln's unconditional surrender on May 12. The Patriots' defeat at Charleston represented the greatest loss of manpower and equipment of the war for the Americans, giving the British almost complete control of the Southern colonies. After the British victory at Charleston, General Clinton placed General Cornwallis in charge of British forces in the South and returned to New York City.

THE BATTLE OF CAMDEN (AUGUST 16, 1780)

In the summer of 1780, the Continental Congress appointed General Gates to form a new southern army to replace the forces lost at Charleston. Gates arrived in the South with plans to repeat the quick victorious campaign at Saratoga. He hastily assembled an army of mostly untrained militiamen and immediately marched to Camden, South Carolina, to capture the British outpost there. When General Cornwallis, still in Charleston, heard of Gates's march, he and his forces quickly left for Camden themselves.

The Battle of Camden
Library of Congress, Prints and Photographs Division [LC-USZ62-50450]

On the evening of August 15, the British and American armies literally ran into each other near Camden. The following morning they met on the battlefield. Although the American forces actually outnumbered the British, the experienced British regulars intimidated the untrained militiamen that composed two-thirds of Gates's forces. In fact, many of those militiamen panicked and turned and ran without firing a shot. General Gates himself fled the field and retreated forty miles on the same day. Gates would never again command an army, and this disaster at Camden marked a low point in the Revolution for the Patriots. In three months, the British had captured

Death of Major Ferguson at Kings Mountain
Library of Congress, Prints and Photographs Division [LC-USZ62-21072]

Major General Nathanael Greene
Library of Congress, Prints and Photographs Division [LC-USZ62-121991]

two American armies and solidified their hold on South Carolina. They had made great progress in their goal of splitting the colonies into northern and southern halves.

BATTLE OF KINGS MOUNTAIN (OCTOBER 7, 1780)

After the Patriot defeats at Charleston and Camden, General Cornwallis appeared to have a clear path all the way to Virginia. In September, Cornwallis invaded North Carolina and gave orders to Major Patrick Ferguson to guard his left flank. When the activities of Ferguson and his men threatened a group known as the Overmountain Men living in the area, they began to pursue Ferguson. Militiamen from Virginia, North Carolina, and South Carolina soon joined the Overmountain Men in their pursuit.

Eventually, they caught up with Ferguson at Kings Mountain near the border of North Carolina and South Carolina. Ferguson and his men found the higher position impossible to defend; they were in the open and the Patriots had cover. British forces under Ferguson were soon defeated, destroying one whole section of Cornwallis's army and forcing him to retreat to South Carolina to wait for reinforcements.

Meanwhile, the Continental Congress had named Major General Nathanael Greene to replace Gates as commander of the Southern army. The victory at Kings Mountain gave Greene time to reorganize and rebuild. Deciding to split his forces, Greene assigned command of the more mobile unit to General Daniel Morgan. He recognized that the Patriots needed to make use of hit-and-run tactics to harass the British and force them to head north.

BATTLE OF COWPENS (JANUARY 17, 1781)

Recognizing Greene's strategy, General Cornwallis set up his own mobile unit under Lieutenant Colonel Banastre Tarleton and sent it out after Morgan's forces. After several weeks of maneuvering, General Morgan was forced to choose his ground before Tarleton's troops overran him. Morgan decided on a cattle-grazing area, known as Cowpens, in northern South Carolina.

Although the Americans were outnumbered and ill prepared, Morgan's sharp-shooting riflemen were quickly able to kill or capture almost all the onrushing British soldiers. A fierce bayonet charge by the Patriots then led to a mass British surrender. This devastating British defeat enraged Cornwallis, who pursued Morgan with even greater determination. Greene and his forces rushed to join Morgan. The tide of the war in the South had turned toward the Americans.

BATTLE OF GUILFORD COURTHOUSE (MARCH 15, 1781)

Two months after the American victory at Cowpens, Greene returned to North Carolina and began maneuvering against Cornwallis. Greene finally decided to take a stand near Guilford

Final battles in the South

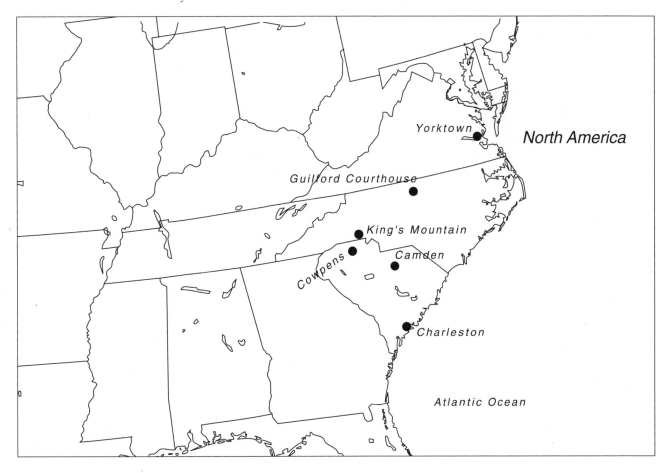

Battle of Cowpens
*Library of Congress, Prints and Photographs
Division [LC-USZ62-55195]*

**Lee's cavalry at the
Battle of Guilford Courthouse**
*Library of Congress, Prints and Photographs
Division [LC-USZ62-12274]*

Courthouse. Although the Patriot forces inflicted a devastating first attack, Cornwallis was able to steady his troops. Greene then withdrew from the field rather than take any more casualties.

At Guilford Courthouse, British casualties outnumbered American losses. Cornwallis and his men were tired and dangerously weakened, and their supplies were running low. At first, Cornwallis withdrew to the safety of the coast, near Wilmington, North Carolina. He eventually decided to abandon the Carolinas and marched for Virginia. Believing that the British southern campaign was now doomed, General Clinton feared that the Americans would next move to attack his base at New York City. Therefore, Clinton ordered Cornwallis to adopt a defensive position along the Virginia coast and to be prepared to send his troops north.

BATTLE OF YORKTOWN (OCTOBER 20, 1781)

Cornwallis and his troops arrived in Yorktown, Virginia, a port located on a peninsula in the Chesapeake Bay, in late May of 1781. There, the British awaited reinforcements and supplies by sea from New York, promised by General Clinton but slow in coming. Cornwallis spent the next several months maneuvering against the Marquis de Lafayette's roving forces in the area.

Meanwhile, Washington received word that the French fleet under Admiral de Grasse was on its way to the Chesapeake Bay area. With this news, Washington began planning a bold land-sea operation to trap Cornwallis in Yorktown. He sent orders to Lafayette to seal off the neck of the peninsula. Then Washington led his troops on a three-hundred-mile march from West Point, New York, to Virginia.

By late August, the French fleet (twenty-eight warships carrying three hundred troops) had arrived from the West Indies and established control of the Chesapeake Bay. General Washington and his men, as well as French troops under Count de Rochambeau, assembled in Virginia by late September. Washington spread the combined American and French forces of more than sixteen thousand soldiers in a semicircle across the neck of the peninsula. Cornwallis and his men were trapped on all sides, hemmed in by land and cut off by sea.

The American troops slowly and steadily closed in on the trapped British soldiers. Cornwallis made a desperate attempt to ferry his forces across the York River to safety on the night of October 16, but a storm drove them back. The following day, Cornwallis asked for surrender. Terms of surrender were negotiated on the eighteenth, and the official surrender ceremony was held on October 19, 1781.

At two o'clock in the afternoon on the nineteenth, more than eight thousand British soldiers marched onto the field, with drums beating a solemn march. Facing the American army, they lay down their arms as the British band played "The World Turned Upside Down." This song told the story of a mother and daughter who quarreled, with the mom eventually getting down on her knees to beg her daughter's forgiveness. General Cornwallis, claiming illness, did not attend but sent his sword by his brigadier general, Charles O'Hara. General Benjamin Lincoln accepted Cornwallis's sword for the Americans.

The Battle of Yorktown turned out to be the last major engagement of the American Revolution. Sporadic fighting dragged on in other areas of America for more than two years as peace discussions between the Americans and the British took place in Paris. Three thousand British troops remained in America; and the British still controlled New York City, Long Island, Charleston, and Georgia. The last British soldiers were withdrawn from New York City in November of 1783.

Marquis de Lafayette
Library of Congress, Prints and Photographs Division [LC-USC4-572]

THE TREATY OF PARIS (SEPTEMBER 3, 1783)

Benjamin Franklin, John Adams, and John Jay negotiated for the United States in Paris. The Continental Congress had instructed these delegates to consult with the French before they took any action. However, the Americans disregarded these instructions and concluded a preliminary peace treaty with Britain on November 30, 1782. Congress approved the treaty on April 15, 1783, and the formal signing of the treaty took place on September 3, 1783. By this point, Britain was beset with problems from France and Spain, and its Parliament was led by men willing to recognize America's independence.

Under the terms of the Treaty of Paris, which bore the same name as the treaty that ended the French and Indian War twenty

Surrender at Yorktown
Line drawing courtesy of Amy Pak

John Jay
Library of Congress, Prints and Photographs
Division [LC-USZ61-295]

Signing of the Treaty of Paris
Library of Congress, Prints and Photographs
Division [LC-USZ6-279]

years earlier, the British recognized American independence and promised to withdraw all troops from America as soon as possible. The boundaries of the United States were established—west to the Mississippi River, north to Canada, east to the Atlantic Ocean, and south to about Florida. The American Congress was instructed to recommend that the colonies restore property taken from Loyalists during the war. They agreed not to persecute Loyalists and to allow those who fled the colonies to return. The new nation also assumed all debts owed to England.

The American Revolution ended two centuries of British rule over its American colonies and resulted in the birth of a new nation—the United States of America. However, even though the Treaty of Paris formally ended the fighting in 1783, the future of the American nation was unsettled until 1787, the year that the United States Constitution was written. Without the establishment of a stable system of government, the new nation could easily have come unraveled.

IMPACT

- The Patriots' defeat by the British at Charleston in the spring of 1780 represented the greatest loss of manpower and equipment of the Revolution for the Americans.

- Following the devastating Patriot defeats at Charleston and the disastrous defeat of General Gates at Camden, the British under General Cornwallis appeared to have a clear path all the way to Virginia. However, a Patriot victory at Kings Mountain, North Carolina, in October 1780, gave American forces an opportunity to reorganize and rebuild.

- The tide of war turned toward the Americans after a devastating British defeat at the Battle of Cowpens in January 1781. Although outnumbered and ill prepared, American sharp-shooting riflemen, under the command of General Daniel Morgan, were instrumental in this American victory.

- After heavy casualties at the Battle of Guilford Courthouse, the British under Cornwallis were dangerously weakened. The British believed that their southern campaign was doomed and feared that the Americans would attack their base in New York City.

- American and French troops and a French fleet slowly closed in on Cornwallis and his forces, trapped on the Yorktown peninsula. Terms of surrender were negotiated in Virginia in October 1781, but sporadic fighting dragged on in other areas of America for more than two years.

- The Treaty of Paris of 1783 recognized American independence and established the boundaries of the new nation. Withdrawal of all British troops from America was promised as soon as possible, and Loyalists were protected from persecution and promised the restoration of any property confiscated during the war.

UNIT FOUR
THE PERIOD OF ESTABLISHMENT AND EXPANSION

Lessons 25 — 32

With the ratification of the country's new constitution and the election of its first president, the United States began its history as a federal republic of states. Growing in size from the thirteen original colonies in 1790 to thirty states by 1848, the new American nation underwent many challenges and changes in the first sixty years of its existence, such as:

- The test of two wars (the War of 1812 and the Mexican War) and many violent clashes with Native Americans
- The country's first financial crises
- The start of the Industrial Revolution and the emergence of a distinctly American culture

The Northwest Territory became a U.S. possession following the American Revolution, moving the boundaries of the new nation westward. The greatest expansion of land occurred in the first years of the nineteenth century as a result of the purchase of the Louisiana Territory from France, doubling the young country's size. This resulted in a wave of pioneers moving westward that continued for most of the nineteenth century. The dream of Manifest Destiny — U.S. possession of the entire American continent — quickly became a very real possibility.

Although the first U.S. president, George Washington, warned the American people against forming political parties, little time elapsed before two distinct political factions emerged. Two members of Washington's cabinet, Alexander Hamilton and Thomas Jefferson, held opposing points of view concerning the nature of the national government. Hamilton favored a strong national government, managed by well-educated and prosperous men, and believed that government should encourage business and industry. Those following Hamilton, including the second U.S. president, John Adams, became known as Federalists. These men advocated flexibility in interpreting the nation's Constitution, and they were known as broad or loose constructionists.

Jefferson, on the other hand, feared a powerful national government and had faith in the ordinary people of America. He hoped to keep the United States a nation of farmers and landowners, and he was concerned with liberty and justice for the individual. Those supporting Jefferson became the founders of the Democratic-Republican Party. These men, known as strict constructionists, did not advocate flexibility in interpreting the country's new Constitution. The third, fourth, and fifth U.S. presidents (Jefferson, Madison, and Monroe) were Democratic-Republicans.

By 1824, the Federalist political party no longer existed in the United States. The Democratic-Republican Party splintered into several factions. The factions led by John Quincy Adams and Henry Clay would become the short-lived National Republican Party and later the Whigs. The faction led by Andrew Jackson became the Democratic Party, and the faction led by William Crawford was not significant. Four of these factions ran candidates for president in 1824. Although Andrew Jackson won the most popular votes, no candidate received a majority of the electoral votes, so the U.S. House of Representatives chose John Quincy Adams to serve as the nation's sixth president. In 1828, Adams and Jackson engaged in a bitter rematch, with Jackson positioning himself as a friend of the common man. This time Jackson won, calling his election a "democratic revolution," a new "Jeffersonianism." For the next twelve years, national politics polarized around Jackson and his opponents. This period in American history ended with the election of James Polk, who became known as the last of the Jacksonians. He is also considered the last strong presidential leader before the Civil War.

All American History

LESSON 25

A New Nation Is Born . . . . 1783 — 1789 A.D.

ATMOSPHERE

RESULTS OF THE WAR FOR INDEPENDENCE

The Revolutionary War gave birth to the United States of America. Thirteen British colonies threw off royal rule and in its place established governments ruled by law and dedicated to the guarantee of certain basic rights and liberties. According to Thomas Paine, the American Revolution "contributed more to enlighten the world, and diffuse a spirit of freedom and liberality among mankind, than any human event that ever preceded it."[15] In fact, the success of the American Patriots set in motion a chain of revolutions that continues to this day.

Most historians estimate that about 7,200 Americans were killed in action during the Revolution and approximately 8,200 were wounded. As many as 10,000 others died in military camps from disease or exposure, and some 8,500 died in prison after being captured by the British. The total American military deaths numbered around 27,500. Many American soldiers were penniless after the war ended because they received little or no pay while serving in the army. Soldiers who enlisted for the entire war were given certificates for western land, but many of them had to sell the certificates because they needed money before the western lands were available to them.

The American colonies went deeply into debt to finance the Revolution. Even after the war was over, inflation, the destruction and plunder caused by military action, and the disruption of normal trade inflicted losses on many American families. Under the Articles of Confederation the United States Congress had no power to tax to raise money to repay American loans, and the thirteen states continued to print worthless paper money. After the Revolution, the American nation suffered a severe economic depression.

The Articles of Confederation had created a "firm league of friendship among the thirteen states." The national government that it established was not as powerful as the thirteen state governments. Rather, it had only the powers granted to it by the states, which viewed themselves as basically independent of each other. In the years immediately following the American Revolution, the newly formed nation came to realize that it did not have a good working plan for its government.

EVENT

NATIONAL INSTABILITY

The period from 1783 to 1789 was a critical period in American history. During this time, the thirteen newly formed states constantly squabbled among themselves and grew increasingly suspicious and jealous of each other. They argued over boundary lines and charged each other import taxes. The states also refused to support the national government financially — and in almost any other way.

Since the national government of the United States was obviously weak, other nations treated the new country with little respect. For example, the national government was unable to defend U.S. borders from British and Spanish aggression because the states would not contribute the money needed for military protection. George Washington's assessment, written in a letter to James Madison in 1785, was that "We are either a United people, or we are not. If the former, let us, in matters of general concern act as a nation, which have national objects to promote, and a national character to support. If we are not, let us no longer act a farce by pretending to it. For whilst we are playing a d[ou]ble game, or playing a game between the two, we shall never be consistent or respectable — but may become the dupes of some powers, and most assuredly, the contempt of all."[16]

The Articles of Confederation, submitted for ratification while the Revolution was still being fought, reflected the reluctance of the new American states to give too much power to a central governmental authority. At the time, most Americans were fearful of the possibility that the new national government would become as tyrannical as they considered the British government to be, meaning the war would have been fought in vain. However, in the years immediately following the Revolution, many Americans became frustrated with the ineffective Confederation government as they faced political confusion and economic chaos.

James Madison
Library of Congress, Prints and Photographs Division [LC-USZ62-16960]

STATE CONSTITUTIONS

The Continental Congress had suggested that each new state write a state constitution. State leaders drafted documents that divided governmental power among a governor, a state assembly, and state courts — reflecting the principles of separation of powers and checks and balances. Each state constitution also contained a bill of rights. These state constitutions established precedents important to the writing of the Constitution of the United States.

MOUNT VERNON (VIRGINIA) CONFERENCE (1785 – 1786)

Under the Articles of Confederation, the thirteen American states were often involved in trade disputes. Each state could tax the goods of another state or even refuse to trade with that state. This created many conflicts, and there was no federal court system to settle these conflicts. In 1785, the states of Maryland and Virginia agreed to meet at Mount Vernon to discuss their trade differences. The Mount Vernon Conference was successful in solving some of their disputes. In

Alexander Hamilton
Library of Congress, Prints and Photographs
Division [LC-USZ62-125560]

January 1786, the state of Virginia invited the other eleven states to send representatives to a conference in Annapolis to discuss regulation of trade among the states.

ANNAPOLIS CONFERENCE (1786)

Only five states accepted Virginia's invitation and sent delegates to the Annapolis Conference in 1786. Thus, no real business regarding national trade regulations could take place. However, at the urging of James Madison and Alexander Hamilton, a call was issued to all of the states to send delegates to a convention in Philadelphia in 1787. This convention was planned to provide an opportunity for all the states to discuss how to improve the general condition of the national government.

SHAYS'S REBELLION (1786 – 1787)

Massachusetts was especially hard hit by the economic hardships facing the new nation. The British cut off trade between the United States and the British West Indies, hurting Massachusetts's distillers, shipbuilders, and lumbermen who depended on that trade. Many Massachusetts farmers were heavily in debt and faced with the seizure of their farms by their creditors. Farmers and other workers unable to pay their debts were sent to debtor prisons and not released until their debts were paid. The Massachusetts state legislature responded to this economic crisis by raising taxes and increasing court costs.

In August 1786, mobs of Massachusetts's farmers and workers decided to congregate and bar access to the courthouses of several towns. An important leader of this rebellion was Captain Daniel Shays, a Revolutionary War veteran and farmer. Most of the rebels' actions during Shays's Rebellion were not violent. However, on January 25, 1787, Shays and two thousand men attempted to seize a federal arsenal in Springfield in order to capture weapons. The defending state militia killed three of these rebels with cannon shot and quickly put down the uprising. When the rebels were captured in February, they were sentenced to death for treason. The newly elected governor, John Hancock, subsequently pardoned the rebels.

Shays's Rebellion visibly demonstrated the weakness of America's Confederation government. Uprisings occurred in other states, creating a crisis atmosphere and fear of mob rule. Just a short time after Shays's Rebellion, the Constitutional Convention convened in order to strengthen the central government and to prevent such anarchy in the future.

Constitutional Convention
Line drawing courtesy of Amy Pak

CONSTITUTIONAL CONVENTION (MAY – SEPTEMBER, 1787)

In late May of 1787, the Constitutional Convention was officially called to order in Philadelphia, at the time the largest city in the United States. The convention completed its business in September, just as the heat began to break. In addition to the heat, the delegates contended with biting flies as well as mosquitoes that bit right through the silk stockings that they wore. These mosquitoes led to much illness throughout the city.

Seventy-four men were chosen as delegates to the Constitutional Convention. Only fifty-five actually came, but all of them were not present at the same time. By the end of the convention, there were only thirty-nine men left to sign the finished document. Of the thirteen states, only Rhode Island did not send any delegates to the convention. The men gathered in Philadelphia in the summer of 1787 were members of America's upper and middle classes. Well-educated and widely read, thirty-one of these men had earned a college degree. The group included successful lawyers, bankers, merchants, planters, educators, and doctors. Many had also served in the American Revolution or as members of the Continental Congress or Confederation Congress. Eight of them had signed the Declaration of Independence. Most of the delegates were young men in their mid-thirties. The youngest, Jonathan Dayton, was twenty-six years old; the oldest, Ben Franklin, was eighty-one.

George Washington was unanimously chosen as president of the convention. His calm presence kept the proceedings running smoothly. The convention met 89 of the 116 days from May 25 until September 17. James Madison from Virginia attended every day of the convention and took notes. Sitting close to the front, Madison never

Roger Sherman
Library of Congress, Prints and Photographs Division [LC-USZ62-111793]

missed sessions and copied down all the speeches. Today he is known as the Father of the Constitution.

The convention debates were endless. Washington at one point said, "I see no end to my staying here."[17] To prevent the pressure and influence of public opinion, the convention voted to keep its proceedings secret. When Thomas Jefferson, who was serving as American ambassador to France, heard about this, he was quite upset. He and others felt that democracy worked best in an atmosphere of openness. Others said that the convention could never have accomplished what it did if everyone in Philadelphia had known what was going on.

Throughout the summer of 1787, everyone in the colonies was curious about what was happening at the convention. James Madison's father tried to get his son to tell him at least what had not been decided. However, George Washington rigorously enforced the secrecy rule. At the State House the delegates even kept the windows shut so that no one could listen to the proceedings. Finally, they moved to the second floor so that they could open the windows and speak without fear of being heard.

There were several major issues debated at the Constitutional Convention. A principal dispute between the large and small states concerned the national legislative branch. The Virginia plan called for the number of congressmen from each state to be decided by population. This proposal, of course, favored states with large populations. The New Jersey plan insisted that each state should have an equal number of congressmen, favoring states with small populations. Neither side wanted to give in. Finally, Roger Sherman of Connecticut came up with a compromise.

At age sixty-six, Sherman was the second oldest man at the convention. He had signed both the Declaration of Independence and the Articles of Confederation. Supposedly Thomas Jefferson once pointed to Roger Sherman and said, "There is Mr. Sherman of Connecticut, who never said a foolish thing in his life."[18] Sherman's compromise, known as the Connecticut Plan or the Great Compromise, proposed that one house of the national legislature should reflect a state's population and the other house should have an equal number of representatives from each state.

Another point of contention at the Constitutional Convention was whether slaves would be counted as part of a state's population. Northern delegates to the convention felt that southern states should not be allowed to count their slave population in order to determine legislative representation. The dispute was settled with the Three-Fifths Compromise, which stated that three-fifths of the slave population would be counted when determining representation.

The delegates to the Constitutional Convention developed a constitution that established a three-branch federal government (legislative, executive, and judicial) with checks and balances. Power was balanced between the national and state governments. By September 17, the Constitution was finished and ready to be signed. Two Virginians, Edmund Randolph and George Mason, and one delegate from Massachusetts, Elbridge Gerry, refused to sign it. According to James Madison, Benjamin Franklin was looking at the President's chair while the last delegates were signing the Constitution. At the back of the chair was painted a sun. Madison reported that Franklin commented, "I have often in the course of the session... looked at that sun behind the President without being able to tell whether it was rising or setting. But now at length I have the happiness to know it is a rising and not a setting sun."[19]

At last, American newspapers could print the text of the Constitution and write about it. Everyone could read it and form an opinion. The group of American leaders who supported the Constitution and worked to get it ratified were known as the Federalists. Those who opposed the Constitution and worked to get it defeated were known as the Anti-Federalists. Those who opposed the Constitution believed that it gave too much power to the national government at the expense of the states.

We the People of the United States, in Order to form a more perfect Union, establish Justice, insure domestic Tranquility, provide for the common defense, promote the general Welfare, and secure the

Edmund Randolph
Library of Congress, Prints and Photographs Division [LC-USZ62-3761]

George Mason
Library of Congress, Prints and Photographs Division [LC-USZ62-3759]

Blessings of Liberty to ourselves and our Posterity, do ordain and establish this Constitution for the United States of America.

— the preamble of the Constitution

Each state called a special convention to decide whether or not to ratify the Constitution. Debate was hot and spirited at these conventions. In Virginia, Patrick Henry became so excited in his attempt to defeat the Constitution that he twirled his wig around on his head more than once. The Anti-Federalists in Virginia almost won, but James Madison persuaded the delegates that their liberties would be safe under the new Constitution.

Two-thirds (nine) of the states had to ratify the Constitution before it could be put into effect. However, if the American government were to succeed, the support of all thirteen states was necessary. By 1790, all of the thirteen states had ratified the Constitution. Meanwhile, the first federal elections were held. George Washington was unanimously elected the first president of the United States under the new Constitution and was inaugurated in 1789.

IMPACT

- The thirteen original colonies became the United States, and they are listed here in the order that they agreed to ratify the Constitution between 1787 and 1790: Delaware, Pennsylvania, New Jersey, Georgia, Connecticut, Massachusetts, Maryland, South Carolina, New Hampshire, Virginia, New York, North Carolina, and Rhode Island.

- In the years immediately following the American Revolution, the United States faced major political and economic problems. The national government established under the Articles of Confederation proved to be ineffective in meeting the challenges faced by the new nation. Shays's Rebellion (1786 – 1787) was a visible demonstration of the weakness of America's Confederation government.

- State constitutions, written during the American Revolution, established precedents important to the writing of the new U.S. Constitution. The conferences held at Mt. Vernon and Annapolis in 1785 and 1786 also paved the way for the Constitutional Convention in 1787.

- Meeting in Philadelphia, the delegates to the Constitutional Convention worked in secrecy throughout the hot summer months of 1787. George Washington served as president of the convention, and James Madison became known as the Father of the Constitution.

- Compromises reached at the Constitutional Convention dealt with such issues as representation in the national legislature and the counting of slaves as part of a state's population. The new U.S. Constitution established a three-branch federal government with checks and balances and with power divided between the national and state governments.

- Those supporting ratification of the Constitution were known as Federalists, and those opposing ratification were known as Anti-Federalists. By 1790, all thirteen states had ratified the new constitution, and George Washington had been unanimously elected the first president of the United States.

LESSON 26

ATMOSPHERE

DETERMINED TO SUCCEED

The newly formed United States experienced rapid economic and population growth during the first years of its existence. Politically, the young nation faced the fundamental question of whether its newly adopted Constitution was actually a workable plan of government.

Although political party divisions and conflicts would arise and foreign nations would interfere with American shipping and commerce, the new nation seemed determined to succeed. In fact, these early achievements were quite impressive — the establishment of a new Constitution, the adoption of the Bill of Rights protecting individual freedoms, the building of a new national capital in Washington, D.C., and the implementation of successful financial policies.

George Washington
National Archives print [148-GW]

EVENT

GEORGE WASHINGTON (1789 — 1797)

At the end of the American Revolution, Washington returned to his home at Mount Vernon. When a new national government was

Washington's inauguration
National Archives print [148-GW-557]

John Jay
*Library of Congress, Prints and Photographs
Division [LC-USZ61-295]*

established under the Constitution, Washington was unanimously elected its first president. According to Richard Henry Lee, Washington was "first in war, first in peace, and first in the hearts of his countrymen."[20]

John Adams was selected to be the first American vice president. Washington's inauguration as the first president of the United States occurred on April 30, 1789, in New York City. He took the oath of office with his hand resting on a Bible, setting a precedent for all future presidents. In 1790, the nation's capital was moved from New York City to Philadelphia. Eventually, the decision was made to establish a permanent national capital named the District of Columbia on a piece of land granted by Virginia and Maryland along the Potomac River. When Washington died suddenly in 1799, the Federal City was named Washington to honor him.

With the approval of Congress, Washington organized three departments in the nation's new executive branch—the departments of State, Treasury, and War. He selected Thomas Jefferson as secretary of state, Alexander Hamilton as secretary of the treasury, and Henry Knox as secretary of war. Washington also appointed Edmund Randolph to serve as his attorney general. Collectively, these advisors became known as the president's cabinet.

During Washington's first administration, the United States Congress established the national judicial branch under the provisions of the Judiciary Act of 1789. John Jay was appointed to serve as the first chief justice of the Supreme Court. In addition to the appointment of six justices to the Supreme Court, Congress set up thirteen federal district courts (one per state) and three federal circuit courts (for appeals). Congress also adopted the first ten amendments to the Constitution, introduced by James Madison in 1789. These amendments became known as the Bill of Rights. The Eleventh Amendment, limiting the national judiciary in suits brought against states, was passed in 1795.

When France went to war with Britain in 1793, the United States was obligated to come to the aid of the French according to the terms of the 1778 Treaty of Alliance. The Federalists were pro-British, and the Democratic-Republicans were pro-French. Washington responded to this foreign policy crisis with the 1793 Proclamation of Neutrality, stating that the United States would not take sides in the war. Further tension with the British was avoided when John Jay negotiated a treaty with Great Britain, which became known as the Jay Treaty. The British agreed to evacuate redcoats from the Northwest Territory in America and to compensate for British raiding of American ships. The Democratic-Republicans were critical of the Jay Treaty, believing that the United States had not been hard enough on the British.

Washington's secretary of the treasury, Alexander Hamilton, decided to tax the production of whiskey in order to raise revenue to

Washington laying the District of Columbia cornerstone
Library of Congress, Prints and Photographs Division [LC-USZ62-13343]

pay off government debts. When backcountry farmers in western Pennsylvania refused to pay the tax, the Whiskey Rebellion erupted in violence in 1794. President Washington responded to this revolt by calling up thirteen thousand troops, personally riding out in uniform with Hamilton by his side to confront the rebels. Although this action alienated many, Washington wanted to make the point that the national government had the strength to enforce the law.

Because the federal and state governments still faced huge debts, Washington's administration continued to wrestle with inflation and the inability to obtain foreign credit. To deal with this ongoing economic struggle, Secretary of the Treasury Hamilton proposed that the national government assume all of the remaining federal and state debts. However, some of the states (Maryland, Virginia, North Carolina, and Pennsylvania) had already finished paying off their debts and didn't want to be taxed to pay off the debts of other states. Finally, a compromise was reached in Congress. Hamilton's debt program would be approved if the nation's capital would be built on the Potomac River between Virginia and Maryland. This new debt policy proved to be successful, and foreign investors began to show an interest in the new nation.

Hamilton also proposed the creation of a Bank of the United States, which would serve as a depository for government funds, make loans, and collect taxes. Both Thomas Jefferson and James Madison maintained that such a national bank was unconstitutional since the U.S. Constitution did not give the Congress specific authority to create such a bank. Hamilton, on the other hand, appealed to the "necessary and proper clause" in the Constitution, which he believed gave Congress the power to do whatever was needed to carry out its responsibilities. In 1791 Congress voted to charter a national bank for a period of twenty years.

Washington refused to seek election for a third term in office, setting a precedent that was followed by all succeeding presidents until Franklin Roosevelt. In his Farewell Address Washington urged his fellow Americans to lay aside partisan divisions and to steer clear of foreign alliances, cultivating economic ties with Europe but not political ties. American foreign policy would follow Washington's counsel until the twentieth century.

FRIENDS AND FELLOW-CITIZENS: The period for a new election of a citizen, to administer the executive government of the United States, being not far distant, and the time actually arrived, when your thoughts must be employed designating the person, who is to be clothed with that important trust, it appears to me proper, especially as it may conduce to a more distinct expression of the public voice, that I should now apprize you of the resolution I have formed, to decline being considered among the number of those out of whom a choice is to be made....

In looking forward to the moment, which is intended to terminate the career of my public life, my feelings do not permit me to suspend the deep acknowledgment of that debt of gratitude, which I owe to my beloved country for the many honors it has conferred upon me; still more for the steadfast confidence with which it has supported me; and for the opportunities I have thence enjoyed of manifesting my inviolable attachment, by services faithful and persevering, though in usefulness unequal to my zeal. If benefits have resulted to our country from these services, let it always be remembered to your praise... Profoundly penetrated with this idea, I shall carry it with me to my grave, as a strong incitement to unceasing vows that Heaven may continue to you the choicest tokens of its beneficence; that your union and brotherly affection may be perpetual; that the free constitution, which is the work of your hands, may be sacredly maintained; that its administration in every department may be stamped with wisdom and virtue; than, in fine, the happiness of the people of these States, under the auspices of liberty, may be made complete, by so careful a preservation and so prudent a use of this blessing, as will acquire to them the glory of recommending it to the applause, the affection, and adoption of every nation, which is yet a stranger to it....

Observe good faith and justice towards all Nations; cultivate peace and harmony with all. Religion and Morality enjoin this conduct;

and can it be, that good policy does not equally enjoin it? It will be worthy of a free, enlightened, and, at no distant period, a great Nation, to give to mankind the magnanimous and too novel example of a people always guided by an exalted justice and benevolence. Who can doubt, that, in the course of time and things, the fruits of such a plan would richly repay any temporary advantages, which might be lost by a steady adherence to it? Can it be, that Providence has not connected the permanent felicity of a Nation with its Virtue? The experiment, at least, is recommended by every sentiment which ennobles human nature. Alas! is it rendered impossible by its vices?...

Though, in reviewing the incidents of my administration, I am unconscious of intentional error, I am nevertheless too sensible of my defects not to think it probable that I may have committed many errors. Whatever they may be, I fervently beseech the Almighty to avert or mitigate the evils to which they may tend. I shall also carry with me the hope, that my Country will never cease to view them with indulgence; and that, after forty-five years of my life dedicated to its service with an upright zeal, the faults of incompetent abilities will be consigned to oblivion, as myself must soon be to the mansions of rest.

Relying on its kindness in this as in other things, and actuated by that fervent love towards it, which is so natural to a man, who views it in the native soil of himself and his progenitors for several generations; I anticipate with pleasing expectation that retreat, in which I promise myself to realize, without alloy, the sweet enjoyment of partaking, in the midst of my fellow-citizens, the benign influence of good laws under a free government, the ever favorite object of my heart, and the happy reward, as I trust, of our mutual cares, labors, and dangers.

—from George Washington's Farewell Address
given on September 17, 1796

JOHN ADAMS (1797 – 1801)

The first real contest for the American presidency took place in 1796. Alexander Hamilton was not chosen to be the Federalist presidential nominee because he had alienated too many people.

John Adams
National Archives print

Instead, the Federalists nominated John Adams. The Democratic-Republicans selected Thomas Jefferson as their candidate. Under the rules of the Electoral College prior to the passage of the Twelfth Amendment (ratified in 1804), Adams was elected president and Jefferson, vice president. Before 1804, U.S. electors listed their top two choices for president, and there was no mention of a vice president on the ballot. The person with the majority of votes was named president, and the person with the next highest number of votes was named vice president.

The election of 1796 demonstrated that a peaceful transfer of power could occur in the new nation. Although Adams was the first president to live in the Federal City, he spent much time back home in Quincy, Massachusetts. Having served his country as a diplomat in Europe, Adams had grown to admire the British. As the British and French continued to fight each other, Adams decided to keep the United States neutral. This policy angered the French, who seized three hundred American ships and severed diplomatic ties with the United States in 1797. Although the British were also capturing American ships, Hamilton and other Federalists pushed for the Americans to enter the war on the British side. However, Adams believed that going to war would destroy the young American nation. In 1799, the United States negotiated a treaty with the French, which ended the previous French-American treaty of alliance and called upon the French to leave American ships alone. The United States was not allowed to seek compensation for previous French damage to American shipping.

In 1798 the Federalist-controlled Congress passed two controversial acts — the Alien Act and the Sedition Act. The Alien Act gave the president greatly expanded powers to imprison or expel any immigrants (aliens) considered to be dangerous. The Democratic-Republicans believed that the Alien Act particularly targeted French and Irish immigrants, who were strong supporters of their party. The Sedition Act made it illegal to write anything false or malicious against the United States government and outlined penalties for anti-government activities.

John Marshall
Line drawing courtesy of Amy Pak

In response to these acts, Thomas Jefferson authored the *Kentucky Resolutions* and James Madison penned the *Virginia Resolutions*. According to these resolutions, the Alien and Sedition acts were unconstitutional violations of First Amendment freedoms. Jefferson and Madison believed that the national government existed by the consent of the states, thus giving states the right to judge the constitutionality of a national law. During this same period, the state of Massachusetts passed a resolution declaring that states could not declare federal laws unconstitutional. When the Alien and Sedition acts expired, they were not renewed. However, the issue of states' rights continue to play an important role in American politics until the Civil War.

John Adams was an intelligent and honest man, but many saw him as argumentative and elitist. His efforts to make peace with France had divided the Federalist Party, and passage of the Alien and Sedition acts had strengthened opposition to his leadership. In the election of 1800, Adams again ran as the Federalist nominee and Jefferson as the Democratic-Republican. Because there was a tie for the highest number of votes, the United States House of Representatives was forced to select the president. They chose Thomas Jefferson.

Before leaving office, Adams appointed John Marshall to be chief justice of the Supreme Court, Marshall would serve as chief justice for the next thirty-five years, working to make the federal judiciary an equal branch of the government. The Judiciary Act of 1801, passed just as Adams was leaving office, increased the number of federal judges. Adams's last-minute attempts to appoint Federalists to fill these new positions became known as his midnight appointments.

THOMAS JEFFERSON (1801 – 1809)

With the election of Thomas Jefferson, the Federalist period of the American presidency (1789 – 1801) ended. The next three presidents would be Democratic-Republicans, all from Virginia. These presidents believed that they were involved in a "revolution" that would take the federal government back to the "democratic spirit of 1776." Their desire was to cut taxes, balance the budget, and reduce the size of the

Thomas Jefferson
National Archives print

military. The period in American history from 1801 to 1825 has often been called the Jeffersonian era.

The Anti-Federalists soon began to call themselves Republicans or Jeffersonians. Over time, they also became known as the Democratic-Republicans. Today, historians usually refer to them as Democratic-Republicans in order to avoid confusion with the modern Republican Party. The Federalist Party, which had prevailed under Washington and Adams, began to disappear during Jefferson's term in office. However, throughout the Jeffersonian era, the Supreme Court under John Marshall remained a stronghold of Federalist beliefs. In 1803 during Jefferson's first term in office, a landmark Supreme Court decision, *Marbury vs. Madison*, established the Supreme Court's right of judicial review, which is the authority to declare a law passed by Congress unconstitutional.

The President's House
Library of Congress, Prints and Photographs Division [LC-USZC4-1495]

Thomas Jefferson was the first president to be inaugurated in Washington, D.C. His vice president during his first term was Aaron Burr, a man he did not trust. In 1804, Burr killed Alexander Hamilton in a duel. During Jefferson's second term in office, George Clinton, the governor of New York, served as his vice president.

During Jefferson's first administration, the Republicans moved quickly to repeal the Judiciary Act of 1801. The Twelfth Amendment to the Constitution was also passed, calling for the casting of separate ballots for president and vice president. Jefferson's secretary of the treasury drew up a plan to reduce taxes and to pay off the national debt. However, Jefferson made no attempt to eliminate Hamilton's national bank. He and his followers decided just to allow it to quietly die in 1811 when its charter expired.

In 1803, Jefferson agreed to the Louisiana Purchase, paying France fifteen million dollars for the Louisiana Territory. This land, which stretched from the Mississippi River to the Rocky Mountains, would later be carved into thirteen states. The French dictator Napoleon sold the land because he needed money to fight the British. But he also wanted to create a maritime rival for Great Britain in the United States. Although Jefferson did not seek direct constitutional authority for the federal government to make this purchase, he moved to accept the French

Meriwether Lewis
Library of Congress, Prints and Photographs Division [LC-USZC4-2970]

William Clark
Library of Congress, Prints and Photographs Division [LC-USZ62-10609]

offer because he feared French restrictions on American trade on the Mississippi River. Although many Americans at the time believed this land to be worthless and unnecessary, the Louisiana Purchase proved to be a phenomenal bargain. From 1804 until 1806, Meriwether Lewis and William Clark were commissioned by President Jefferson to explore this territory that more than doubled the size of the American nation.

During Jefferson's presidency, the United States was involved in a naval war with Tripoli. This Muslim kingdom in North Africa had been capturing American merchant ships, enslaving their crews and demanding ransoms. Even though Jefferson had planned to reduce the size of the American navy, he felt compelled to send a squadron of American warships to the Mediterranean to deal with Tripoli.

In Jefferson's last years in office, the United States also nearly went to war with Britain. The British had been stopping American ships at sea and forcibly removing any British deserters found on these vessels. When an American ship refused to submit to a British search in 1807, the British killed a number of Americans onboard. As a result of this violence, the United States passed the Embargo Act, which banned American trade with the rest of the world. Unfortunately, this piece of legislation really harmed only the Americans, leading to an economic recession that especially hurt New England. The very unpopular Embargo Act was repealed during Jefferson's last week in office.

JAMES MADISON (1809 – 1817)
In 1808, Jefferson persuaded the Republicans to nominate his secretary of state, James Madison, as their presidential candidate. Madison crushed the Federalist nominee, Charles Cotesworth Pinckney, in the election. Although Madison was an exceptional political philosopher, he was a passive political leader, often dominated by Congress. The major event of Madison's administration was American involvement in the War of 1812, which will be discussed in the next lesson.

JAMES MONROE (1817 – 1825)
Madison's secretary of state, James Monroe, was chosen as the Republican presidential nominee in 1816. Monroe reminded many

of George Washington, and he came within one vote of being the only president besides Washington to be elected unanimously. Tall, courtly, and modest, Monroe has been called the "last of the Revolutionary farmers." His two terms in office, known as the era of good feelings, were marked by feelings of postwar triumph following the War of 1812 and the collapse of Federalist opposition to the Republican Party.

Two important treaties were negotiated during Monroe's years in office — the Rush-Bagot Treaty and the Adams-Onis Treaty. The Rush-Bagot Treaty (1817) called for disarmament in the Great Lakes region and established an undefended American border with British Canada. As a follow-up to this treaty, the British and the Americans signed the Convention (treaty) of 1818, which established joint American and British occupation and settlement of Oregon. The Adams-Onis Treaty (1821) allowed the United States to take possession of Florida from Spain at the cost of five million dollars. General Andrew Jackson was named governor of this new American territory, which had been previously inhabited by outlaws, runaway slaves, the Spanish, and Native Americans unfriendly to white settlers.

As a result of the War of 1812, the United States became determined to remain isolated from Europe. The Monroe Doctrine, articulated by the president in 1823 in a speech to Congress, maintained that the American continents were closed to colonization by European nations. Europe was not welcome to intervene in the Western Hemisphere, and the United States would not interfere in European affairs.

James Madison
Library of Congress, Prints and Photographs Division [LC-USZ62-13004]

James Monroe
Library of Congress, Prints and Photographs Division [LC-USZ62-104958]

IMPACT

- New States that were added to the Union during this time: Vermont (1791), Kentucky (1792), Tennessee (1796), Ohio (1803), Louisiana (1812), Indiana (1816), Mississippi (1817), Illinois (1818), Alabama (1819), Maine (1820), and Missouri (1821).

Andrew Jackson
Library of Congress, Prints and Photographs Division [LC-USZ62-435]

- During Washington's administration, the presidential cabinet was organized, the national judiciary was established, and the Bill of Rights and the Eleventh Amendment were ratified. The United States remained neutral as France went to war with Britain, and the failure of the Whiskey Rebellion demonstrated that the federal government had power to enforce the law. Alexander Hamilton's debt assumption program and proposal for a national bank were approved by Congress. In his Farewell Address, Washington urged his fellow Americans to avoid partisan divisions and foreign alliances.

- John Adams's election in 1796 as the second president of the United States demonstrated that a peaceful transfer of political power could occur in the new nation. During his term in office, Adams maintained neutrality in the conflict between Britain and France. Before leaving office (after his unsuccessful bid for re-election), Adams appointed the Federalist John Marshall as chief justice, as well as a number of other Federalists to newly created federal judgeships.

- Under Thomas Jefferson's leadership, plans were made to reduce taxes and pay off the national debt. The Twelfth Amendment to the Constitution was passed, the Louisiana Territory was purchased from France, and Lewis and Clark were commissioned to explore the new land. The United States was involved in a naval war with Tripoli, and the unpopular Embargo Act was responsible for banning American trade with the rest of the world.

- The War of 1812 was the most important event of James Madison's presidency.

- The fifth U.S. president, James Monroe, ushered in an era of good feelings following the War of the 1812. The Monroe Doctrine, reflecting the American desire for isolationism, proclaimed that the American continents were closed to colonization by European nations.

LESSON 27

The War of 1812 . . . . 1812 — 1814 A.D.
Native American Battles in the
Northwest Territory . . . . 1794 — 1811 A.D.

ATMOSPHERE

CAUSES OF WAR

Although the United States had tried to stay neutral in the fighting between France and Britain, neither country respected American neutrality. Most Federalists opposed fighting the British. Many New Englanders opposed it as well because they feared harm to their shipping.

However, westerners and southerners generally favored going to war against Britain. "War hawks," like Henry Clay from Kentucky and Andrew Jackson from Tennessee, worked to convince President Madison to declare war on Britain. They believed that Great Britain's repeated demonstrations of a lack of respect for the United States could not be allowed to continue without a response. Not only had the British continually interfered with American trade and purposefully incited Native Americans to violent attacks, they also had frequently seized men from American ships to serve in their navy. The British justified this practice, known as impressment, as a necessary one because of the increasing number of deserters in their navy. Americans were outraged that the British had impressed thousands of American citizens. Some of the American nationalists pushing for

John Jay
Library of Congress, Prints and Photographs Division [LC-USZ62-37502]

war against the British were also expansionists, looking for an opportunity to add territory to the United States by taking Canada from Great Britain.

When the United States declared war on the British, the American nation was certainly not united behind the war effort and was woefully unprepared for it. American armed forces consisted of only about seven thousand men, and its militia was undependable. Attempts to enlarge the American navy, which consisted of only sixteen warships, were voted down. New Englanders, who labeled the war Mr. Madison's war, resisted contributing men and money to the war effort. Although the War Hawks had pushed for war, even they were reluctant to pay the costs. The only real American advantage was the fact that the British were already occupied with fighting the French under Napoleon.

WARFARE WITH THE NATIVE AMERICANS

The young American nation continued to engage in brutal conflict with Native American tribes over possession of land. In the early 1790s, Indian resistance to the westward expansion of American settlers was fiercest in the Northwest Territory (the area north of the Ohio River). By May 1791, General Charles Scott had issued a warning to tribes in the Northwest Territory that their villages would be ransacked and destroyed, their wives and children brought into captivity, and their warriors slaughtered if they continued to prevent Americans from moving into the Northwest Territory. However, for several years, tribal warriors continued to be victorious over American troops sent to subdue them.

Finally, General "Mad Anthony" Wayne was appointed to lead the American assault against the Native Americans in the Northwest Territory. On August 20, 1794, near Toledo, Ohio, American forces under Wayne succeeded in routing the Indians at the Battle of Fallen Timbers. Under the terms of the Treaty of Fort Greenville, for a token amount of $10,000 the Indians surrendered all rights to the southern two-thirds of an area between Lake Erie and the Ohio River that included present day Ohio, part of Indiana, and other areas in the

"Mad Anthony" Wayne
Line drawing courtesy of Amy Pak

Northwest Territory. Following the Battle of Fallen Timbers, American settlers began to pour into the Ohio region. Between 1800 and 1820 the white population in the Ohio Valley more than doubled. Ohio grew so quickly that Congress separated it from the rest of the Northwest Territory and admitted it as the first state from the region in 1803.

At the Battle of Fallen Timbers, William Henry Harrison served as aide-de-camp to General Wayne. When Harrison resigned from the army in 1798, he served as secretary of the Northwest Territory and then as its first delegate to Congress. In 1801, Harrison became governor of the Indiana Territory, a position that he held for twelve years. As governor, Harrison's primary job was to obtain title to Indian lands so that settlers could press forward into the wilderness. When the Native Americans retaliated against the settlers, Harrison was responsible for defending the American settlements.

An eloquent Native American leader named Tecumseh worked diligently to unite the Shawnee tribes into a confederation that would force the white settlers to leave the Northwest Territory. Aided in this mission by his brother, a religious leader, or shaman, called the Prophet, his hope was to stop American expansion into Indiana and Illinois. William Henry Harrison became fearful that Tecumseh had become too powerful, and in 1811 he received permission to attack the Shawnee Confederacy. When Harrison knew that Tecumseh was away, he marched about one thousand men to the Shawnee camp on the Tippecanoe River.

Before dawn on November seventh, the Shawnee attacked Harrison's camp on the Tippecanoe. After heavy fighting, Harrison and his forces succeeded in repulsing the Shawnee, but 190 Americans lay dead and wounded. Twice as many Shawnee died as Americans, and the Shawnee village was destroyed. Harrison claimed a great victory for the Americans and became known as Old Tippecanoe. Although the victory at Tippecanoe disrupted Tecumseh's confederacy, it did not diminish Indian raids on the frontier.

William Henry Harrison
Library of Congress, Prints and Photographs Division [LC-USZ62-31]

Tecumseh
Line drawing courtesy of Amy Pak

EVENT

CANADIAN AND NAVAL BATTLES

The Americans believed that they would easily take Canada from the British but would have trouble fighting on the seas. The opposite proved to be true. The American army fought poorly in its opening campaign in Canada, whereas the American navy won several surprising victories during the early stages of the war, encouraging the American people to persevere. The USS *Constitution*, nicknamed Old Ironsides, became famous for shattering British ships with devastating broadsides.

Captain Oliver Hazard Perry was also successful against the British invaders at the Battle of Lake Erie. At that battle Perry supposedly said, "We have met the enemy and they are ours." However, the British navy outnumbered the American fleet fifty to one, and eventually the British blockade succeeded in forcing American warships to stay in port or out to sea for the remainder of the war.

BATTLE OF THE THAMES AND THE BATTLE OF BLADENSBURG

In October 1813, William Henry Harrison, who had been given command of the army in the Northwest Territory, led American troops against combined Indian and British forces at the Battle of the Thames. The Americans were victorious, amd the Seminole leader Tecumseh was killed during this battle.

The Shawnee scattered after this defeat and never again offered serious resistance in the Northwest Territory. Between 1817 and 1821 dozens of tribes in the Ohio Valley were forced to live on reservations or move to the wilderness beyond the Mississippi River. This opened up land to white settlers; that land eventually became the states of Illinois, Indiana, and Michigan.

When the war in Europe ended with the defeat and surrender of Napoleon, the British were freed to turn their full attention to the United States. In 1813, the British army sailed into the Chesapeake Bay and landed troops to march on the American capital. Five miles from

**USS *Constitution*,
"Old Ironsides"**
National Archives print [C-R9691]

Captain Oliver Perry
Library of Congress, Prints and Photographs
Division [LC-USZ62-16942]

Washington, D.C., these British forces defeated American forces at the Battle of Bladensburg.

As the British troops marched into Washington, most of the city's residents and soldiers fled. The British invaders proceeded to set fire to the U.S. Capitol, and the resulting blaze devastated the Senate wing of the building. They also torched the U.S. Treasury, the Library of Congress, and a number of other local landmarks. Although President Madison was away for a meeting with his generals, his wife Dolley was at home as word came that the British were on their way to the president's mansion. Hearing of the imminent arrival of the British, she loaded silverware, red velvet drapes, and important papers onto a wagon. She also had a portrait of Washington taken down and packed to be sent to safety. Mrs. Madison fled just as the British arrived and set fire to the mansion. Only thunderstorms prevented the British from burning the entire city to the ground. After the war the president's house was painted white to cover the scorch marks left by the British. During this period Americans began referring to the president's house as the White House.

BATTLE OF FORT McHENRY

After their victory at the Battle of Bladensburg and burning of the capital, the British decided to move on to Baltimore. Private ships from that Maryland port city had been capturing and sinking British ships during the war. The British planned both a land and sea component of their attack upon Baltimore. More than three thousand British troops were landed near North Point, and the British navy prepared to lay siege to Fort McHenry. Meanwhile, American Major-General Samuel Smith had convinced a number of wealthy Baltimore merchants to sink their boats in the harbor to create a barrier to keep away the British navy. They also had fortified the city, digging trenches and putting cannon in place, and had brought in adequate supplies and troops.

Fighting began on Sunday, September 13. The British commander, General Robert Ross, was killed during the conflict. British ships

Battle of the Thames
Library of Congress, Prints and Photographs Division [LC-USZ62-122]

Dolley Madison
Library of Congress, Prints and Photographs Division [LC-USZ62-68175]

Burning of Washington, D.C.
Library of Congress, Prints and Photographs Division [LC-USZ62-117176]

Francis Scott Key
*Library of Congress, Prints and Photographs
Division [LC-USZC4-6200]*

pounded Fort McHenry with rockets and mortar shells for twenty-five hours. The British infantry attempted to march north and west to attack Baltimore. However, thousands of American solders blocked their path so the British army waited for its navy to subdue Fort McHenry and then sail into Baltimore harbor to shell the city. When the attack at Fort McHenry did not succeed, the British navy sailed to North Point to pick up their troops and the Battle of Baltimore was over.

A Washington lawyer, Francis Scott Key, was detained on a truce ship with the British in Baltimore harbor during the bombing. No one knew whether Fort McHenry had been captured by the British until the American flag could still be seen at dawn. Key wrote a poem about this battle, which he entitled "The Defense of Fort McHenry." His poem was published and republished, and eventually the words were set to an old British drinking song. Someone also eventually gave the poem a new name, "The Star-Spangled Banner." A hundred years later this song became the American national anthem.

Oh, say can you see, by the dawn's early light,
What so proudly we hailed at the twilight's last gleaming?
Whose broad stripes and bright stars, through the perilous fight,
O'er the ramparts we watched, were so gallantly streaming?
And the rockets' red glare, the bombs bursting in air,
Gave proof through the night that our flag was still there.
O say, does that star-spangled banner yet wave
O'er the land of the free and the home of the brave?

On the shore, dimly seen through the mists of the deep,
Where the foe's haughty host in dread silence reposes,
What is that which the breeze, o'er the towering steep,
As it fitfully blows, half conceals, half discloses?
Now it catches the gleam of the morning's first beam,
In full glory reflected now shines on the stream:
'Tis the star-spangled banner! O long may it wave
O'er the land of the free and the home of the brave.

And where is that band who so vauntingly swore
That the havoc of war and the battle's confusion
A home and a country should leave us no more?
Their blood has wiped out their foul footstep's pollution.
No refuge could save the hireling and slave
From the terror of flight, or the gloom of the grave:
And the star-spangled banner in triumph doth wave
O'er the land of the free and the home of the brave.

Oh! thus be it ever, when freemen shall stand
Between their loved homes and the war's desolation!
Blest with victory and peace, may the heaven-rescued land
Praise the Power that hath made and preserved us a nation.
Then conquer we must, when our cause it is just,
And this be our motto: "In God is our trust."
And the star-spangled banner in triumph shall wave
O'er the land of the free and the home of the brave!

—Full text of "The Star-Spangled Banner"

Se-loc-ta, a Creek chief
Library of Congress, Prints and Photographs Division [LC-USZC4-8273]

THE BATTLE OF HORSESHOE BEND AND THE BATTLE OF NEW ORLEANS

General Andrew Jackson was commissioned to defend the South against the British and against the Creek tribes (known as Red Sticks) who had allied themselves with the British. Other friendly Creek tribes (known as White Sticks) had sided with the Americans in the hope of being allowed to keep their land. Jackson led the Americans and White Sticks to victory in the Battle of Horseshoe Bend. At the end of the War of 1812, twenty-three thousand acres were seized from the Creek, affecting both White Sticks and Red Sticks.

The American victory at New Orleans was the most stunning of the War of 1812. Within one hour American forces commanded by Andrew Jackson won the battle. Two thousand British were killed, wounded, or listed as missing. Only thirteen Americans were killed, and sixty were wounded. The Battle of New Orleans made a war hero of Old Hickory, Andrew Jackson. Ironically, this battle was fought two

Me-Na-Wa
Library of Congress, Prints and Photographs Division [LC-USZC4-2952]

weeks after the war was already over. Slow communication across the Atlantic had kept news of the treaty from reaching America.

THE TREATY OF GHENT

Signed in 1814, the Treaty of Ghent offered a "peace without victory." The treaty made no reference to impressment, called for no exchange of territory, and referred all boundary disputes to arbitration committees. As a result of the War of 1812, the British did finally realize that they had truly lost their American colonies. For a second time, the United States had fought off the most powerful nation in the world. On the other hand, the United States also realized that it would not be gaining new territory in Canada.

War of 1812 battlesites

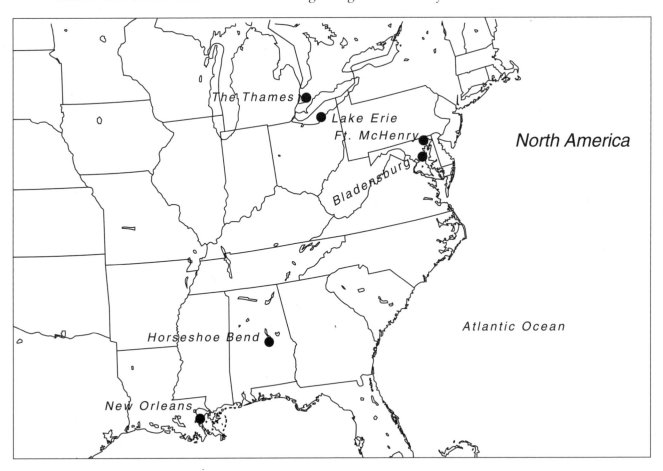

IMPACT

The Battle of New Orleans
*Library of Congress, Prints and Photographs
Division [LC-USZC2-3796]*

- Most westerners and southerners favored going to war against Great Britain, whereas New Englanders opposed war because they feared harm to their shipping. When the United States finally declared war on the British in 1812, the nation was woefully unprepared and not united behind the war effort.

- The young American nation continued to engage in brutal conflict with Native Americans over possession of land. American forces under General "Mad Anthony" Wayne routed Native American forces at the Battle of Fallen Timbers in 1794. Following this victory, the Indians surrendered all rights to their territory in the Ohio River region for a token amount of money and American settlers began pouring into the area.

- Tecumseh, a Native American leader, sought to unite the Shawnee tribes into a confederation for the purpose of forcing the white settlers to leave the Northwest Territory. In 1811, William Henry Harrison, governor of the Indian Territory, received permission to attack the Shawnee Confederacy. After heavy fighting at the Battle of Tippecanoe, Harrison claimed victory for the Americans.

- At the Battle of the Thames, William Henry Harrison led U.S. troops in defeating combined British and Native American forces. Tecumseh was killed in this battle; the Shawnee scattered, never again to offer resistance in the Northwest Territory.

- In 1812, British troops marched to Washington and burned much of the city. The British then proceeded to Baltimore, where they bombed Fort McHenry. However, the Americans succeeded in holding off their attack. American forces under General Andrew Jackson won victories at the Battle of Horseshoe Bend and the Battle of New Orleans.

- The Treaty of Ghent, which ended the War of 1812, is known as a "peace without victory." The treaty called for no exchange of territory, referred boundary disputes to arbitration committees, and did not deal with the issue of impressment. However, the new American nation had succeeded in fighting off the most powerful nation in the world for the second time.

LESSON 28

ATMOSPHERE

A NEW POLITICAL ERA

Democracy as we know it today in the United States did not exist during the Federalist and Jeffersonian periods. In the early 1800s Americans did not vote directly for U.S. senators, governors, and state judges. Almost every state and territory only permitted white men to vote. Accordingly, many states and territories only allowed white men to own property and hold elected offices.

In the decades surrounding the presidency of Andrew Jackson, several political developments expanded democracy in the United States. Many of the states rewrote their constitutions to eliminate property and residency requirements for free white males. Furthermore, direct methods of choosing presidential electors, state judges, and governors replaced indirect methods. The dominant political figure of the era, Andrew Jackson, was also instrumental in instituting the national political nominating convention.

The other major political change in the Jacksonian period was the emergence of a solid national two-party system. Unlike the first two U.S. political parties (the Federalists and the Democratic-Republicans), the Jacksonian Democrats and the Whigs were political parties that had

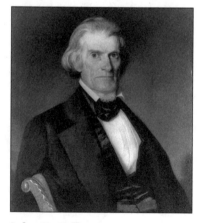

John C. Calhoun
Library of Congress, Prints and Photographs Division [LC-USZ62-44217]

grassroots organizations and support in every part of the nation. Although many political issues have changed since the 1800s, today's Democratic and Republican political parties still have much in common with their predecessors.

THE FIVE CIVILIZED NATIONS

In 1817, Andrew Jackson was sent by the secretary of war, John C. Calhoun, to Florida to capture runaway slaves. The Seminole tribe of Florida had been protecting these runaways, and the Spanish had done nothing to make the Seminole return the fugitives.

When Jackson moved into Florida, he did more than attempt to capture runaway slaves. He also burned down Seminole villages,

Political cartoon entitled, "The Two Bridges"
Library of Congress, Prints and Photographs Division [LC-USZ62-1277]

destroyed their crops, and captured and killed many of them. The Seminole leader Osceola was taken prisoner during this time but later released. As Americans began moving into Florida after the signing of the Adams-Onis Treaty, the Seminole were forced to make way for them.

Jackson forced many tribes to sign treaties surrendering territory that today makes up three-quarters of Florida, one-fifth of Georgia and Mississippi, and small parts of North Carolina and Kentucky. The doom of the tribes known as the Five Civilized Nations (Creek, Cherokee, Choctaw, Chickasaw, and Seminole) was sealed.

EVENT

JOHN QUINCY ADAMS (1825 – 1829)

When no presidential candidate received a majority of the electoral votes in the 1824 election, the House of Representatives had to choose from the top three candidates — Andrew Jackson, John Quincy Adams, and Henry Clay. Clay, who preferred Adams's nationalist policies and considered Jackson unqualified, played an instrumental role in securing Adams's victory in the House. Jackson's supporters believed that he had been cheated of the presidency. When Adams appointed Clay to be his secretary of state, the Jacksonians accused Adams and Clay of making a "corrupt bargain." John C. Calhoun of South Carolina served as Adams's vice president.

Adams's election brought to an end the Virginia dynasty that had lasted for twenty-four years. Born in Quincy, Massachusetts, John Quincy was the son of John Adams, the second president of the United States. The Democratic-Republican Adams was a brilliant, well-educated, and morally upright man who had worked as a lawyer and served as a diplomat. Many historians consider him to be one of America's greatest secretaries of state — a position he held in the Monroe administration. However, Adams had no patience for the ways of politics and always chose to do what he considered to be right even if it was not necessarily popular.

Cherokee chief
Library of Congress, Prints and Photographs Division [LC-USZ62-90958]

Choctaw men
Library of Congress, Prints and Photographs Division [LC-USZ62-70646]

Chickasaw Indian bust
*Library of Congress, Prints and Photographs
Division [LC-USZ6-680]*

Seminole chief
*Library of Congress, Prints and Photographs
Division [LC-USZC4-2904]*

A key emphasis of Adams's administration was Henry Clay's American System. This system of economic nationalism called for Congress to do the following: pass a protective tariff to promote development of American manufacturing; charter a national bank to supply the United States with a uniform and reliable currency; and approve internal improvement projects that would encourage and facilitate trade (roads, canals, harbor developments).

ANDREW JACKSON (1829 – 1837)

The 1828 election was a bitter rematch between Andrew Jackson and John Quincy Adams. Jackson's campaign was managed by Martin Van Buren, a shrewd New York state senator referred to as the Little Magician. Urging the Democrats to avoid divisive issues, Van Buren ran a campaign that emphasized the symbolic image of Jackson as Old Hickory, friend of the common man. Like his father before him, Adams was not re-elected to a second term in office.

The election of 1828 marked the first time that a president was elected who was neither a Virginian nor an Adams. Jackson was also the first American president who was not a well-educated aristocrat. Born to poor Scotch-Irish farmers in a log cabin on the border of North and South Carolina, Jackson had little formal education. However, he was a man of action. By the time he was elected president, he had become a lawyer, plantation owner, governor, judge, military hero, and member of both the United States House of Representatives and Senate.

Seeking to serve as the representative of the common man, Andrew Jackson called his presidency a democratic revolution. Ordinary people flocked to his inauguration. In his first message to Congress, Jackson recommended eliminating the Electoral College. He also believed that public service should not be a lifelong career and called for government offices to be rotated among deserving applicants. When Jackson moved to replace government officeholders with supporters of his administration, his system of patronage became known as the spoils system. Jackson's closest circle of friends, who served as his real advisors, were referred to as his Kitchen Cabinet.

National politics began to polarize around Jackson and his opponents. Over time, two political parties emerged from the old Democratic-Republican Party — the Democrats, who supported Jackson, and the National Republicans (soon to become the Whigs), who opposed him. Some of the leaders in the opposition to Jackson included Daniel Webster, Henry Clay, and Jackson's first vice president, John C. Calhoun. Because Jackson refused to defer to Congress in policymaking and effectively used his veto power, his opponents referred to him as King Andrew.

As president, Jackson faced continuing examples of sectional factionalism on the national political scene. For example, westerners demanded internal improvements, but northeasterners objected to large federal expenditures. Northeasterners demanded a protective tariff, but southerners insisted on tariff reduction. In 1828 Congress, passed an extremely high tariff, which the South referred to as the tariff of abominations. In response to this tariff, John C. Calhoun anonymously published a pamphlet defending the doctrine of nullification —the belief that any state could nullify a national law. Four years later, South Carolina actually nullified the Tariff of 1832, and Jackson sought war powers against the state, which threatened to secede if attempts were made to collect the tariff duties. Finally, Henry Clay, the "Great Compromiser," proposed the Compromise Tariff of 1833, which temporarily defused the crisis.

The major issue faced by Jackson in his bid for re-election in 1832 was the future of the second Bank of the United States. Hoping to help Henry Clay in his run for the presidency, Jackson's political rivals forced the issue by having the charter of the National Bank submitted for early renewal. Jackson considered the National Bank to be unconstitutional despite an 1819 Supreme Court decision (*McCulloch vs. Maryland*) that denied states the power to interfere with Congress's ability to enact a national bank. Jackson also opposed the National Bank because its stock was concentrated in the hands of wealthy individuals in the Northeast and Europe and because the bank was able to influence congressmen through loans.

John Quincy Adams
Library of Congress, Prints and Photographs Division [LC-USZ62-44523]

Andrew Jackson
Library of Congress, Prints and Photographs Division [LC-USZ62-47464]

Therefore, when the National Bank's petition for recharter was submitted, he vetoed it. When two succeeding secretaries of the treasury refused to withdraw federal funds from the National Bank, Jackson appointed a third that was willing to do so. These federal funds were placed in state banks, which Jackson's opponents called pet banks. This controversy rallied Democratic support for Jackson, and he and his second vice president, Martin Van Buren, won an easy victory in 1832.

During his second term in office, Jackson faced spiraling inflation, which he attempted to slow down by issuing an executive decree that became known as the Specie Circular of 1836. This prohibited the use of anything but specie (gold or silver) to purchase public land in the

Political cartoon entitled, "The Vision"
Library of Congress, Prints and Photographs Division [LC-USZ62-1573]

hope of cutting down on western land speculation, which was fueling inflation. As a result of the Specie Circular, there was an increased demand for specie, leading to a money shortage.

MARTIN VAN BUREN (1837 – 1841)

Jackson's hand-picked successor as the Democratic presidential nominee during the 1836 election was his second vice president, Martin Van Buren. By the early 1830s, a loose coalition of anti-Jackson forces had formed a political alliance, which became known as the Whig Party. The Whigs derived their name from the name of the British party that traditionally opposed royal tyranny.

Daniel Webster
Line drawing courtesy of Amy Pak

The strategy of the Whigs in the 1836 election was to run several candidates, each strong in his own region, in order to keep Van Buren from getting a majority of the electoral votes. This would throw the election into the House of Representatives, where the Whigs hoped to be strong enough to maneuver one of their candidates into the presidency. However, these Whig tactics did not succeed, and Van Buren was elected president in 1836. With his election Van Buren would become the last sitting vice president to be elected president until Bush succeeded Reagan in 1989.

Just weeks after Van Buren was inaugurated, the panic of 1837 plunged the country into a five-year depression. Factors contributing to this depression included Jackson's Specie Circular, the inflationary practices of some state banks, and farm disasters (the collapse of cotton prices and massive wheat crop failure). Hundreds of American businesses and banks failed, and thousands of Americans lost their land during the worst depression thus far in the nation's history. Nevertheless, Van Buren opposed the creation of a new Bank of the United States and the placement of government funds in state banks. Instead, he fought for the establishment of an independent treasury system to handle government transactions. Van Buren's decision to continue Jackson's deflationary practices only deepened and prolonged the depression.

King Andrew
Library of Congress, Prints and Photographs Division [LC-USZ62-1562]

When Van Buren ran for re-election in 1840, he was often referred to as Old Kinderhook, (Kinderhook, New York was his birthplace) and

---

Martin Van Buren
Library of Congress, Prints and Photographs
Division [LC-USZ62-13008]

William Henry Harrison
Library of Congress, Prints and Photographs
Division [LC-USZ62-7567]

that nickname was shortened to OK. After the 1840 election, the word *OK* entered the American vocabulary as meaning "all right." Van Buren was defeated by the Whig candidate, William Henry Harrison.

WILLIAM HENRY HARRISON (1841)

Harrison's running mate was John Tyler, a states' rights Virginian and friend of Henry Clay. The Whigs presented their candidate as a humble and heroic backwoodsman and an Indian fighter—in contrast to the "aristocratic" Van Buren. They drew crowds with parades, log cabin floats, and hard cider, and they used campaign slogans such as "Martin Van Ruin" and "Tippecanoe and Tyler, Too."

Although the Whigs presented William Henry Harrison as a simple frontier Indian fighter, in reality he had been born into Virginia planter aristocracy. After his college studies, Harrison obtained a commission in the infantry and headed to the Northwest Territory, where he spent much of his life. Harrison arrived in Washington in February 1841 to prepare for his inauguration, and he asked Daniel Webster to edit his inaugural address. On March 4, Harrison delivered the longest inaugural address ever (105 minutes) on an extremely cold day. He contracted pneumonia and died one month later in the White House.

JOHN TYLER (1841 – 1845)

John Tyler, a former Virginia governor and United States senator, became the first American vice president to take office after the president died in office. The Whigs had nominated Tyler for vice president in hopes of attracting support from Southerners who supported states' rights. When Harrison died, Whig leaders in Congress and the cabinet assumed that Tyler would submit to them, but he refused to do so. In fact, he vetoed Clay's higher tariffs and Clay's plan for a new national bank. As a result of these actions, Tyler's opponents began referring to him as His Accidency.

In the fall of 1841, Tyler's entire cabinet, except for Secretary of State Webster, resigned after he vetoed banking bills supported by the

Whigs. The Whigs also decided to expel Tyler from their party. In 1842, when Tyler vetoed a tariff bill, the first impeachment resolution against a president was introduced in the House of Representatives. The resolution was defeated.

In 1842, Tyler's secretary of state succeeded in negotiating the Webster-Ashburton Treaty with Britain. This treaty gave the United States seven-twelfths of the disputed northern border of Maine, where American and British lumberjacks were clashing over timber claims. Britain received the rest of the twelve-hundred-square-mile area. In addition, by 1844, the Far East had been opened to American traders after a treaty with China was signed.

By the end of his administration, Tyler had replaced his original Whig cabinet with Southern conservatives. From 1844 to 1845, John C. Calhoun served as his secretary of state. These Southern conservatives later returned to the Democratic Party, committed to the preservation of states' rights and slavery. The Whig Party then became more representative of the interests of Northern businessmen and small farmers.

In 1844, Henry Clay emerged as the leading Whig candidate for president. Although Tyler was interested in running as a Democrat, the Democrats chose to nominate a dark horse as their candidate — Andrew Jackson's friend and ally, James K. Polk. Born in North Carolina, Polk had served as both a U.S. representative and the Speaker of the House. The aged Jackson, believing that the American people favored expansion, urged the Democratic convention to nominate a candidate who stood for expansion.

Finally, on the ninth ballot, Polk, who was known as Young Hickory, was chosen as the Democratic nominee. Running on a platform calling for "re-annexation" of Texas, "re-occupation" of Oregon, and acquisition of California, Polk won the 1844 election by a narrow margin. (The Democratic convention of 1844 claimed that Texas had once belonged to the United States, referring to the U.S. claim between 1804 and 1819 that the Louisiana Purchase extended west to the Rio Grande. So the Democrats used "re-annexation" as their campaign

Death of Harrison
Library of Congress, Prints and Photographs Division [LC-USZ62-51523]

John Tyler
Library of Congress, Prints and Photographs Division [LC-USZ62-13010]

James Polk
Library of Congress, Prints and Photographs Division [LC-USZ61-187]

theme. In truth, it was really the annexation of Texas.) This strategy linked an issue popular in the South (Texas re-annexation) with an issue popular in the North (Oregon re-occupation). A third party, the anti-slavery Liberty Party, cost Clay the election. Taking Polk's election as a mandate for Texas annexation, Tyler quickly pushed through a joint resolution of Congress offering annexation to Texas. As a result, Mexico broke off diplomatic relations with the United States. As Tyler left office, war with Mexico seemed inevitable.

JAMES POLK (1845 – 1849)

The 1844 Democratic platform claimed the entire Oregon area for the United States from the boundary of California northward to the southern boundary of Russian Alaska (a latitude of 54° 40'). Some of the Democrats had insisted on "54° 40' or fight." However, Polk offered to settle with the British along the forty-ninth parallel. When the British minister declined, Polk reasserted America's claim to the entire region. The British finally agreed to the forty-ninth parallel, except for the southern tip of Vancouver Island.

As president, Polk succeeded in lowering the tariff and restoring Van Buren's independent treasury system. The most significant development during Polk's term in office was the Mexican War, which will be discussed in the next lesson. A vast amount of territory was added to the United States during Polk's four years in office, but its acquisition caused a widening breach between the North and the South over the expansion of slavery.

James K. Polk was the last of the Jacksonians to serve as president and the last strong chief executive until the Civil War. In the first fifty-two years of American history (1789 – 1841) under the U.S. Constitution, there were only eight presidents. In the next twenty years (1841 – 1861), there were eight presidents. Polk, a very self-disciplined and hard-working president, saw his health decline during his four years in office. He refused to run for a second term and died four months after leaving office.

IMPACT

- New States that were added to the Union from 1825 – 1849: Arkansas (1836), Michigan (1837), Florida (1845), Texas (1845), Iowa (1846), and Wisconsin (1848).

- As a result of Andrew Jackson's violent attacks toward the Seminole in Florida, many tribes signed treaties surrendering territory that today makes up three-fourths of Florida and parts of Georgia, Mississippi, North Carolina, and Kentucky. The humiliating relocation of the Five Civilized Nations (Seminole, Creek, Cherokee, Choctaw, Chickasaw) continued at a rapid pace.

- The winner of the 1824 presidential election, John Quincy Adams, was chosen by the U.S. House of Representatives. His election brought an end to the Virginia dynasty, and his administration focused on the establishment of Henry Clay's American System — protective tariffs, a national bank, and internal improvements.

- The 1828 presidential election was a bitter rematch between Adams and Andrew Jackson, with Jackson the victor. Old Hickory referred to his presidency as a "democratic revolution" and himself as a representative of the "common man." National politics polarized around Jackson, with the Democrats supporting him and the National Republicans opposing him.

- Jackson's hand-picked successor for president was his second vice-president, Martin Van Buren. By the time of the election of 1836, a coalition of anti-Jackson forces had formed a political alliance, which became known as the Whig Party. Just weeks after Van Buren took office, the Panic of 1837 plunged the United States into a five-year depression.

- When Van Buren ran for re-election in 1840, he was defeated by the Whig candidate, William Henry Harrison. Harrison was presented as a heroic backwoodsmen in contrast to the "aristocratic" Van Buren. Just one month after taking office, Harrison died from pneumonia.

- When Harrison died in office, John Tyler became the first American vice president to take office upon the death of the president. Tyler refused to submit to the Whig leaders in Congress and in the cabinet, and all of Tyler's "inherited" Cabinet resigned, except for the secretary of state, Daniel Webster.

- In 1844, the Democrats nominated a dark horse candidate, James K. Polk, who was known as Young Hickory. Polk defeated the Whig candidate, Henry Clay, as well as a candidate of the anti-slavery Liberty Party. Polk was the last of the Jacksonians to serve as president and the last strong chief executive until the Civil War.

LESSON 29

ATMOSPHERE

MANIFEST DESTINY

In an article in the July/August 1845 issue of *The United States Magazine and Democratic Review*, the writer John O'Sullivan asserted that the United States had the right of "Manifest Destiny to overspread and possess the whole of the continent which Providence has given us for the free development of our yearly multiplying millions."[21] However, long before the 1840s, there were many Americans who believed that their nation had been providentially ordained to acquire the entire North American continent.

The westward push
Library of Congress, Prints and Photographs Division [LC-USZ62-94187]

During the first fifty years of its existence, the United States witnessed an amazing migration of pioneers westward, a migration that resulted in the pushing of the nation's borders three thousand miles to the west. The driving force behind this westward expansion and the chief ambition of every American was the opportunity to own land. The American federal government encouraged this westward expansion, promising western land as a military bounty. Unfortunately, Manifest Destiny also led to the destruction of a way of life for millions of Native Americans who faced exploitation and violence as the United States expanded westward.

Immediately following the American Revolution, pioneers began to push west into an area of untamed wilderness that came to be known as the Northwest Territory. This frontier region lay west of Pennsylvania, north of the Ohio River, east of the Mississippi River, and south of the Great Lakes. The Northwest Ordinances of 1787 and 1789 developed a three-stage process for this frontier area to become a state:

- creation of a "territory" by the U.S. Congress and subsequently the appointment of a governor and judges with laws subject to congressional veto
- popular election of a state legislature once territorial population reached five thousand
- eligibility to become a state once territorial population reached sixty thousand

This plan would provide an orderly mechanism for the development of all future states. Free schools were required, as well as freedom of religion. Slavery was not allowed in the Northwest Territory. This region would eventually yield five states — Illinois, Indiana, Michigan, Wisconsin, and Ohio.

During the first decades of the 1800s, mountain men were paving the way for American settlers who wanted to move farther west. These men lived in secluded mountain areas during the winter, trapping beavers to make a living. The remainder of the time they spent exploring unknown areas and mapping mountain passes and trails to the Northwest, Southwest, and Pacific that pioneers would use decades later. Three of the most famous of these mountain men were Zebulon Pike, Jim Beckwourth, and Jedediah Smith.

EVENT

A WESTWARD PUSH

In 1803, the United States gained significant western territory as a result of the Louisiana Purchase. The success of the Lewis and Clark

Expedition sparked much interest in the western frontier, and many Americans began moving westward for available cheap land. By 1810, the American nation had also annexed West Florida (parts of present-day Alabama, Louisiana, and Mississippi) and nine years later, East Florida (present-day Florida).

In 1818, the United States and Great Britain agreed to joint occupation of Oregon. This uneasy truce would last for almost thirty years; the British occupied Oregon territory north of the forty-ninth parallel and the United States occupied territory south of the forty-ninth parallel. The Oregon territory at this point included the present-day states of Oregon, Washington, Idaho, and parts of Montana and Wyoming. In 1832, a Boston businessman named Nathaniel Wyeth traveled to Oregon and brought home favorable reports about the Willamette Valley. He reported that the area had an abundance of beavers and other animals, an abundance of fertile land, and a mild climate. Missionaries began moving west to Oregon to establish missions for the local Native Americans in the mid 1830s. Over time, more and more Americans journeyed west over the Oregon Trail to settle in the Oregon Territory.

Stephen Austin
Library of Congress, Prints and Photographs Division [LC-USZ62-206]

TEXAS AND THE ALAMO

American merchants began trading with the Spanish in Santa Fe. Huge profits were to be made by traders willing to travel the Santa Fe Trail. By 1822, American settlers, led by Stephen Austin, had moved into another region held by the Spanish — Texas — which was part of Mexico and had been controlled by Spain since the sixteenth century. These American immigrants were offered free land for farming and ranching if they agreed to become Mexican citizens and Catholics. By 1824, Mexico had declared its independence from Spain and formed a republic. Texas was a state in the Mexican Republic.

But in 1834, a dictator named Santa Ana took control of Mexico. Santa Ana became increasingly suspicious of the growing American population in Texas and declared martial law there. The Americans, in turn, resented being governed by the corrupt and inefficient Mexican government. Santa Ana eventually declared that no more

Davy Crockett
Library of Congress,
Prints and Photographs Division

The Alamo
Library of Congress, Prints and Photographs
Division [LC-USZ6-197]

Santa Ana surrendering
to Sam Houston
Library of Congress, Prints and Photographs
Division [LC-USZ62-65432]

Americans could settle in Texas, but people from the United States continued to cross the border into Texas illegally.

In February 1836, the Mexican army under Santa Ana recaptured San Antonio, which had been taken by the Americans four months earlier. They then laid siege to the Alamo, a Catholic mission that had been turned into a fort by the Americans. The American defenders at the Alamo, including such well-known figures as Davy Crockett and Jim Bowie, held out for thirteen days. Although they succeeded in killing hundreds of Mexicans, eventually all but fifteen of the Americans died. The survivors were mostly women and children.

In April 1836, eight hundred outraged Americans, led by Sam Houston, won the Battle of San Jacinto with the battle cry, "Remember the Alamo!" Santa Ana was captured and forced to sign a peace treaty recognizing Texas's independence.

When Texas became an independent republic in 1836, President Jackson refused to annex it to the United States. He feared doing so might spark a war with Mexico. Texas became established as a republic, which lasted for almost ten years.

THE CALIFORNIA GOLD RUSH AND THE FORTY-NINERS

By the 1830s, there were many Americans who believed that the United States was large enough. However, there were also many other Americans who believed that the rightful destiny of the United States included westward expansion. Their desire to extend the boundaries of the United States to the Pacific encouraged America's pushing the British out of Oregon, taking over California and New Mexico, and pursuing war with Mexico.

In 1849, an estimated eighty thousand people from the eastern United States and many foreign countries traveled to California as part of the great California gold rush. A few miners, who are often referred to as forty-niners, did strike it rich; but most prospectors earned at most only an adequate living. Many towns near the mining areas became ghost towns once the gold and silver deposits ran out. When California gold production began to decline, prospectors who did not strike it rich began scouting other western areas. Many eventually settled in the Great Plains (present-day Wyoming, Colorado, North and South Dakota, Montana, Kansas, Nebraska, and Oklahoma).

NATIVE AMERICANS

During the administration of Andrew Jackson, the Indian Removal Act of 1830 made it legal for the president to move Indian tribes west. This act granted the president both the funds and the authority to remove Native Americans by force if necessary. With this authorization Jackson began a determined effort to coerce Indian tribes in the East to move to lands west of the Mississippi River and east of the Rockies. In 1831 and 1832, two Supreme Court decisions, *Cherokee Nation v. Georgia* and *Worcester v. Georgia*, protected Indian land from aggressive actions of the federal government. Jackson ignored these decisions and proceeded to seize millions of acres of tribal lands. Eventually five Indian nations were removed from their homes—the Choctaw, the Chickasaw, the Creek, the Cherokee, and the Seminole.

The Cherokee decided to go to court, rather than to war, in an attempt to resist westward removal. Although Chief Justice Marshall handed down a decision in favor of the Cherokee, Jackson ignored it. Between 1835 and 1838, the United States Army forcibly removed more than fifteen thousand Cherokee from their homes and forced them to march westward to Indian Territory. This was the territory set aside for Native Americans by the Indian Intercourse Act of 1834, and it included present-day Oklahoma north and east of the Red River, Kansas, and Nebraska. The Cherokee called this journey the Trail of Tears. One out of four Cherokee died during the march from starvation or disease. The six million dollar cost of the removal was deducted from the nine million dollars offered the Cherokee in the treaty that they were forced to sign.

As a result of American victory in the Seminole War (1835–1842), most of the Seminole nation was rounded up and sent west. At first the Seminole agreed to move west if the government would provide them with a special agent to protect them from their Creek enemies. When the government refused to do this, the Seminole decided to

Panning for gold
National Archives print [53-1900]

Panning for gold
National Archives print [53-1901]

resist all attempts to move them. War broke out. Seminole raiding parties attacked and killed white Americans and destroyed the sugar cane industry. Several companies of American soldiers under different commanders unsuccessfully tried to capture Osceola, the Seminole's daring chief. By the time it was over, the Seminole War had cost the lives of fifteen hundred American soldiers and more than twenty million dollars. This war had also become immensely unpopular with the American public. Osceola was finally overwhelmed and captured when the Seminole raised the white flag of truce to exchange prisoners. He died from malaria in prison, and most Seminole ended up going west. However, some still refused to go, and in 1842 the American government finally gave up fighting them. About three hundred Seminole remained in Florida.

THE MEXICAN WAR

Causes for the Mexican War

Mexico and the United States had a long history of hostility, which exploded as James Polk began his presidency. Three days before Polk's inauguration, the outgoing president, John Tyler, signed a joint congressional resolution annexing Texas. To protest this action, Mexico severed diplomatic ties with the United States. American expansionists were insisting that Mexico cede New Mexico and California to the United States and extend the southern border of Texas by 150 miles southward to the Rio Grande. The Americans also demanded that the Mexicans repay money they owed Americans.

In September 1845, President Polk ordered John Slidell to Mexico City. There he was to offer the Mexican government thirty million dollars to settle the border dispute, purchase New Mexico and California, and satisfy American claims against the Mexicans. However, Mexican governmental leaders refused to meet with Slidell.

Early Skirmishes, a Declaration from Polk, and Opposition

By the spring of 1846, American military troops under the leadership of General Zachary Taylor had been sent to the Rio Grande. Skirmishes broke out almost immediately between American and Mexican forces there. On April 25, a reconnoitering party of sixty-three American soldiers was attacked on the north side of the Rio Grande by sixteen hundred Mexican cavalry. Although only eleven Americans died, the remaining soldiers were captured by the Mexicans. By May 13, Polk had signed a declaration of war against Mexico.

The United States was unprepared for a war with Mexico. It possessed only a small army of unruly volunteers. Mexico had a larger army than the United States, but it was equally unprepared for war. The United States had a superior navy, better military leadership, more accurate weapons, and greater financial resources — and all of these factors led to American victory.

Mexican War battlesites

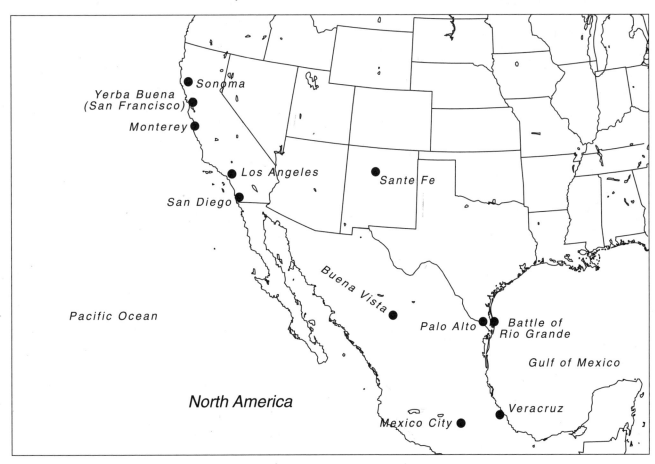

General Zachary Taylor
Library of Congress, Prints and Photographs
Division [LC-USZ62-1193]

General Winfield Scott
Library of Congress, Prints and Photographs
Division [LC-USZC4-9950]

A sizeable minority of Americans opposed the war. These Americans considered the war to be unjust—a brazen attempt by the United States to seize territory from a weaker neighbor. Abraham Lincoln, Frederick Douglass, Henry Clay, Henry Thoreau, and Walt Whitman all opposed the Mexican War.

Northern and Central Campaigns

The commander of approximately six thousand American troops in northern Mexico was General Zachary Taylor, who was nicknamed Old Rough and Ready. Although he was not an organized commander or a disciplined strategist, Taylor exhibited great bravery and enjoyed the devotion of the soldiers under his command. After driving the Mexicans from the Rio Grande, Taylor and his troops moved south. They won victories at Palo Alto on May 8, 1846, and Buena Vista in February of 1847.

In 1847, President Polk sent ten thousand American soldiers under the command of General Winfield Scott by sea from New Orleans to Veracruz, Mexico. These American forces succeeded in capturing Veracruz and then marched inland. By September 14, 1847, Scott's troops had captured Mexico City. Although he was not particularly warm or popular with his soldiers, Winfield Scott was a brilliant strategist. Under Scott's direction, the American forces outwitted the Mexican commander, Santa Ana, forcing him to abandon Mexico City. Because both Scott and Taylor were Whigs, their success in Mexico created jealousy among Polk and the other Democrats.

New Mexico and California Campaigns

Immediately after war was declared, Brigadier General Stephen Kearney was ordered by President Polk to occupy New Mexico and California. With a small force of fewer than two thousand men, Kearney moved down the Santa Fe Trail into New Mexico in the summer of 1846. The Mexican governor there could offer no resistance, and Kearney and his men took the city without fighting. Kearney then divided his command into three groups and set out with one of the groups to California.

Meanwhile, American settlers in Sonoma, California, had revolted against Mexican rule in June 1846, even before news of the war had reached them. They then established the Bear Flag Republic under the leadership of John C. Frémont. However, all of California was by no means under U.S. control. In early July, U.S. Commodore John Sloat landed at Monterey, California, and two days later occupied San Francisco (Yerba Buena). Later in July, Americans sailed down the coast and landed troops at San Diego and near Los Angeles. After more fighting between the Americans and Mexicans, a provisional U.S. government in California was established under the leadership of Stephen Kearney in 1847.

John C. Frémont
Public Domain

Treaty of Guadalupe Hidalgo

On February 2, 1848, Mexico and the United States signed the Treaty of Guadalupe Hidalgo, which ended the Mexican War. Under the terms of this treaty, the United States gave Mexico fifteen million dollars and assumed all debts that Mexico owed American citizens. The border between Texas and Mexico was set at the Rio Grande, and the United States received all or part of present-day New Mexico, Utah, Nevada, California, Arizona, Colorado, and Wyoming.

Approximately thirteen thousand American soldiers died in the Mexican War, and one hundred million dollars was spent to wage this war. A number of American soldiers gained distinction in the Mexican War — Robert E. Lee, Ulysses S. Grant, Thomas Jackson, and George B. McClellan. In fact, the Mexican War ironically served as a training ground for the Civil War.

Brigadier General Stephen Kearney
Library of Congress, Prints and Photographs Division [LC-USZ62-17905]

IMPACT

- The driving force behind the westward expansion of the United States was the ambition of every American to own land. This westward movement was encouraged by the U.S. government. Unfortunately, it led to the destruction of the way of life for millions of Native Americans.

- The Northwest Ordinances of 1787 and 1789 established a three-stage process for statehood for frontier territory, which proved helpful in the development of all future states.

- American settlers moved into Texas, a region held by the Spanish, in 1822. When Mexico became independent in 1824, Texas became a state in the new Mexican Republic. Ten years later, Santa Ana became the Mexican dictator and declared martial law in Texas. In 1836, the Mexican army under Santa Ana recaptured San Antonio and laid siege to the Alamo. Several months later, the Americans defeated Santa Ana at the Battle of San Jacinto. Texas became an independent republic in 1836.

- In 1849 approximately eighty thousand people traveled to California as part of the California gold rush. When California gold production began to decline, prospectors who had not struck it rich began scouting other western areas. Eventually, many settlers began moving into the Great Plains region.

- Using the Indian Removal Act of 1830, Andrew Jackson initiated a determined effort to force Native American tribes to lands west of the Mississippi and east of the Rockies. From 1835 to 1838, the U.S. Army forcibly removed more than fifteen thousand Cherokee westward to Oklahoma in a journey called the Trail of Tears.

- When Congress voted to annex Texas, Mexico severed diplomatic ties with the United States. By the spring of 1846, U.S. military troops under General Zachary Taylor had been sent to the Rio Grande. Not long afterward, President Polk signed a declaration of war against Mexico. Both countries were unprepared for this war.

- The Treaty of Guadalupe Hidalgo, ending the Mexican War in 1848, gave Mexico fifteen million dollars and the United States all or part of present-day New Mexico, Utah, Nevada, California, Arizona, Colorado, and Wyoming.

LESSON 30

The Industrial Revolution . . . . 1790 — 1850 A.D.

ATMOSPHERE

ADVANCES IN MANUFACTURING PROCESSES

As Britain began to industrialize in the years leading up to the American Revolution, she used her American colonies for her benefit. The British obtained many of the raw materials for their industries from the colonists and also sold many of the goods that they manufactured in America. At the same time, the mother country prohibited many kinds of manufacturing in the colonies. Britain also forbid the export of its industrial machines and the plans for building them as well as the emigration of engineers and other individuals with technological knowledge.

In 1789, a British mechanic named Samuel Slater, who has been called the Father of American Industry, secretly immigrated to the United States. Before leaving Britain, Slater worked for a partner of Richard Arkwright, the inventor of a water-powered spinning machine. During this time Slater learned about every aspect of textile production — from construction and use of the machinery to the management of labor. Although others who had manufacturing experience immigrated to the United States before Slater, he was

Eli Whitney
*Library of Congress, Prints and Photographs
Division [LC-USZC4-12270]*

the first who knew how to build the Arkwright model of textile machinery.

After securing financial backing from several American investors, Samuel Slater constructed the first successful American cotton-spinning mill in Pawtucket, Rhode Island. As Slater's business grew, additional textile mills were soon built in Massachusetts and Connecticut. The organizational system that Slater developed for these factories became known as the Rhode Island System. This system, a model for many other manufacturers, involved recruiting families (including children) to work in Slater's mills. These families often lived in company-owned houses near the mills, attended company churches and schools, and shopped at company stores.

Another factory system that developed in the early nineteenth century was known as the Lowell System. Developed by Francis Cabot Lowell, a wealthy Boston merchant, this system primarily employed girls and woman age twelve to twenty–five. Most of this female labor force came from New England farms. They lived in company-owned boardinghouses. Unlike Slater's factories, Lowell's mills included power looms and his operations combined the spinning of yarn and the weaving of cloth. When a downturn in the textile industry led to a cut in their wages, the Lowell women went on strike in the mid-1830s.

EVENT

EARLY AMERICAN INDUSTRIALIZATION

The textile industry grew rapidly in New England and also flourished in Mid-Atlantic cities like Philadelphia and Paterson, New Jersey. During these early years of American industrial development, the nation's leaders debated the nature of government involvement in manufacturing. In his *1791 Report on Manufactures*, Alexander Hamilton, the secretary of the treasury, listed the advantages of industrial development for the new American nation and advocated government assistance for industry.

During the years that followed, federal assistance to American manufacturing primarily took two forms — protective tariffs and patent protection to inventors (the first national patent law was passed in 1790). Because most early European industrial goods were of better quality and less expensive than those produced in the United States, American factory owners believed that they really needed protective tariffs. These tariffs made the price of imported goods higher than the cost of the same products manufactured in the United States. Although protective tariffs helped northern industries, they also meant that American consumers were forced to pay more for lower quality products.

Important American inventors during the early Industrial Revolution included Eli Whitney, who not only invented the cotton gin but also popularized the use of interchangeable parts in his manufacture of muskets. By the mid-1840s, Elias Howe had developed the sewing machine, which was improved and marketed by Isaac Singer. During the Mexican War, a six-shooter designed by Samuel Colt became the standard sidearm of the American army. This era in American history also saw the accidental invention of vulcanization by Charles Goodyear. In this process, sulfur and heat were used to create rubber, a waterproof product flexible at all temperatures.

During this period of early industrialization in the United States, the American nation began moving from a subsistence or self-sufficient farm economy with few cash transactions to a capitalistic market economy based on money and jobs. This new type of economy grew more quickly, provided more services, and caused people to become more interdependent. However, it also was more prone to boom and bust cycles, such as the panics of 1819 and 1837.

New technology did not automatically replace the old during this early American industrial period. The "putting out" or domestic production system continued for a time, even as factories grew in number and importance. The domestic system involved an employer "putting out" raw materials to rural employees who worked from their homes to produce goods and then returned the finished products to the employer for payment. By the 1840s and 1850s, European

Elias Howe
Library of Congress, Prints and Photographs Division [LC-USZ61-96]

Charles Goodyear
Library of Congress, Prints and Photographs Division [LC-D416-15]

Eli Whitney's cotton gin
Line drawing courtesy of Amy Pak

Cyrus McCormick
Library of Congress, Prints and Photographs Division [LC-USZ62-27710]

immigration to the United States had caused the nation's labor force to become plentiful. With the increased availability of cheap labor came deteriorating conditions for workers. Employers no longer felt pressured to provide good wages and a safe, clean working environment because any worker who complained could easily be replaced. The Lowell System and others like it came to an end. Labor unions began to organize, although they were strongly opposed by industry management.

INDUSTRIAL ADVANCES FOR AGRICULTURE

According to U.S. census figures, 95 percent of Americans lived on farms in 1790. By 1850, that figure had dropped to 85 percent. Although agriculture did remain the primary occupation of most Americans during the first half of the nineteenth century, it would definitely be impacted by the nation's new industrial revolution. The first major technological development that affected American agriculture was the invention of the cotton gin by Eli Whitney in 1793. This machine, which removed seeds from cotton bolls in a much shorter time than human workers could, caused southern cotton production once again to become enormously profitable. This increased profitability revitalized slavery in the South, where it had appeared to be dying out. It also caused the South to become reliant upon one cash crop, thus hampering that region's industrial growth.

There were other inventions that revolutionized American agriculture. Improved iron plows as well as John Deere's invention of a steel plow in 1830 made plowing new lands much easier. Cyrus McCormick's mechanical reaper, developed in 1834, reduced the labor needed for harvesting. The growing use of factory-made agricultural machinery meant American farmers needed more cash in order to purchase the machines. These new agricultural inventions along with changes in land laws that made land easier and cheaper to purchase encouraged westward migration.

Although most Americans continued to live on farms during the first half of the nineteenth century, the United States began moving slowly toward greater urbanization during this period. In 1790, the six largest cities in the United States were all ports — Philadelphia, New York City, Boston, Charleston, Baltimore, and Salem. Of these cities, only Philadelphia and New York City had populations of twenty thousand or more. By 1860 there were forty-three American cities with a population of at least two hundred thousand.

INDUSTRIAL ADVANCES IN TRANSPORTATION

Before 1830, the major means of transportation in the United States was by horse or by mule- and ox-drawn wagon. People also paid to ride in horse-pulled enclosed wagons called stagecoaches, which were cramped and uncomfortable. Stagecoach drivers changed horses in stages along the way to their destinations (hence, the name *stagecoach*). The roads were usually not well maintained. Many of America's early roads were called "corduroy" roads because their beds were made of round logs cut in half lengthwise and laid end to end. In later years a new type of road was constructed using a process developed in Scotland called macadam. Macadamized roads consisted of a crushed stone and clay base with asphalt or tar on top.

In the first half of the nineteenth century, many American roads were constructed by private developers, who then charged fees or tolls for the use of their roads. These toll roads, also called turnpikes, were helpful in improving communication and commerce between settlements. One of the few road projects subsidized by the federal government during this period was the National Road (also

The Cumberland Road
National Archives print [38-784]

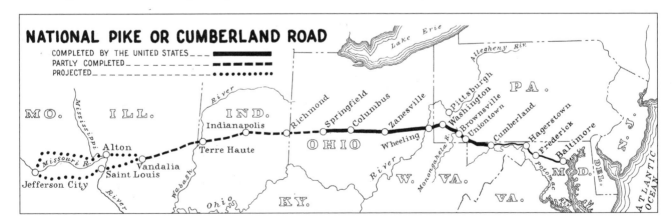

Lesson 30: The Industrial Revolution

Robert Fulton's steamboat, the _Clermont_
Library of Congress, Prints and Photographs Division [LC-D4-5429]

The Erie Canal
Library of Congress, Prints and Photographs Division [LC-D4-17914]

known as the Cumberland Road), which extended from Maryland westward. By 1850, this road had reached Vandalia, Illinois. Although people in the West lobbied for roads subsidized by federal money, many southerners did not favor the use of federal taxes for road construction.

When water transportation was possible, it was often preferable to land travel for transporting heavy loads. However, navigable rivers often had waterfalls and other obstacles that had to be overcome. In 1807, Robert Fulton unveiled the first effective steamboat (the _Clermont_) with his partner, Robert Livingston. Steamboats revolutionized river travel because they could move rapidly upstream. However, they were also dangerous to operate and were only able to operate on major rivers. For travel on smaller rivers and streams, flatboats were still used.

By the 1820s, canals were being built in the American North and Northwest. Canals provided a way to get around river obstacles without off-loading and reloading. The first American canal project was the 363-mile Erie Canal, built from Albany to Buffalo and linking the Hudson River to Lake Erie. Although the Erie Canal started a canal-building frenzy in the 1820s and 1830s, no other canal was ever as successful as the Erie was. Most canals were built by private developers without financial help from the federal government, although some states provided subsidies. Because canals were so expensive to build and were inoperable during winter freezes, the canal craze ended in the 1840s.

Transportation by rail was a dream of many Americans, who believed that vehicles running on rails would provide a smoother ride than those on a corduroy road. Early experiments with rail transportation used railroad cars pulled by horses. By 1830, a steam-powered train named the _Tom Thumb_ had been built for the Baltimore and Ohio Railroad. The earliest steam-powered trains were fueled by wood, but eventually the wood was replaced by coal. Nicknamed the "iron horsemen," trains could be used year-round to carry heavy loads. Between 1830 and 1860, railroad lines were laid up and down the eastern seaboard of the United States and gradually pushed westward. By 1860, more than thirty thousand miles of railroad track had been laid in the United States, and trains could travel up to thirty miles per hour. Like turnpikes and canals, railroads were first developed with private capital.

INDUSTRIAL ADVANCES IN COMMUNICATION

In the first half of the nineteenth century, stagecoaches were used to carry mail across the United States. By the 1830s, a new type of fast sailing vessel, the clipper ship, was being used to transport mail from the East around Cape Horn to California. This voyage took eight to nine months. In 1856, seventy-five thousand Californians signed petitions to the United States Congress, demanding faster mail service. On September 16, 1858, John Butterfield began fulfilling a government contract that called for transporting mail and passengers in coaches between Tipton, Missouri, and San Francisco in twenty-five days.

Less than two years later in the spring of 1860, the Pony Express began using speedy horseback riders to transport mail in ten days or less from St. Joseph, Missouri, to Sacramento, California. Pony Express riders were required to be eighteen years of age or younger, skinny, and willing to risk death. They stopped only to eat, sleep, and change horses. The Pony Express lasted only until October of 1861, when they were put out of business by the transcontinental telegraph. Invented by Samuel F.B. Morse, the telegraph made possible the sending of messages from coast to coast in just seconds.

The number of newspapers in the United States multiplied enormously during the first half of the nineteenth century. The development of the steam printing press in the 1830s dramatically cut printing costs and speeded production, making it possible for the first mass-circulation newspapers to appear. The number of American magazines also increased dramatically — from just six American magazines in 1794 to six hundred in 1850. Two of the more popular magazines were the *Atlantic Monthly* and *Harper's New Monthly*. However, there were magazines for every imaginable audience — scientific journals, literary reviews, women's magazines, religious periodicals, children's magazines, and comics.

Pony Express rider
Library of Congress, Prints and Photographs Division [LC-USZC4-2458]

Samuel F. B. Morse with his invention, the telegraph
Library of Congress, Prints and Photographs Division [LC-USZ62-2188]

**Cover of *Harper's
New Monthly* magazine**
*Library of Congress, Prints and Photographs
Division [LC-USZ62-57743]*

IMPACT

- Samuel Slater, known as the Father of American Industry, secretly immigrated to the United States from Great Britain in 1789 and constructed the first successful American cotton-spinning mill in Rhode Island.

- The American textile industry grew rapidly in New England and the Mid-Atlantic states. During the early years, federal assistance to American manufacturing primarily took two forms — protective tariffs and patent protection to inventors.

- During the first half of the nineteenth century, the United States began moving from a subsistence or self-sufficient farm economy to a capitalistic market economy based on money and jobs. Although this type of economy grew more quickly and provided more services, it was also more prone to boom and bust cycles.

- Technological developments that impacted American agriculture included improved iron plows as well as the invention of the cotton gin, steel plows, and mechanical reapers. Farmers needed more cash to be able to purchase the factory-made machinery.

- Before 1830, the major means of transportation in the United States was by horse, mule- and ox-drawn wagon, or stagecoach. Robert Fulton's invention of the first effective steamboat revolutionized river travel in 1807. By the 1830s, steam-powered trains, which could be used year-round to carry heavy loads, had been developed.

- Mail service from the East Coast to the West Coast was quite slow until 1860 when the Pony Express began employing speedy horseback riders to transport mail across the country.

This service was put out of business in just a few years by the transcontinental telegraph.

- The number of newspapers and magazines in the United States multiplied enormously during the first half of the nineteenth century. The development of the steam printing press cut printing costs and speeded production. For the first time, mass-circulation newspapers appeared.

LESSON 31

Early Nineteenth Century
Family Life . . . . LATE 1700s — EARLY 1800s A.D.

ATMOSPHERE

A TYPICAL NINETEENTH CENTURY AMERICAN FAMILY

At the beginning of the nineteenth century, the average life span in the United States was less than forty years. The average American man married at age twenty-six. The average American woman married at age twenty-two and gave birth to a child every other year, for a total of seven or eight children.

Child mortality rates were still quite high; one out of every ten American children did not survive past childhood. During the first half of the nineteenth century, there were few American parents who divorced. Although families differed in their methods of discipline and the emotional tone of their households, there was typically more formality and restraint between American parents and children during this period than there is today. Middle- and lower- class parents often needed their children to work in their fields to help the family survive. As the country became more industrialized, children worked in factories for the same reason.

EVENT

**Elizabeth Cody Stanton
and Lucretia Mott**
Line drawing courtesy of Amy Pak

Horace Mann
*Library of Congress, Prints and Photographs
Division [LC-USZ62-60506]*

MARRIAGE AND CHILDREN

During the nineteenth century, when an American woman married, she gave up her legal identity. Everything that she had now belonged to her husband. She was not allowed to own property or vote. Most middle- and lower-class American women worked diligently in their homes from sunup to sundown—feeding their families, making clothes, and keeping their houses clean without benefit of indoor plumbing or running water. However, during the first half of the nineteenth century, there were some American women who ventured outside the home to write for newspapers and work for reform causes. Also, as the United States became more industrialized and urbanized, many American women were forced to leave their homes to work in factories to help their families survive financially.

In the summer of 1848, approximately three hundred people (including nearly forty men) assembled in a Methodist church in Seneca Falls, New York, to discuss the unequal status of women in America. Elizabeth Cady Stanton, Lucretia Mott, and others had worked for eight years to make this convention a reality. The delegates to the Seneca Falls convention adopted a statement, deliberately modeled on the Declaration of Independence, that proclaimed, "these truths to be self-evident: that all men and women are equal." Other resolutions called for reform in property and marital laws and for women's suffrage — the right for women to vote. Following the Seneca Falls convention, many religious leaders and most of the press denounced its activities; some of the original signers of the declaration eventually withdrew their names.

EDUCATION FOR NINETEENTH CENTURY CHILDREN

During the first years of the nineteenth century, almost one-half of the children in the United States did not attend a school. In fact, before 1830 there were only a few free public schools outside of New England. Wealthy children in the South were taught by private tutors or attended private academies. In some areas of the country, parents combined their resources and hired a teacher. Nevertheless, many children who did not attend school did learn to read — from their parents at home and at Sunday school. Surprisingly, by 1840 there was a 78 percent literacy rate in the United States.

During the 1840s and 1850s, more and more states began to establish public school systems. One of the leading figures in this drive for public education was the head of the Massachusetts Board of Education, Horace Mann. Mann believed that public schools made it possible to improve and equalize educational opportunities for American children, and he eventually became known as the Father of American Education. He worked to establish training institutes for teachers; to raise more funds for teacher salaries, books, and school construction; and to increase the length of the school year to six months.

Another important figure in American education during this period was William McGuffey. Although he worked as a college professor and president and helped to organize the public school system of Ohio, McGuffey is primarily remembered as the compiler of the *McGuffey Eclectic Readers*. The *First* and *Second Readers* were published in 1836, the *Third* and *Fourth Readers* in 1837, the *Fifth Reader* in 1844, and the *Sixth Reader* in 1857. McGuffey's readers, which were filled with literature and exercises that taught traditional moral values, played an influential role in American education for nearly two generations. Frequently revised and printed in new editions, these readers had estimated sales totaling over 120 million copies.

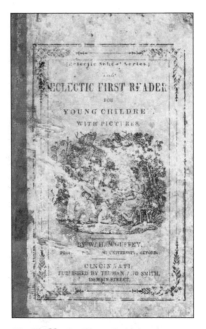

McGuffey's *First Reader*
Public Domain

NINETEENTH CENTURY CLOTHING

During the first half of the nineteenth century, the average American owned one outfit for everyday wear, one for church, and possibly one other for a seasonal change. All of the clothing was hand-sewn. Sewing machines were not invented until about 1850, and when they became available, they were very expensive to own. Even wealthier Americans did not necessarily own extensive wardrobes. However, their financial resources did make it possible for them to buy ready-made clothes at a store or pay to have their clothes custom-sewn.

Americans living in cities and towns usually bought the fabrics for their clothing from stores. Those in rural areas still frequently went through the entire process of producing their own fabric (shearing, carding, spinning, and weaving). Wool and linen were the most common fabrics used for clothing; cotton and silk were scarcer and more expensive. Even before synthetic dyes were developed in the late 1850s, a variety of natural dyes could be made from plant parts. Americans during this era spent a significant amount of time producing and caring for their clothes, even though they did not frequently launder them.

Nineteenth century dress
Library of Congress, Prints and Photographs Division [LC-USZ62-3332]

Clothing Styles for Men

Everyday shirts for American men during this period were linen pullovers with large collars, full sleeves, buttoned cuffs, and long tails to tuck into their trousers. Since men did not wear underwear, the tails of their shirts helped to protect them from the scratchy wool of their trousers. Men's everyday trousers, made with straight, slim legs, were held up by suspenders rather than belts. They almost always wore a single or double-breasted vest.

Several different styles of coats were worn by American men of the period — tailcoats (waist length in front with thigh-length tails in back), frock coats (thigh-length all around), and roundabouts (cropped at the waist). During the early 1800s, overcoats were introduced for cold weather. All coats were either single- or double-breasted and always fully lined.

Leather boots served as everyday shoe wear for American men of the period. For formal wear, gentlemen often wore shoes with pointy toes and high arches. Men's stockings were usually hand-knit from wool or linen, although the wealthy often purchased machine-knit stockings. A variety of men's hat styles were available, including top hats (previously worn only when riding horseback). By the 1830s, silk hats were becoming increasingly popular because beaver pelts had grown scarcer and more expensive.

Wealthy American gentlemen frequently chose finer fabrics for their clothing and finer leather for their boots. Their shirts might have ruffles at the neck and sleeve, and their vests might be made from embroidered silk satin. Their trousers and coats were well tailored and typically black, dark blue, gray, or tan. Only the wealthy owned enough shirts to set one or more aside as just "night shirts." Most men simply went to bed wearing the same shirt that they had worn during the day.

Clothing Styles for Women

Everyday clothing for American women during this period consisted of one-piece, dark-colored wool, cotton, or silk dresses. Dresses worn for house and farm work opened down the front. They were pinned

Nineteenth century clothing catalog page
Library of Congress, Prints and Photographs Division [LC-USZ62-1084]

---

closed or fastened with hooks and eyes. Dresses worn outside the home opened down the back. They were always closed with hooks and eyes. Dress sleeves were usually long, skirts were very full, and waists were slightly higher than the natural waistline. Aprons were always worn at home.

For an undergarment, American women of this period wore a linen or cotton chemise (shift) with short sleeves and a neckline gathered up with a drawstring. Over the chemise, a woman wore a cotton corset seamed with whalebone to achieve a small waist (the ideal was twenty inches) and a high bust. Every American woman was expected to wear her corset year-round. At least three petticoats were also worn at all times — sometimes more when the dress required it or when it was cold.

Nineteenth century women's clothing style
Library of Congress, Prints and Photographs Division [LC-USZ62-64654]

Footwear for American women living in rural areas was usually simple work boots. Upper-class women living in the city wore light-weight leather slippers—black for everyday wear and pastel colors to match their party dresses for formal wear. Women's stockings, generally about knee high, were knit from black or white wool, cotton, or linen. All American women, rich or poor, kept their heads covered most of the time. For sleeping, most women wore cotton or linen nightgowns and a nightcap.

American women grew increasingly interested in fashion during the first half of the nineteenth century. Fashions from London, Paris, and large eastern U.S. cities were pictured in monthly magazines, and upper-class American women had their dresses remade to reflect current trends. Very wealthy women also might change their dresses as many as six times a day, depending on the social events that they attended.

Clothing Styles for Children

Nineteenth century boy in waistcoat and tie
National Archives print [33-30]

Until the age of six, most American girls and boys during this period wore a cotton, linen, or wool "dress." The dress was long or short to suit the season. A boy might also wear matching drawers underneath his dress, and girls would often wear pantalets. Corsets for young children had gone out of style by the 1830s, and children's fashions had begun to allow more freedom of movement and to be more comfortable and convenient.

An interesting boy's fashion from this period was the skeleton suit. This outfit consisted of a tight jacket, usually with two rows of ornamental buttons in front, high-waisted ankle-length trousers that buttoned onto the jacket, and a white shirt with an open-necked collar. During the 1830s and 1840s, military-style uniforms were popular for boys and bustles and crinolines were popular for girls.

During this time in history, there was no teen culture, and there were no particular styles of teen clothing. Teenagers usually wore hand-me-down clothing from their parents, unless their family was very wealthy.

NINETEENTH CENTURY HEALTH AND HYGIENE

American medical practices did not change much throughout the eighteenth century. Perhaps the foremost medical practitioner of that period was Benjamin Rush, who believed in the Enlightenment's philosophy of natural law. According to this philosophy, the human body was a machine and all diseases were due to the overstimulation of blood and nerves. Treatments primarily involved "heroic" medicine — bleeding, blistering, purging, and vomiting. *Heroic medicine* is a term for aggressive medical practices or methods of treatment that were later overcome by scientific advances. In medical history, this time was the age of heroic medicine.

In the first half of the nineteenth century, surgery was usually the last resort for any medical problem because it was always painful and often fatal. The only anesthetics available were alcohol and opium. By the 1840s, a number of wealthy Americans were experimenting with ether, chloroform, and nitrous oxide as social drugs, and these drugs eventually were tried as anesthetics in surgery. Because surgeons often wore filthy coats and had little regard for cleanliness, deadly infections like gangrene or septicemia were often spread.

As the nineteenth century progressed, many Americans began to lose faith in the ability of physicians to cure using heroic treatments and turned to alternative treatments. Two examples of such

Nineteenth century boy in leg-of-mutton trousers
National Archives print [33-27]

treatments included hydropathy (natural healing powers of water) and homeopathy (using extremely small doses of drugs to produce similar symptoms to the original disease). Jacksonian America began believing that every man could be his own doctor, and by the 1840s many states had repealed their physician licensing laws, making it possible for anyone to be free to practice medicine.

NINETEENTH CENTURY NUTRITION, EATING, AND COOKING HABITS

Although there was an abundance of edible plants and animals in the United States, American food remained grounded in British food traditions until well into the nineteenth century. Meats and breads predominated in American cuisine, and few green vegetables and fruits were eaten. Before the Civil War there were four principal American food traditions: southern (emphasis on frying, simmering, and high seasonings), New England (emphasis on boiled and baked meats, boiled vegetables, and baked breads), Mid Atlantic (emphasis on Quaker simplicity — boiled puddings and dumplings), and frontier/backcountry (emphasis on ingredients that others used as animal feed — corn, potatoes, and various greens).

As America began to develop its own political and cultural traditions in the 1800s, American food began to distinguish itself from its British origins. As the nineteenth century progressed, American cookbooks reflected the use of native ingredients, such as squash, corn, and cranberries. *Not by Bread Alone*, an American cookbook published in 1847, had a patriotic cover and a distinctly native approach to food. It also contained advice on such things as how to revive tainted meat, how to rid the house of rats, and how to jump out of a wagon.

During the nineteenth century, American cooking also was influenced by the influx of European immigrants, especially those from Germany. The German emphasis on beer, marinated meats, wursts, and sour flavors was gradually assimilated into the mainstream American diet, seen in such foods as barbeque, coleslaw, and donuts. Until the last decades of the nineteenth century, most

Dr. Benjamin Rush
Library of Congress, Prints and Photographs Division [LC-USZ62-28646]

American cookbooks emphasized economy and practicality rather than elegance and luxury.

The American diet during the nineteenth century included an abundance of meat and distilled liquor. Having so much fertile land allowed Americans to raise corn and feed it to livestock as fodder. Much of the rest of the corn was converted into whiskey. By the early nineteenth century, the average adult American man was drinking more than seven gallons of pure alcohol a year.

IMPACT

- In 1800, the average American life span was less than forty years. Most families had seven or eight children, but child mortality rates were high. Divorce rates were low. During the first half of the nineteenth century, the relationship between American parents and children was typically more formal than it is today.

- American women of this period were generally not allowed to own property or vote. The Seneca Falls Convention of 1848 adopted a statement proclaiming that men and women were equal.

- Before 1830, only a few free public schools existed in the United States outside of New England. Wealthy southern children were usually taught by private tutors or in private academies. Many children who did not attend school did learn to read from their parents or at Sunday school.

- Most Americans in the early nineteenth century had very limited wardrobes. All clothing was sewn by hand until the invention of the sewing machine around 1850. Linen and wool were the most common fabrics used, although more wealthy families could afford cotton and silk. Clothing for men, women, and children followed definite styles and trends, which differed somewhat according to social class and location.

- Surgery was usually the last resort for anyone dealing with a medical problem during this period in American history because it was always painful and often fatal. Deadly infections were often spread because surgeons did not realize that they needed to be concerned about cleanliness.

- American food remained grounded in British food traditions until well into the nineteenth century. Breads and meats predominated, and few fruits and green vegetables were eaten. As the century wore on, American cookbooks began to reflect the use of native ingredients, and the influx of European immigrants also affected the American diet.

LESSON 32

Early Nineteenth Century
Culture . . . . LATE 1700s — EARLY 1800s A.D.

ATMOSPHERE

THE VARIOUS ASPECTS OF
NINETEENTH CENTURY CULTURE

During the first fifty years of its history as a nation, the United States continued the process of establishing itself as culturally distinct from Great Britain. Despite their political and economic ups and downs, the American people possessed a growing sense of nationalism and optimism about the future of their young country.

American authors and artists began creating literature and works of art that reflected American scenes and important national figures. The minstrel show emerged as the first uniquely American entertainment form. New American religions, such as Mormonism and transcendentalism, developed. The Second Great Awakening, with its emphasis on evangelical revivalism, was also a distinctively American experience.

EVENT

NINETEENTH CENTURY SOCIETY

Although the United States remained a primarily agricultural nation during the first half of the nineteenth century, the Industrial Revolution definitely had an impact upon American society. Increasing industrialization and urbanization in the North brought with it a tremendous growth in the working class in that region. As a result, northern society in this era continued moving more and more away from customs that emphasized the importance of one's family name or one's "gentlemanly honor." Instead, the emphasis shifted to the importance of getting ahead materially in a capitalist economy.

The South, on the other hand, continued to be predominantly agricultural during this period and southern society did not move away from an emphasis on family honor and the aura of power. Of course, the ultimate expression of southern servility during this period was the relationship of a slave to his master. However, southern expressions of social control were also seen in a southerner's willingness to risk his life in a duel rather than to endure an insult and the southern use of mob justice, such as lynching and tarring and feathering.

From 1800 to 1850, a tremendous wave of European immigrants entered the United States. Over time, their increasing numbers caused concern on the part of those already settled in the new American nation. This tension would increase over time (and is still experienced to the present day). In addition to this constant stream of newcomers from across the ocean, Americans from different regions and social classes moved often (usually westward)—settling and resettling, while confronting their differences and working together to survive on the frontier. Of course, a tragic result of this westward expansion was the forced removal of Native Americans from their homes to reservations, with the resulting loss of life and dignity.

NINETEENTH CENTURY RELIGION

The dominant form of Christian religious expression in early nineteenth century America was revivalism. Highly emotional meetings, known as revivals, were held in all sections of the country, calling Americans to awaken to their need for spiritual rebirth. During some years in the first half of the nineteenth century, revivals occurred so frequently that religious publications that specialized in tracking them lost count. In fact, these revivals were so widespread that this period became known as the Second Great Awakening.

On the American frontier, the most famous of these camp meeting revivals occurred in Cane Ridge, Kentucky, in August 1801. Between August 6 and August 12 as many as twenty-five thousand people gathered to pray in Cane Ridge, a town of only about eighteen hundred people. Many who attended these meetings exhibited physical manifestations such as uncontrollable shaking, jumping and dancing, and even collapse. The original sponsors of these meetings, the Presbyterians, soon repudiated them because of their intense emotionalism. However, the Methodists embraced these camp meetings and introduced them into the eastern United States. In 1811, one observer estimated that three to four million Americans attended camp meetings annually.

Revivals in the East tended to be more subdued than those on the frontier, although the eastern revivals also witnessed large numbers of conversions to Christianity. For example, Yale University, under the leadership of President Timothy Dwight (Jonathan Edwards's grandson), underwent a revival in which at least half of the student body was converted to Christianity. The denominations that had predominated in colonial America (Episcopal, Presbyterian, and Congregationalist) grew very slowly during this period, whereas the Baptist, Methodist, Catholic, and African Methodist Episcopal denominations grew at a phenomenal rate.

From 1824 to 1837, a preacher named Charles Finney held a series of revivals that introduced new features. Finney advertised his revival meetings and organized choirs to sing at them. He prayed to God

Charles Finney
Library of Congress, Prints and Photographs Division [LC-USZ62-27692]

Henry David Thoreau
*Library of Congress, Prints and Photographs
Division [LC-USZ61-361]*

Minstrel show poster
*Library of Congress, Prints and Photographs
Division [LC-USZC4-4558]*

using informal and emotional language, preached for his listeners to make an immediate decision to accept Christ, and provided an "anxious bench" for those responding to his public invitation. As a result of Finney's revivals, thousands of Americans converted to Christ. Finney was also a committed abolitionist who encouraged Christians to become involved in the anti-slavery movement.

Several unorthodox religions developed during this period of American history. Unitarianism, which was centered at Harvard University, denied the deity of Christ and the Trinity. Deism, the religion of Thomas Jefferson and Benjamin Franklin, taught that God created the universe, set it in operation, and then stood back to allow it to work on its own. Deists denied essential doctrines of orthodox Christianity, such as the deity of Christ, the inspiration of the Bible, and the reality of miracles. Transcendentalism, primarily the creation of Ralph Waldo Emerson, taught that man is good and ultimately perfectible. According to transcendentalists, God dwells within every man and everything is part of God. The transcendentalists also glorified nature as a creative force in which an individual could discover his true self and commune with the supernatural.

Another distinctive religious group that arose in the first half of the nineteenth century was the Church of Jesus Christ of Latter-Day Saints, or the Mormons. Founded by Joseph Smith in 1830, this group grew to thousands within just a few years and formed a tight community with strong leaders. According to Smith, an angel revealed to him the location of the Book of Mormon, buried near Palmrya, New York, which he translated and published in 1830. Smith believed that his new church, based on this Book of Mormon, was a restoration of primitive Christianity, which he thought other churches had deserted. The Mormon community was persecuted from the beginning because of its different practices (including polygamy and the zeal to convert others) and was forced to move from New York to Ohio to Missouri to Illinois. In 1844, the Illinois settlement was destroyed, and Smith and his brothers were murdered. The new Mormon leader, Brigham Young, led his followers west to Utah in 1847.

NINETEENTH CENTURY RECREATION AND THE ARTS

Games, Entertainment, and Music

Doll making had reached quite a high state of art by the nineteenth century. Although children in the lower class could not afford dolls with heads and hands made of porcelain, it was not unusual for a little girl to own a doll with a head made of papier-mâché or cloth. Even slave children had dolls, sometimes made of nothing more than a corncob with a strip of cloth wrapped around it.

During this period, American children also played dominoes, checkers (called draughts), pickup sticks (called jackstraws), cup and ball, marbles, blind man's bluff, tag, kick the can, ring toss, and

Dolls and other toys
Library of Congress, Prints and Photographs Division [LC-USZ62-113460]

Stephen Foster
*Library of Congress, Prints and Photographs
Division [LC-USZ62-56944]*

Washington Irving
Line drawing courtesy of Amy Pak

hopscotch. They experimented with a variety of different types of tops, skipped rope, chased hoops, and enjoyed Jacob's Ladder — a series of thin, flat blocks that seemed to magically flip over when held on its end.

An important form of adult entertainment during the first half of the nineteenth century was attending the theater. A typical night at an American theater before the Civil War included not only the play but musical interludes and a comic opera. In addition, there might be demonstrations of magic tricks, acrobatics, tightrope walking, fireworks, or pantomime. Melodramas, emphasizing action over characterization, were very popular. They were filled with thrilling fights and daring escapes and were staged with elaborate scenery.

American theaters in the years before the Civil War were rowdy places. The audiences interacted directly with the actors and musicians and liquor flowed freely. Spectators expressed their approval with boisterous clapping and their disapproval with yelling and hissing and by pelting actors with rotten eggs. Some theatrical performances actually led to riots. However, Americans during this era also attended sedate poetry readings, sermons, and public lectures with great enthusiasm. The lyceum movement, which was started by Josiah Holbrook in 1826, sponsored traveling lectures on religion, philosophy, science, the arts, and literature.

During this period, the first uniquely American entertainment form emerged — the minstrel show. Providing music, dance, comedy, and novelty acts, minstrel shows offered humor that ranged from slapstick and one-liners to comedy skits. Many of America's most enduring popular songs were introduced in minstrel shows, including "Turkey in the Straw," "Dixie," and the songs of Stephen Foster. Foster, the most acclaimed American composer of the mid-nineteenth century, wrote more than two hundred songs, mostly love songs and sentimental ballads, such as "Beautiful Dreamer" and "Old Folks at Home" as well as up-tempo comic songs, such as "Oh! Susanna" and "Camptown Races." During an era when the United States was undergoing industrialization and urbanization, Foster's songs reflected nostalgia for a simpler time and stirred popular enthusiasm for American music.

Literature

In the early nineteenth century a number of authors in the United States began to create literary works that emphasized American scenes and characters. One of the first Americans to write in this style was Washington Irving, author of the *Sketch Book* and the *Knickerbocker History*. The *Sketch Book* contained fictional accounts of life in New York's Hudson River valley, such as "The Legend of Sleepy Hollow" and "The Story of Rip Van Winkle." Irving's *Knickerbocker History* poked fun at the lives of early Dutch settlers in Manhattan.

An American poet of the period, Henry Wadsworth Longfellow, became well known for his lengthy narrative poems about important national figures, such as Miles Standish, Paul Revere, John Alden, Priscilla Mullins, and Hiawatha. Meanwhile, the author James Fenimore Cooper created an enduring American archetype, the frontier hero at home in the wilderness — Natty Bumpo — in his *Leatherstocking Tales*.

Henry Wadsworth Longfellow
National Archives print [111-BA-1081]

In the 1840s and 1850s, American writers continued to move toward creating a distinctly American literature. During a period that became known as the Romantic era of literature, American authors emphasized the colorful, the imaginative, and the emotional. They also put greater stress on the individual and a love of nature.

Three important American writers during the Romantic period were Edgar Allen Poe, Nathaniel Hawthorne, and Herman Melville. The young literary genius Edgar Allan Poe became known for "inventing" the detective novel, writing frightening horror tales, and creating masterful poetry. Nathaniel Hawthorne, perhaps best remembered as the author of *The Scarlet Letter*, wrote perceptively about the problem of sin and the effects of guilt. Hawthorne challenged a growing American belief in man's essential goodness and the progress of American society in science and technology. The other important novelist of this period was Herman Melville, who belonged to a New York literary circle known as Young America. Melville's well-known novel, *Moby Dick*, was an epic allegory demonstrating the consequences of human arrogance.

James Fenimore Cooper
National Archives print [306-PS-A-59-1526]

Nathaniel Hawthorne
National Archives print [200(s) FL-13]

Edgar Allen Poe
National Archives print [111-B-3794]

Two New Englanders and transcendentalists, Ralph Waldo Emerson and Henry David Thoreau, wrote of the goodness of man and the glory of nature. Emerson became known for his works *Nature* and *Self-Reliance*, and Thoreau became known for *Walden* and *Civil Disobedience.* According to Emerson, the ideal native American poet of the era was Walt Whitman, a New York printer and carpenter's son with only five years of schooling. Whitman's lengthy volume of poetry entitled *Leaves of Grass* was quite unconventional in style, using free verse rather than rhymed or regularly metered verse.

Art

At the end of the eighteenth century, there were few professional artists in the United States. Americans of the Revolutionary War generation had associated art with luxury, corruption, and aristocracy. During the early 1800s, however, American artists began to overcome the American public's hostility toward the visual arts. The American people of this time were especially eager for paintings of the great events of the American Revolution.

The period in American art history from Washington to Jackson (1791 – 1828) has become known as the Federalist era. Perhaps the greatest Federalist artist was John Trumbull, who was known for his realistic historical paintings. Two of Trumbull's most famous works include *The Battle of Bunker Hill* and *The Signing of the Declaration of Independence*. Charles Wilson Peale, another Federalist painter, was known for his portraits of famous American officers (fourteen of George Washington alone) and for his establishment of America's first museum of the natural world in Philadelphia. Another successful and prolific portrait painter of the Federalist period was Gilbert Stuart—famous for his paintings of George Washington.

The Jacksonian period of American art history (1828 – 1850) demonstrated a growing sense of nationalism and optimism about the future of the United States. American artists during this era became known for their portrayal of American scenes and peoples. Thomas Cole and other artists in the Hudson River School painted landscapes that showed the power and grandeur of nature not yet tamed by

American civilization. George Caleb Bingham gained fame for his paintings depicting the American West, George Catlin for his paintings of Native Americans, and John James Audubon for his many paintings of the birds of America.

Architecture

At the time of the American Revolution, architectural styles based on ancient Greek and Roman buildings began to appear in Europe. This neoclassical style became closely identified with the political ideals of the new American republic. This style of architecture, dominant in the United States, was known as the American Federal style. Its identifying features included classical Greek detailing in entryways, Palladian windows, balustrades, sidelights, and oval/circular rooms. Examples of this type of architecture include the White House (with the most famous Federal-style oval room, the Oval Office) and the Massachusetts State House. Prominent American architects from the Federal period were Charles Bullfinch from Boston and Samuel McIntire from Salem.

From 1820 until 1850, the dominant architectural style in the United States was referred to as Greek Revival. In fact, this style became so popular that it became known as the National style. The model for the National style was the ancient Greek temple, in which a horizontal superstructure supported a series of columns. Identifying features included square or rounded columns (usually Doric), a gable front floor plan (with the gable end facing the street), and a temple-front entryway with an entry door surrounded by a rectangular transom and sidelights. Stone and brick were the favored building materials. Wood was often covered with a thin coat of plaster and scored to resemble stone. Examples of this type of architecture include the U.S. Capitol, the U.S. Supreme Court building, and the Cathedral of St. Paul in Boston.

As a result of the economic opportunities of the Industrial Revolution, the growing American middle class had more money to spend on housing by the 1830s and 1840s. They often chose to build attractive homes outside the city, and horse-drawn railcars brought

Herman Melville
National Archives print [208-N-32456-PME]

***The Battle of Princeton
by John Trumbull***
Library of Congress, Prints and Photographs Division [LC-USZC4-7646]

Summer Red Bird
by John J. Audubon
*Library of Congress, Prints and Photographs
Division [LC-USZC4-722]*

Supreme Court building
*Library of Congress, Prints and Photographs
Division [LC-USZ62-106476]*

the man of the house back and forth to work. Indoor plumbing and gas lights were becoming available to those who could afford them, as well as all kinds of new household machines.

IMPACT

- The dominant form of Christian religious expression in early nineteenth century America was revivalism. Charles Finney was the most famous U.S. revivalist preacher during this time period. Unitarianism, Deism, transcendentalism, and Mormonism were four unorthodox religions that developed in this era.

- An important form of American entertainment during the first half of the nineteenth century was going to the theater. Poetry readings, sermons, and public lectures were also enthusiastically attended. The first uniquely American entertainment form, the minstrel show, emerged during this period.

- In the early nineteenth century, a group of American authors wrote literature that emphasized American scenes and characters. By the 1840s and 1850s, Romantic authors were emphasizing the individual and a love of nature.

- During the early 1800s, American painters began to overcome the hostility of the American public toward the visual arts. Federalist painters became famous for their realistic historical paintings and portraits of famous Americans. During the Jacksonian period, artists gained recognition for their portrayal of American scenes and peoples.

We the People

Article 1

AFTERWORD

This first volume of *All American History* spans three and a half centuries of the history of the nation now known as the United States of America. This study has occurred within the framework of four distinct time periods — the Age of European Exploration, the period of colonization, the period of revolution, and the period of establishment and expansion.

THE AGE OF EUROPEAN EXPLORATION

Adventurers sponsored by Spain, Portugal, England, France, and the Netherlands journeyed westward across the Atlantic Ocean, prompted by the goal of finding a western trade route to the Far East and the treasures (gold) that would result from such a discovery. Many competed in this quest to gain glory for the monarchs and countries that they represented. Some even ventured forth with a desire to glorify God and spread the Gospel.

Their efforts, made possible by the development of new navigational instruments and better mapmaking skills, were responsible for a revolutionary redrawing of the world map, the creation of many new trade routes and markets, and the downfall of a number of ancient Native American civilizations. Eventually, the nations of

Europe realized that they had not succeeded in finding a new western trade route but that they had discovered a New World.

THE PERIOD OF COLONIZATION

By the beginning of the seventeenth century, England, Spain, France, the Netherlands, and Sweden had all claimed land in North America. Over the next century and a half, settlers from these nations crossed the Atlantic Ocean in the hopes of establishing colonies, or at least fur-trading outposts, in the New World. There were two primary motivating factors behind the establishment of these colonies — religious (the desire to escape religious persecution) and economic (the hope of making a profit).

During this period of colonization, thirteen English colonies grew up along the Atlantic seaboard from Maine to Georgia. Spain held present-day Florida and attempted to extend into Georgia and the Carolinas. The Swedish and Dutch planted colonies in what is now New York, New Jersey, and Delaware, while the French took control of most of eastern Canada. Inevitably, disputes arose among these nations over territorial boundaries, and wars occurred to settle those claims. The Swedish and Dutch colonies were eventually taken over by the English. At the end of the seventeenth century, only England and France remained as colonial powers in North America. By 1763, the English had triumphed over the French in the French and Indian War and taken control of French territories in North America.

THE PERIOD OF REVOLUTION

Following the French and Indian War, the British government angered its American colonies with its efforts to regulate them more rigidly. Parliament's decision to levy taxes on the colonists particularly aroused their anger, making them feel that their rights as Englishmen had been violated. Colonial leaders arose to organize colonial resistance to Parliamentary actions that they considered to be unjust, but the British were determined not to back down.

Despite the strong attachment between the English colonies and the mother country, a series of incidents escalated the tension between them, and war broke out in 1774. The colonies banded together through their representatives in the Continental Congress and declared their independence in a declaration on July 4, 1776. Under the leadership of General George Washington, the Continental army, supported by many units of colonial militiamen, managed to outlast the British regulars and the various generals appointed to command them. Eventually, David (the thirteen colonies) defeated Goliath (Great Britain), bringing about the recognition of a newly independent nation — the United States of America.

THE PERIOD OF ESTABLISHMENT AND EXPANSION
The first government established for the former thirteen colonies, organized under the Articles of Confederation in 1783, did not prove to be a workable one. Fearful of granting too much power to a central authority, the colonists had not given their national government enough power to keep the country together.

Eventually, the Constitutional Convention was called in Philadelphia in 1787, and a new U.S. Constitution was adopted by all thirteen states by 1790. The election of the nation's first president, George Washington, occurred peacefully in 1788, and the United States began its history as a federal republic. However, continuing debate took place concerning the balance of power between the national and state governments, leading to the formation of political parties — first the Federalists and Democratic-Republicans (Jeffersonians) and then the Whigs and Democrats (Jacksonians). By 1848 the new American nation had grown from thirteen to thirty states. This tremendous westward expansion was fueled by acquisition of new territory and a belief in Manifest Destiny.

During the first half of the nineteenth century, the United States also emerged victorious from two wars — the War of 1812 and the Mexican War — and pushed tribe after tribe of Native Americans off of their land. With the coming of the Industrial Revolution, the United States grew stronger economically and technologically and a distinctly American culture began to emerge.

By 1850, however, there were dark clouds looming on the horizon for the United States. The second volume of *All American History* will begin with a look at the nation's growing sectionalism and the explosive issues of slavery and states' rights—which became the prelude to a civil war that would threaten to undo all the years of nation building following the American Revolution and the Constitutional Convention.

APPENDIX

CHARTER DOCUMENTS OF THE UNITED STATES

DECLARATION OF INDEPENDENCE

Note: The following text from the National Archives is a transcription of the Declaration of Independence.

IN CONGRESS, JULY 4, 1776

The unanimous Declaration of the thirteen united States of America, When in the Course of human events, it becomes necessary for one people to dissolve the political bands which have connected them with another, and to assume among the powers of the earth, the separate and equal station to which the Laws of Nature and of Nature's God entitle them, a decent respect to the opinions of mankind requires that they should declare the causes which impel them to the separation.

We hold these truths to be self-evident, that all men are created equal, that they are endowed by their Creator with certain unalienable Rights, that among these are Life, Liberty and the pursuit of Happiness.—That to secure these rights, Governments are instituted among Men, deriving their just powers from the consent of the governed,—That whenever any Form of Government becomes destructive of these ends, it is the Right of the People to alter or to abolish it, and to institute new Government, laying its foundation on such principles and organizing its powers in such form, as to them shall seem most likely to effect their Safety and Happiness. Prudence, indeed, will dictate that Governments long established should not be changed for light and transient causes; and accordingly all experience hath shewn, that mankind are more disposed to suffer, while evils are sufferable, than to right themselves by abolishing the forms to which they are accustomed. But when a long train of abuses and usurpations, pursuing invariably the same Object evinces a design to reduce them under absolute Despotism, it is their right, it is their duty, to throw off such Government, and to provide new Guards for their future security.—Such has been the patient sufferance of these Colonies; and such is now the necessity which constrains them to alter their former Systems of Government. The history of the present King of Great Britain is a history of repeated injuries and usurpations, all having in direct object the establishment of an absolute Tyranny over these States. To prove this, let Facts be submitted to a candid world.

He has refused his Assent to Laws, the most wholesome and necessary for the public good.

He has forbidden his Governors to pass Laws of immediate and pressing importance, unless suspended in their operation till his Assent should be obtained; and when so suspended, he has utterly neglected to attend to them.

He has refused to pass other Laws for the accommodation of large districts of people, unless those people would relinquish the right of Representation in the Legislature, a right inestimable to them and formidable to tyrants only.

He has called together legislative bodies at places unusual, uncomfortable, and distant from the depository of their public Records, for the sole purpose of fatiguing them into compliance with his measures.

He has dissolved Representative Houses repeatedly, for opposing with manly firmness his invasions on the rights of the people.

He has refused for a long time, after such dissolutions, to cause others to be elected; whereby the Legislative powers, incapable of Annihilation, have returned to the People at large for their exercise; the State remaining in the mean time exposed to all the dangers of invasion from without, and convulsions within.

He has endeavoured to prevent the population of these States; for that purpose obstructing the Laws for Naturalization of Foreigners; refusing to pass others to encourage their migrations hither, and raising the conditions of new Appropriations of Lands.

He has obstructed the Administration of Justice, by refusing his Assent to Laws for establishing Judiciary powers.

He has made Judges dependent on his Will alone, for the tenure of their offices, and the amount and payment of their salaries.

He has erected a multitude of New Offices, and sent hither swarms of Officers to harrass our people, and eat out their substance.

He has kept among us, in times of peace, Standing Armies without the Consent of our legislatures.

He has affected to render the Military independent of and superior to the Civil power.

He has combined with others to subject us to a jurisdiction foreign to our constitution, and unacknowledged by our laws; giving his Assent to their Acts of pretended Legislation:

For Quartering large bodies of armed troops among us:

For protecting them, by a mock Trial, from punishment for any Murders which they should commit on the Inhabitants of these States:

For cutting off our Trade with all parts of the world:

For imposing Taxes on us without our Consent:

For depriving us in many cases, of the benefits of Trial by Jury:

For transporting us beyond Seas to be tried for pretended offences:

For abolishing the free System of English Laws in a neighbouring Province, establishing therein an Arbitrary government, and enlarging its Boundaries so as to render it at once an example and fit instrument for introducing the same absolute rule into these Colonies:

For taking away our Charters, abolishing our most valuable Laws, and altering fundamentally the Forms of our Governments:

For suspending our own Legislatures, and declaring themselves invested with power to legislate for us in all cases whatsoever.

He has abdicated Government here, by declaring us out of his Protection and waging War against us.

He has plundered our seas, ravaged our Coasts, burnt our towns, and destroyed the lives of our people.

He is at this time transporting large Armies of foreign Mercenaries to compleat the works of death, desolation and tyranny, already begun with circumstances of Cruelty & perfidy scarcely paralleled in the most barbarous ages, and totally unworthy the Head of a civilized nation.

He has constrained our fellow Citizens taken Captive on the high Seas to bear Arms against their Country, to become the executioners of their friends and Brethren, or to fall themselves by their Hands.

He has excited domestic insurrections amongst us, and has endeavoured to bring on the inhabitants of our frontiers, the merciless Indian Savages, whose known rule of warfare, is an undistinguished destruction of all ages, sexes and conditions.

In every stage of these Oppressions We have Petitioned for Redress in the most humble terms: Our repeated Petitions have been answered only by repeated injury. A Prince whose character is thus marked by every act which may define a Tyrant, is unfit to be the ruler of a free people.

Nor have We been wanting in attentions to our Brittish brethren. We have warned them from time to time of attempts by their legislature to extend an unwarrantable jurisdiction over us. We have reminded them of the circumstances of our emigration and settlement here. We have appealed to their native justice and magnanimity, and we have conjured them by the ties of our common kindred to disavow these usurpations, which, would inevitably interrupt our connections and correspondence. They too have been deaf to the voice of justice and of consanguinity. We must, therefore, acquiesce in the necessity, which denounces our Separation, and hold them, as we hold the rest of mankind, Enemies in War, in Peace Friends.

We, therefore, the Representatives of the united States of America, in General Congress, Assembled, appealing to the Supreme Judge of the world for the rectitude of our intentions, do, in the Name, and by Authority of the good People of these Colonies, solemnly publish and declare, That these United Colonies are, and of Right ought to be Free and Independent States; that they are Absolved from all Allegiance to the British Crown, and that all political connection between them and the State of Great Britain, is and ought to be totally dissolved; and that as Free and Independent States, they have full Power to levy War, conclude Peace, contract Alliances, establish Commerce, and to do all other Acts and Things which Independent States may of right do. And for the support of this Declaration, with a firm reliance on the protection of divine Providence, we mutually pledge to each other our Lives, our Fortunes and our sacred Honor.

Column 1, Georgia: Button Gwinnett, Lyman Hall, George Walton; Column 2, North Carolina: William Hooper, Joseph Hewes, John Penn; South Carolina: Edward Rutledge, Thomas Heyward, Jr., Thomas Lynch, Jr., Arthur Middleton; Column 3, Massachusetts: John Hancock; Maryland: Samuel Chase, William Paca, Thomas Stone, Charles Carroll of Carrollton; Virginia: George Wythe, Richard Henry Lee, Thomas Jefferson, Benjamin Harrison, Thomas Nelson, Jr., Francis Lightfoot Lee, Carter Braxton; Column 4, Pennsylvania: Robert Morris, Benjamin Rush, Benjamin Franklin, John Morton, George Clymer, James Smith, George Taylor, James Wilson, George Ross; Delaware: Caesar Rodney, George Read, Thomas McKean; Column 5, New York: William Floyd, Philip Livingston, Francis Lewis, Lewis Morris; New Jersey: Richard Stockton, John Witherspoon, Francis Hopkinson, John Hart, Abraham Clark; Column 6, New Hampshire: Josiah Bartlett, William Whipple; Massachusetts: Samuel Adams, John Adams, Robert Treat Paine, Elbridge Gerry; Rhode Island: Stephen Hopkins, William Ellery; Connecticut: Roger Sherman, Samuel Huntington, William Williams, Oliver Wolcott; New Hampshire: Matthew Thornton

THE CONSTITUTION OF THE UNITED STATES

Note: The following text from the National Archives is a transcription of the Constitution in its original form. Items that are italicized have since been amended or superseded.

We the People of the United States, in Order to form a more perfect Union, establish Justice, insure domestic Tranquility, provide for the common defense, promote the general Welfare, and secure the Blessings of Liberty to ourselves and our Posterity, do ordain and establish this Constitution for the United States of America.

ARTICLE. I.
Section. 1.
All legislative Powers herein granted shall be vested in a Congress of the United States, which shall consist of a Senate and House of Representatives.

Section. 2.
The House of Representatives shall be composed of Members chosen every second Year by the People of the several States, and the Electors in each State shall have the Qualifications requisite for Electors of the most numerous Branch of the State Legislature.

No Person shall be a Representative who shall not have attained to the Age of twenty five Years, and been seven Years a Citizen of the United States, and who shall not, when elected, be an Inhabitant of that State in which he shall be chosen.

Representatives and direct Taxes shall be apportioned among the several States which may be included within this Union, according to their respective Numbers, which shall be determined by adding to the whole Number of free Persons, including those bound to Service for a Term of Years, and excluding Indians not taxed, three fifths of all other Persons. The actual Enumeration shall be made within three Years after the first Meeting of the Congress of the United States, and within every subsequent Term of ten Years, in such Manner as they shall by Law direct. The Number of Representatives shall not exceed one for every thirty Thousand, but each State shall have at Least one Representative; and until such enumeration shall be made, the State of New Hampshire shall be entitled to chuse three, Massachusetts eight, Rhode-Island and Providence Plantations one, Connecticut five, New-York six, New Jersey four, Pennsylvania eight, Delaware one, Maryland six, Virginia ten, North Carolina five, South Carolina five, and Georgia three.

When vacancies happen in the Representation from any State, the Executive Authority thereof shall issue Writs of Election to fill such Vacancies.

The House of Representatives shall chuse their Speaker and other Officers; and shall have the sole Power of Impeachment.

Section. 3.

The Senate of the United States shall be composed of two Senators from each State, chosen by the Legislature thereof for six Years; and each Senator shall have one Vote.

Immediately after they shall be assembled in Consequence of the first Election, they shall be divided as equally as may be into three Classes. The Seats of the Senators of the first Class shall be vacated at the Expiration of the second Year, of the second Class at the Expiration of the fourth Year, and of the third Class at the Expiration of the sixth Year, so that one third may be chosen every second Year; *and if Vacancies happen by Resignation, or otherwise, during the Recess of the Legislature of any State, the Executive thereof may make temporary Appointments until the next Meeting of the Legislature, which shall then fill such Vacancies.*

No Person shall be a Senator who shall not have attained to the Age of thirty Years, and been nine Years a Citizen of the United States, and who shall not, when elected, be an Inhabitant of that State for which he shall be chosen.

The Vice President of the United States shall be President of the Senate, but shall have no Vote, unless they be equally divided.

The Senate shall chuse their other Officers, and also a President pro tempore, in the Absence of the Vice President, or when he shall exercise the Office of President of the United States.

The Senate shall have the sole Power to try all Impeachments. When sitting for that Purpose, they shall be on Oath or Affirmation. When the President of the United States is tried, the Chief Justice shall preside: And no Person shall be convicted without the Concurrence of two thirds of the Members present.

Judgment in Cases of Impeachment shall not extend further than to removal from Office, and disqualification to hold and enjoy any Office of honor, Trust or Profit under the United States: but the Party convicted shall nevertheless be liable and subject to Indictment, Trial, Judgment and Punishment, according to Law.

Section. 4.

The Times, Places and Manner of holding Elections for Senators and Representatives, shall be prescribed in each State by the Legislature thereof; but the Congress may at any time by Law make or alter such Regulations, except as to the Places of chusing Senators.

The Congress shall assemble at least once in every Year, and such Meeting shall *be on the first Monday in December,* unless they shall by Law appoint a different Day.

Section. 5.

Each House shall be the Judge of the Elections, Returns and Qualifications of its own Members, and a Majority of each shall constitute a Quorum to do Business; but a smaller Number may adjourn from day to day, and may be authorized to compel the Attendance of absent Members, in such Manner, and under such Penalties as each House may provide.

Each House may determine the Rules of its Proceedings, punish its Members for disorderly Behaviour, and, with the Concurrence of two thirds, expel a Member.

Each House shall keep a Journal of its Proceedings, and from time to time publish the same, excepting such Parts as may in their Judgment require Secrecy; and the Yeas and Nays of the Members of either House on any question shall, at the Desire of one fifth of those Present, be entered on the Journal.

Neither House, during the Session of Congress, shall, without the Consent of the other, adjourn for more than three days, nor to any other Place than that in which the two Houses shall be sitting.

Section. 6.

The Senators and Representatives shall receive a Compensation for their Services, to be ascertained by Law, and paid out of the Treasury of the United States. They shall in all Cases, except Treason, Felony and Breach of the Peace, be privileged from Arrest during their Attendance at the Session of their respective Houses, and in going to and returning from the same; and for any Speech or Debate in either House, they shall not be questioned in any other Place.

No Senator or Representative shall, during the Time for which he was elected, be appointed to any civil Office under the Authority of the United States, which shall have been created, or the Emoluments whereof shall have been encreased during such time; and no Person holding any Office under the United States, shall be a Member of either House during his Continuance in Office.

Section. 7.

All Bills for raising Revenue shall originate in the House of Representatives; but the Senate may propose or concur with Amendments as on other Bills.

Every Bill which shall have passed the House of Representatives and the Senate, shall, before it become a Law, be presented to the President of the United States: If he approve he shall sign it, but if not he shall return it, with his Objections to that House in which it shall have originated, who shall enter the Objections at large on their Journal, and proceed to reconsider it. If after such Reconsideration two thirds of that House shall agree to pass the Bill, it shall be sent, together with the Objections, to the other House, by which it shall likewise be reconsidered, and if approved by two thirds of that House, it shall become a Law. But in all such Cases the Votes of both Houses shall be determined by yeas and Nays, and the Names of the Persons voting for and against the Bill shall be entered on the Journal of each House respectively. If any Bill shall not be returned by the President within ten Days (Sundays excepted) after it shall have been presented to him, the Same shall be a Law, in like Manner as if he had signed it, unless the Congress by their Adjournment prevent its Return, in which Case it shall not be a Law.

Every Order, Resolution, or Vote to which the Concurrence of the Senate and House of Representatives may be necessary (except on a question of Adjournment) shall be presented to the President of the United States; and before the Same shall take Effect, shall be approved by him, or being disapproved by him, shall be repassed by two thirds of the Senate and House of Representatives, according to the Rules and Limitations prescribed in the Case of a Bill.

Section. 8.

The Congress shall have Power To lay and collect Taxes, Duties, Imposts and Excises, to pay the Debts and provide for the common Defence and general Welfare of the United States; but all Duties, Imposts and Excises shall be uniform throughout the United States;

To borrow Money on the credit of the United States;

To regulate Commerce with foreign Nations, and among the several States, and with the Indian Tribes;

To establish an uniform Rule of Naturalization, and uniform Laws on the subject of Bankruptcies throughout the United States;

To coin Money, regulate the Value thereof, and of foreign Coin, and fix the Standard of Weights and Measures;

To provide for the Punishment of counterfeiting the Securities and current Coin of the United States;

To establish Post Offices and post Roads;

To promote the Progress of Science and useful Arts, by securing for limited Times to Authors and Inventors the exclusive Right to their respective Writings and Discoveries;

To constitute Tribunals inferior to the supreme Court;

To define and punish Piracies and Felonies committed on the high Seas, and Offences against the Law of Nations;

To declare War, grant Letters of Marque and Reprisal, and make Rules concerning Captures on Land and Water;

To raise and support Armies, but no Appropriation of Money to that Use shall be for a longer Term than two Years;

To provide and maintain a Navy;

To make Rules for the Government and Regulation of the land and naval Forces;

To provide for calling forth the Militia to execute the Laws of the Union, suppress Insurrections and repel Invasions;

To provide for organizing, arming, and disciplining, the Militia, and for governing such Part of them as may be employed in the Service of the United States, reserving to the States respectively, the Appointment of the Officers, and the Authority of training the Militia according to the discipline prescribed by Congress;

To exercise exclusive Legislation in all Cases whatsoever, over such District (not exceeding ten Miles square) as may, by Cession of particular States, and the Acceptance of Congress, become the Seat of the Government of the United States, and to exercise like Authority over all Places purchased by the Consent of the Legislature of the State in which the Same shall be, for the Erection of Forts, Magazines, Arsenals, dock-Yards, and other needful Buildings;—And

To make all Laws which shall be necessary and proper for carrying into Execution the foregoing Powers, and all other Powers vested by this Constitution in the Government of the United States, or in any Department or Officer thereof.

Section. 9.

The Migration or Importation of such Persons as any of the States now existing shall think proper to admit, shall not be prohibited by the Congress prior to the Year one thousand eight hundred and eight, but a Tax or duty may be imposed on such Importation, not exceeding ten dollars for each Person.

The Privilege of the Writ of Habeas Corpus shall not be suspended, unless when in Cases of Rebellion or Invasion the public Safety may require it.

No Bill of Attainder or ex post facto Law shall be passed.

No Capitation, or other direct, Tax shall be laid, *unless in Proportion to the Census or enumeration herein before directed to be taken.*

No Tax or Duty shall be laid on Articles exported from any State.

No Preference shall be given by any Regulation of Commerce or Revenue to the Ports of one State over those of another; nor shall Vessels bound to, or from, one State, be obliged to enter, clear, or pay Duties in another.

No Money shall be drawn from the Treasury, but in Consequence of Appropriations made by Law; and a regular Statement and Account of the Receipts and Expenditures of all public Money shall be published from time to time.

No Title of Nobility shall be granted by the United States: And no Person holding any Office of Profit or Trust under them, shall, without the Consent of the Congress, accept of any present, Emolument, Office, or Title, of any kind whatever, from any King, Prince, or foreign State.

Section. 10.

No State shall enter into any Treaty, Alliance, or Confederation; grant Letters of Marque and Reprisal; coin Money; emit Bills of Credit; make any Thing but gold and silver Coin a Tender in Payment of Debts; pass any Bill of Attainder, ex post facto Law, or Law impairing the Obligation of Contracts, or grant any Title of Nobility.

No State shall, without the Consent of the Congress, lay any Imposts or Duties on Imports or Exports, except what may be absolutely necessary for executing it's inspection Laws: and the net Produce of all Duties and Imposts, laid by any State on Imports or Exports, shall be for the Use of the Treasury of the United States; and all such Laws shall be subject to the Revision and Controul of the Congress.

No State shall, without the Consent of Congress, lay any Duty of Tonnage, keep Troops, or Ships of War in time of Peace, enter into any Agreement or Compact with another State, or with a foreign Power, or engage in War, unless actually invaded, or in such imminent Danger as will not admit of delay.

ARTICLE. II.
Section. 1.
The executive Power shall be vested in a President of the United States of America. He shall hold his Office during the Term of four Years, and, together with the Vice President, chosen for the same Term, be elected, as follows:

Each State shall appoint, in such Manner as the Legislature thereof may direct, a Number of Electors, equal to the whole Number of Senators and Representatives to which the State may be entitled in the Congress: but no Senator or Representative, or Person holding an Office of Trust or Profit under the United States, shall be appointed an Elector.

The Electors shall meet in their respective States, and vote by Ballot for two Persons, of whom one at least shall not be an Inhabitant of the same State with themselves. And they shall make a List of all the Persons voted for, and of the Number of Votes for each; which List they shall sign and certify, and transmit sealed to the Seat of the Government of the United States, directed to the President of the Senate. The President of the Senate shall, in the Presence of the Senate and House of Representatives, open all the Certificates, and the Votes shall then be counted. The Person having the greatest Number of Votes shall be the President, if such Number be a Majority of the whole Number of Electors appointed; and if there be more than one who have such Majority, and have an equal Number of Votes, then the House of Representatives shall immediately chuse by Ballot one of them for President; and if no Person have a Majority, then from the five highest on the List the said House shall in like Manner chuse the President. But in chusing the President, the Votes shall be taken by States, the Representation from each State having one Vote; A quorum for this purpose shall consist of a Member or Members from two thirds of the States, and a Majority of all the States shall be necessary to a Choice. In every Case, after the Choice of the President, the Person having the greatest Number of Votes of the Electors shall be the Vice President. But if there should remain two or more who have equal Votes, the Senate shall chuse from them by Ballot the Vice President.

The Congress may determine the Time of chusing the Electors, and the Day on which they shall give their Votes; which Day shall be the same throughout the United States.

No Person except a natural born Citizen, or a Citizen of the United States, at the time of the Adoption of this Constitution, shall be eligible to the Office of President; neither shall any Person be eligible to that Office who shall not have attained to the Age of thirty five Years, and been fourteen Years a Resident within the United States.

In Case of the Removal of the President from Office, or of his Death, Resignation, or Inability to discharge the Powers and Duties of the said Office, the Same shall devolve on the Vice President, and the Congress may by Law provide for the Case of Removal, Death, Resignation or Inability, both of the President and Vice President, declaring what Officer shall then act as President, and such Officer shall act accordingly, until the Disability be removed, or a President shall be elected.

The President shall, at stated Times, receive for his Services, a Compensation, which shall neither be increased nor diminished during the Period for which he shall have been elected, and he shall not receive within that Period any other Emolument from the United States, or any of them.

Before he enter on the Execution of his Office, he shall take the following Oath or Affirmation:—"I do solemnly swear (or affirm) that I will faithfully execute the Office of President of the United States, and will to the best of my Ability, preserve, protect and defend the Constitution of the United States."

Section. 2.

The President shall be Commander in Chief of the Army and Navy of the United States, and of the Militia of the several States, when called into the actual Service of the United States; he may require the Opinion, in writing, of the principal Officer in each of the executive Departments, upon any Subject relating to the Duties of their respective Offices, and he shall have Power to grant Reprieves and Pardons for Offences against the United States, except in Cases of Impeachment.

He shall have Power, by and with the Advice and Consent of the Senate, to make Treaties, provided two thirds of the Senators present concur; and he shall nominate, and by and with the Advice and Consent of the Senate, shall appoint Ambassadors, other public Ministers and Consuls, Judges of the supreme Court, and all other Officers of the United States, whose Appointments are not herein otherwise provided for, and which shall be established by Law: but the Congress may by Law vest the Appointment of such inferior Officers, as they think proper, in the President alone, in the Courts of Law, or in the Heads of Departments.

The President shall have Power to fill up all Vacancies that may happen during the Recess of the Senate, by granting Commissions which shall expire at the End of their next Session.

Section. 3.

He shall from time to time give to the Congress Information of the State of the Union, and recommend to their Consideration such Measures as he shall judge necessary and expedient; he may, on extraordinary

Occasions, convene both Houses, or either of them, and in Case of Disagreement between them, with Respect to the Time of Adjournment, he may adjourn them to such Time as he shall think proper; he shall receive Ambassadors and other public Ministers; he shall take Care that the Laws be faithfully executed, and shall Commission all the Officers of the United States.

Section. 4.

The President, Vice President and all civil Officers of the United States, shall be removed from Office on Impeachment for, and Conviction of, Treason, Bribery, or other high Crimes and Misdemeanors.

ARTICLE. III.

Section. 1.

The judicial Power of the United States shall be vested in one supreme Court, and in such inferior Courts as the Congress may from time to time ordain and establish. The Judges, both of the supreme and inferior Courts, shall hold their Offices during good Behaviour, and shall, at stated Times, receive for their Services a Compensation, which shall not be diminished during their Continuance in Office.

Section. 2.

The judicial Power shall extend to all Cases, in Law and Equity, arising under this Constitution, the Laws of the United States, and Treaties made, or which shall be made, under their Authority;—to all Cases affecting Ambassadors, other public Ministers and Consuls;—to all Cases of admiralty and maritime Jurisdiction;—to Controversies to which the United States shall be a Party;—to Controversies between two or more States;— *between a State and Citizens of another State;*—between Citizens of different States;—between Citizens of the same State claiming Lands under Grants of different States, and between a State, or the Citizens thereof, and foreign States, Citizens or Subjects.

In all Cases affecting Ambassadors, other public Ministers and Consuls, and those in which a State shall be Party, the supreme Court shall have original Jurisdiction. In all the other Cases before mentioned, the supreme Court shall have appellate Jurisdiction, both as to Law and Fact, with such Exceptions, and under such Regulations as the Congress shall make.

The Trial of all Crimes, except in Cases of Impeachment, shall be by Jury; and such Trial shall be held in the State where the said Crimes shall have been committed; but when not committed within any State, the Trial shall be at such Place or Places as the Congress may by Law have directed.

Section. 3.

Treason against the United States, shall consist only in levying War against them, or in adhering to their Enemies, giving them Aid and Comfort. No Person shall be convicted of Treason unless on the Testimony of two Witnesses to the same overt Act, or on Confession in open Court.

The Congress shall have Power to declare the Punishment of Treason, but no Attainder of Treason shall work Corruption of Blood, or Forfeiture except during the Life of the Person attainted.

ARTICLE. IV.

Section. 1.

Full Faith and Credit shall be given in each State to the public Acts, Records, and judicial Proceedings of every other State. And the Congress may by general Laws prescribe the Manner in which such Acts, Records and Proceedings shall be proved, and the Effect thereof.

Section. 2.

The Citizens of each State shall be entitled to all Privileges and Immunities of Citizens in the several States.

A Person charged in any State with Treason, Felony, or other Crime, who shall flee from Justice, and be found in another State, shall on Demand of the executive Authority of the State from which he fled, be delivered up, to be removed to the State having Jurisdiction of the Crime.

No Person held to Service or Labour in one State, under the Laws thereof, escaping into another, shall, in Consequence of any Law or Regulation therein, be discharged from such Service or Labour, but shall be delivered up on Claim of the Party to whom such Service or Labour may be due.

Section. 3.

New States may be admitted by the Congress into this Union; but no new State shall be formed or erected within the Jurisdiction of any other State; nor any State be formed by the Junction of two or more States, or Parts of States, without the Consent of the Legislatures of the States concerned as well as of the Congress.

The Congress shall have Power to dispose of and make all needful Rules and Regulations respecting the Territory or other Property belonging to the United States; and nothing in this Constitution shall be so construed as to Prejudice any Claims of the United States, or of any particular State.

Section. 4.

The United States shall guarantee to every State in this Union a Republican Form of Government, and shall protect each of them against Invasion; and on Application of the Legislature, or of the Executive (when the Legislature cannot be convened), against domestic Violence.

ARTICLE. V.

The Congress, whenever two thirds of both Houses shall deem it necessary, shall propose Amendments to this Constitution, or, on the Application of the Legislatures of two thirds of the several States, shall call a Convention for proposing Amendments, which, in either Case, shall be valid to all Intents and Purposes, as Part of this Constitution, when ratified by the Legislatures of three fourths of the several States, or by Conventions in three fourths thereof, as the one or the other Mode of Ratification may be proposed by the Congress; Provided that no Amendment which may be made prior to the Year One thousand eight hundred and eight shall in any Manner affect the first and fourth Clauses in the Ninth Section of the first Article; and that no State, without its Consent, shall be deprived of its equal Suffrage in the Senate.

ARTICLE. VI.

All Debts contracted and Engagements entered into, before the Adoption of this Constitution, shall be as valid against the United States under this Constitution, as under the Confederation.

This Constitution, and the Laws of the United States which shall be made in Pursuance thereof; and all Treaties made, or which shall be made, under the Authority of the United States, shall be the supreme Law of the Land; and the Judges in every State shall be bound thereby, any Thing in the Constitution or Laws of any State to the Contrary notwithstanding.

The Senators and Representatives before mentioned, and the Members of the several State Legislatures, and all executive and judicial Officers, both of the United States and of the several States, shall be bound by Oath or Affirmation, to support this Constitution; but no religious Test shall ever be required as a Qualification to any Office or public Trust under the United States.

ARTICLE. VII.

The Ratification of the Conventions of nine States, shall be sufficient for the Establishment of this Constitution between the States so ratifying the Same.

The Word, "the," being interlined between the seventh and eighth Lines of the first Page, the Word "Thirty" being partly written on an Erazure in the fifteenth Line of the first Page, The Words "is tried" being interlined between the thirty second and thirty third Lines of the first Page and the Word "the" being interlined between the forty third and forty fourth Lines of the second Page.

Attest William Jackson Secretary

Done in Convention by the Unanimous Consent of the States present the Seventeenth Day of September in the Year of our Lord one thousand seven hundred and Eighty seven and of the Independence of the United States of America the Twelfth In witness whereof We have hereunto subscribed our Names,

George Washington, Presidt and deputy from Virginia

Delaware: Geo: Read, Gunning Bedford jun, John Dickinson, Richard Bassett, Jaco: Broom; Maryland: James McHenry, Dan of St Thos. Jenifer, Danl. Carroll; Virginia: John Blair, James Madison Jr.; North Carolina: Wm. Blount, Richd. Dobbs Spaight, Hu Williamson; South Carolina: J. Rutledge, Charles Cotesworth Pinckney, Charles Pinckney, Pierce Butler; Georgia: William Few, Abr Baldwin; New Hampshire: John Langdon, Nicholas Gilman; Massachusetts: Nathaniel Gorham, Rufus King; Connecticut: Wm. Saml. Johnson, Roger Sherman; New York: Alexander Hamilton; New Jersey: Wil: Livingston, David Brearley, Wm. Paterson, Jona: Dayton; Pennsylvania: B Franklin, Thomas Mifflin, Robt. Morris, Geo. Clymer, Thos. FitzSimons, Jared Ingersoll, James Wilson, Gouv Morris

THE BILL OF RIGHTS

Note: The following text from the National Archives is a transcription of the first ten amendments to the Constitution in their original form. These amendments were ratified December 15, 1791, and they form what is known as the "Bill of Rights." Amendments 11 - 27 are listed below and include the dates that they were passed by Congress and ratified.

Amendment I
Congress shall make no law respecting an establishment of religion, or prohibiting the free exercise thereof; or abridging the freedom of speech, or of the press; or the right of the people peaceably to assemble, and to petition the Government for a redress of grievances.

Amendment II
A well regulated Militia, being necessary to the security of a free State, the right of the people to keep and bear Arms, shall not be infringed.

Amendment III
No Soldier shall, in time of peace be quartered in any house, without the consent of the Owner, nor in time of war, but in a manner to be prescribed by law.

Amendment IV
The right of the people to be secure in their persons, houses, papers, and effects, against unreasonable searches and seizures, shall not be violated, and no Warrants shall issue, but upon probable cause, supported by Oath or affirmation, and particularly describing the place to be searched, and the persons or things to be seized.

Amendment V

No person shall be held to answer for a capital, or otherwise infamous crime, unless on a presentment or indictment of a Grand Jury, except in cases arising in the land or naval forces, or in the Militia, when in actual service in time of War or public danger; nor shall any person be subject for the same offence to be twice put in jeopardy of life or limb; nor shall be compelled in any criminal case to be a witness against himself, nor be deprived of life, liberty, or property, without due process of law; nor shall private property be taken for public use, without just compensation.

Amendment VI

In all criminal prosecutions, the accused shall enjoy the right to a speedy and public trial, by an impartial jury of the State and district wherein the crime shall have been committed, which district shall have been previously ascertained by law, and to be informed of the nature and cause of the accusation; to be confronted with the witnesses against him; to have compulsory process for obtaining witnesses in his favor, and to have the Assistance of Counsel for his defence.

Amendment VII

In Suits at common law, where the value in controversy shall exceed twenty dollars, the right of trial by jury shall be preserved, and no fact tried by a jury, shall be otherwise re-examined in any Court of the United States, than according to the rules of the common law.

Amendment VIII

Excessive bail shall not be required, nor excessive fines imposed, nor cruel and unusual punishments inflicted.

Amendment IX

The enumeration in the Constitution, of certain rights, shall not be construed to deny or disparage others retained by the people.

Amendment X

The powers not delegated to the United States by the Constitution, nor prohibited by it to the States, are reserved to the States respectively, or to the people.

Amendment XI

Passed by Congress March 4, 1794. Ratified February 7, 1795.
Note: Article III, section 2, of the Constitution was modified by amendment 11.

The Judicial power of the United States shall not be construed to extend to any suit in law or equity, commenced or prosecuted against one of the United States by Citizens of another State, or by Citizens or Subjects of any Foreign State.

Amendment XII

Passed by Congress December 9, 1803. Ratified June 15, 1804.
Note: A portion of Article II, section 1 of the Constitution was superseded by the 12th amendment.

The Electors shall meet in their respective states and vote by ballot for President and Vice-President, one of whom, at least, shall not be an inhabitant of the same state with themselves; they shall name in their ballots the person voted for as President, and in distinct ballots the person voted for as Vice-President, and they shall make distinct lists of all persons voted for as President, and of all persons voted for as Vice-President, and of the number of votes for each, which lists they shall sign and certify, and transmit sealed to the seat of the government of the United States, directed to the President of the Senate;—the President of the Senate shall, in the presence of the Senate and House of Representatives, open all the certificates and the votes shall then be counted;—The person having the greatest number of votes for President, shall be the President, if such number be a majority of the whole number of Electors appointed; and if no person have such majority, then from the persons having the highest numbers not exceeding three on the list of those voted for as President, the House of Representatives shall choose immediately, by ballot, the President. But in choosing the President, the votes shall be taken by states, the representation from each state having one vote; a quorum for this purpose shall consist of a member or members from two-thirds of the states, and a majority of all the states shall be necessary to a choice. [And if the House of Representatives shall not choose a President whenever the right of choice shall devolve upon them, before the fourth day of March next following, then the Vice-President shall act as President, as in case of the death or other constitutional disability of the President. —]* The person having the greatest number of votes as Vice-President, shall be the Vice-President, if such number be a majority of the whole number of Electors appointed, and if no person have a majority, then from the two highest numbers on the list, the Senate shall choose the Vice-President; a quorum for the purpose shall consist of two-thirds of the whole number of Senators, and a majority of the whole number shall be necessary to a choice. But no person constitutionally ineligible to the office of President shall be eligible to that of Vice-President of the United States. *Superseded by section 3 of the 20th amendment.

Amendment XIII

Passed by Congress January 31, 1865. Ratified December 6, 1865.
Note: A portion of Article IV, section 2, of the Constitution was superseded by the 13th amendment.

Section 1.

Neither slavery nor involuntary servitude, except as a punishment for crime whereof the party shall have been duly convicted, shall exist within the United States, or any place subject to their jurisdiction.

Section 2.

Congress shall have power to enforce this article by appropriate legislation.

Amendment XIV
Passed by Congress June 13, 1866. Ratified July 9, 1868.
Note: Article I, section 2, of the Constitution was modified by section 2 of the 14th amendment.

Section 1.

All persons born or naturalized in the United States, and subject to the jurisdiction thereof, are citizens of the United States and of the State wherein they reside. No State shall make or enforce any law which shall abridge the privileges or immunities of citizens of the United States; nor shall any State deprive any person of life, liberty, or property, without due process of law; nor deny to any person within its jurisdiction the equal protection of the laws.

Section 2.

Representatives shall be apportioned among the several States according to their respective numbers, counting the whole number of persons in each State, excluding Indians not taxed. But when the right to vote at any election for the choice of electors for President and Vice-President of the United States, Representatives in Congress, the Executive and Judicial officers of a State, or the members of the Legislature thereof, is denied to any of the male inhabitants of such State, being twenty-one years of age,* and citizens of the United States, or in any way abridged, except for participation in rebellion, or other crime, the basis of representation therein shall be reduced in the proportion which the number of such male citizens shall bear to the whole number of male citizens twenty-one years of age in such State.

Section 3.

No person shall be a Senator or Representative in Congress, or elector of President and Vice-President, or hold any office, civil or military, under the United States, or under any State, who, having previously taken an oath, as a member of Congress, or as an officer of the United States, or as a member of any State legislature, or as an executive or judicial officer of any State, to support the Constitution of the United States, shall have engaged in insurrection or rebellion against the same, or given aid or comfort to the enemies thereof. But Congress may by a vote of two-thirds of each House, remove such disability.

Section 4.

The validity of the public debt of the United States, authorized by law, including debts incurred for payment of pensions and bounties for services in suppressing insurrection or rebellion, shall not be questioned. But neither the United States nor any State shall assume or pay any debt or obligation incurred in aid of insurrection or rebellion against the United States, or any claim for the loss or emancipation of any slave; but all such debts, obligations and claims shall be held illegal and void.

Section 5.

The Congress shall have the power to enforce, by appropriate legislation, the provisions of this article. *Changed by section 1 of the 26th amendment.

Amendment XV
Passed by Congress February 26, 1869. Ratified February 3, 1870.

Section 1.

The right of citizens of the United States to vote shall not be denied or abridged by the United States or by any State on account of race, color, or previous condition of servitude—

Section 2.

The Congress shall have the power to enforce this article by appropriate legislation.

Amendment XVI
Passed by Congress July 2, 1909. Ratified February 3, 1913.
Note: Article I, section 9, of the Constitution was modified by amendment 16.

The Congress shall have power to lay and collect taxes on incomes, from whatever source derived, without apportionment among the several States, and without regard to any census or enumeration.

Amendment XVII
Passed by Congress May 13, 1912. Ratified April 8, 1913.
Note: Article I, section 3, of the Constitution was modified by the 17th amendment.

The Senate of the United States shall be composed of two Senators from each State, elected by the people thereof, for six years; and each Senator shall have one vote. The electors in each State shall have the qualifications requisite for electors of the most numerous branch of the State legislatures.

When vacancies happen in the representation of any State in the Senate, the executive authority of such State shall issue writs of election to fill such vacancies: Provided, That the legislature of any State may empower the executive thereof to make temporary appointments until the people fill the vacancies by election as the legislature may direct.

This amendment shall not be so construed as to affect the election or term of any Senator chosen before it becomes valid as part of the Constitution.

Amendment XVIII
Passed by Congress December 18, 1917. Ratified January 16, 1919. Repealed by amendment 21.

Section 1.
After one year from the ratification of this article the manufacture, sale, or transportation of intoxicating liquors within, the importation thereof into, or the exportation thereof from the United States and all territory subject to the jurisdiction thereof for beverage purposes is hereby prohibited.

Section 2.
The Congress and the several States shall have concurrent power to enforce this article by appropriate legislation.

Section 3.
This article shall be inoperative unless it shall have been ratified as an amendment to the Constitution by the legislatures of the several States, as provided in the Constitution, within seven years from the date of the submission hereof to the States by the Congress.

Amendment XIX
Passed by Congress June 4, 1919. Ratified August 18, 1920.

The right of citizens of the United States to vote shall not be denied or abridged by the United States or by any State on account of sex.

Congress shall have power to enforce this article by appropriate legislation.

Amendment XX
Passed by Congress March 2, 1932. Ratified January 23, 1933.
Note: Article I, section 4, of the Constitution was modified by section 2 of this amendment. In addition, a portion of the 12th amendment was superseded by section 3.

Section 1.

The terms of the President and the Vice President shall end at noon on the 20th day of January, and the terms of Senators and Representatives at noon on the 3d day of January, of the years in which such terms would have ended if this article had not been ratified; and the terms of their successors shall then begin.

Section 2.

The Congress shall assemble at least once in every year, and such meeting shall begin at noon on the 3d day of January, unless they shall by law appoint a different day.

Section 3.

If, at the time fixed for the beginning of the term of the President, the President elect shall have died, the Vice President elect shall become President. If a President shall not have been chosen before the time fixed for the beginning of his term, or if the President elect shall have failed to qualify, then the Vice President elect shall act as President until a President shall have qualified; and the Congress may by law provide for the case wherein neither a President elect nor a Vice President shall have qualified, declaring who shall then act as President, or the manner in which one who is to act shall be selected, and such person shall act accordingly until a President or Vice President shall have qualified.

Section 4.

The Congress may by law provide for the case of the death of any of the persons from whom the House of Representatives may choose a President whenever the right of choice shall have devolved upon them, and for the case of the death of any of the persons from whom the Senate may choose a Vice President whenever the right of choice shall have devolved upon them.

Section 5.

Sections 1 and 2 shall take effect on the 15th day of October following the ratification of this article.

Section 6.

This article shall be inoperative unless it shall have been ratified as an amendment to the Constitution by the legislatures of three-fourths of the several States within seven years from the date of its submission.

Amendment XXI

Passed by Congress February 20, 1933. Ratified December 5, 1933.

Section 1.

The eighteenth article of amendment to the Constitution of the United States is hereby repealed.
Section 2.

The transportation or importation into any State, Territory, or Possession of the United States for delivery or use therein of intoxicating liquors, in violation of the laws thereof, is hereby prohibited.

Section 3.

This article shall be inoperative unless it shall have been ratified as an amendment to the Constitution by conventions in the several States, as provided in the Constitution, within seven years from the date of the submission hereof to the States by the Congress.

Amendment XXII

Passed by Congress March 21, 1947. Ratified February 27, 1951.

Section 1.

No person shall be elected to the office of the President more than twice, and no person who has held the office of President, or acted as President, for more than two years of a term to which some other person was elected President shall be elected to the office of President more than once. But this Article shall not apply to any person holding the office of President when this Article was proposed by Congress, and shall not prevent any person who may be holding the office of President, or acting as President, during the term within which this Article becomes operative from holding the office of President or acting as President during the remainder of such term.

Section 2.

This article shall be inoperative unless it shall have been ratified as an amendment to the Constitution by the legislatures of three-fourths of the several States within seven years from the date of its submission to the States by the Congress.

Amendment XXIII

Passed by Congress June 16, 1960. Ratified March 29, 1961.

Section 1.

The District constituting the seat of Government of the United States shall appoint in such manner as Congress may direct:

A number of electors of President and Vice President equal to the whole number of Senators and Representatives in Congress to which the District would be entitled if it were a State, but in no event more than the least populous State; they shall be in addition to those appointed by the States, but they shall be considered, for the purposes of the election of President and Vice President, to be electors appointed by a State; and they shall meet in the District and perform such duties as provided by the twelfth article of amendment.

Section 2.

The Congress shall have power to enforce this article by appropriate legislation.

Amendment XXIV
Passed by Congress August 27, 1962. Ratified January 23, 1964.

Section 1.

The right of citizens of the United States to vote in any primary or other election for President or Vice President, for electors for President or Vice President, or for Senator or Representative in Congress, shall not be denied or abridged by the United States or any State by reason of failure to pay poll tax or other tax.

Section 2.

The Congress shall have power to enforce this article by appropriate legislation.

Amendment XXV
Passed by Congress July 6, 1965. Ratified February 10, 1967.
Note: Article II, section 1, of the Constitution was affected by the 25th amendment.

Section 1.

In case of the removal of the President from office or of his death or resignation, the Vice President shall become President.

Section 2.

Whenever there is a vacancy in the office of the Vice President, the President shall nominate a Vice President who shall take office upon confirmation by a majority vote of both Houses of Congress.

Section 3.

Whenever the President transmits to the President pro tempore of the Senate and the Speaker of the House of Representatives his written declaration that he is unable to discharge the powers and duties of his office, and until he transmits to them a written declaration to the contrary, such powers and duties shall be discharged by the Vice President as Acting President.

Section 4.

Whenever the Vice President and a majority of either the principal officers of the executive departments or of such other body as Congress may by law provide, transmit to the President pro tempore of the Senate and the Speaker of the House of Representatives their written declaration that the President is unable to discharge the powers and duties of his office, the Vice President shall immediately assume the powers and duties of the office as Acting President.

Thereafter, when the President transmits to the President pro tempore of the Senate and the Speaker of the House of Representatives his written declaration that no inability exists, he shall resume the powers and duties of his office unless the Vice President and a majority of either the principal officers of the executive department or of such other body as Congress may by law provide, transmit within four days to the President pro tempore of the Senate and the Speaker of the House of Representatives their written declaration that the President is unable to discharge the powers and duties of his office. Thereupon Congress shall decide the issue, assembling within forty-eight hours for that purpose if not in session. If the Congress, within twenty-one days after receipt of the latter written declaration, or, if Congress is not in session, within twenty-one days after Congress is required to assemble, determines by two-thirds vote of both Houses that the President is unable to discharge the powers and duties of his office, the Vice President shall continue to discharge the same as Acting President; otherwise, the President shall resume the powers and duties of his office.

Amendment XXVI

Passed by Congress March 23, 1971. Ratified July 1, 1971.
Note: Amendment 14, section 2, of the Constitution was modified by section 1 of the 26th amendment.

Section 1.

The right of citizens of the United States, who are eighteen years of age or older, to vote shall not be denied or abridged by the United States or by any State on account of age.

Section 2.

The Congress shall have power to enforce this article by appropriate legislation.

Amendment XXVII

Originally proposed Sept. 25, 1789. Ratified May 7, 1992.

No law, varying the compensation for the services of the Senators and Representatives, shall take effect, until an election of representatives shall have intervened.

ENDNOTES

1. Peter and Connie Roop, ed., *I,Columbus: My Journal 1492-1493* (New York: Walker and Company, 1990) 15.

2. Polydore Vergil, *The Anglica Historia of Polydore Vergil A.D. 1485–1537* (translated by Denys Hay) (London: Office of the Royal Historical Society, Camden Series, 1950) 117.

3. Susan Korman, *Sir Walter Raleigh* (Philadelphia: Chelsea House Publishers, 2001) 69.

4. John A. Garraty and Mark C. Carnes, eds., *American National Biography*, Vol. 16 (New York: Oxford University Press, 1999) 839.

5. Joy Hakim, *History of US: From Colonies to Country 1710–1791* (New York: Oxford University Press, 1999) 50.

6. Russell B. Adams, Jr., ed., *The Revolutionaries* (Alexandria, VA: Time-Life Books, 1996) 75.

7. http://www.pbs.org/wnet/historyofus/web01/segment3.html

8. Thomas Paine, *Common Sense, The Rights of Man, and Other Essential Writings of Thomas Paine* (New York: New American Library, 1969) 75.

9. Harvey J. Kaye, *Thomas Paine: Firebrand of the Revolution* (New York: Oxford University Press, 2000) 144.

10. Thomas Fleming, *Liberty! The American Revolution* (New York: Penguin Putnam, 1997) 169.

11. Carl Becker, *The Declaration of Independence: A Study in the History of Political Ideas* (New York: Alfred Knopf, 1942) 208.

12. Michael. V. Uschan, *America's Founders* (San Diego: Lucent Books, 2000) 58.

13. http://www.valleyforge.org/Patriots/index.cfm?action=PorTTimeline

14. Richard B. Morris, *The Making of a Nation* (New York: Time, Inc., 1963) 66.

15.   Thomas Paine, *The American Crisis* "Thoughts on the Peace, and the probable Advantages thereof," December 9, 1783.

16.   Richard Bernstein with Kym S. Rice, *Are We to Be a Nation? The Making of the Constitution* (Cambridge: Harvard University Press, 1987) 85.

17.   Joy Hakim, *From Colonies to Country A History of U.S. — Book 3* (New York: Oxford University Press, 1993) 160.

18.   Ibid., 169.

19.   Catherine Drinker Bowen, *Miracle at Philadelph8ia* (Boston: Little Brown and Company, 1966) 269.

20.   Peter Hannaford, ed., *The Essential George Washington: Two Hundred Years of Observations on the Man, the Myth, the Patriot* (Bennington, VT: Images from the Past, Inc., 1999) 47.

21.   Michael V. Uschan, *Westward Expansion* (San Diego: Lucent Books, 2001) 51.

INDEX

G

Gage, Thomas, 222, 238
Games, 198–199, 389–390
Gaspee, 227–228
Gates, Horatio, 268–269
Geography (Ptolemy), 1
George III, King of England, 218, 234
Georgia, 169–171
Georgia Charter, 164
Gerry, Elbridge, 307
Gil Eannes, 21
Glorious Revolution, 124, 159
Gold, cities of, 66, 72
Gold rush, 354–355, 360
Golden Hind, 79
Goose Creek Men, 168
Govenorship, 191–192
Government
    proprietary, 145–146, 163–164, 191
    representative, 191–193
Grand Canyon, 73
Grasse, Admiral comte de, 292
Great Awakening, 197–198
Great Compromise, 306–307
Great Migration, 122
Green Mountain Boys, 240, 267
Greene, Nathanael, 278, 290
Greenland, 6–7
Grenville, Sir Richard, 82
Guam, 57
Guerilla warfare, 288
Guilford Courthouse, Battle of, 291–292
Gulf Stream, 55
Gullah, 168

H

Hamilton, Alexander, 298, 319, 364
Hancock, John, 253, 254
Harriot, Thomas, *A Briefe and True Report of the New Found Land of Virginia,* 84, 85

Harrison, William Henry, 327, 333, 344
Hawkins, Sir John, 78
Hawthorne, Nathaniel, 391
Health, 181–182, 379–380
Henry, Patrick, 221, 308
Henry the Navigator
    founding of Sagres by, 14–15
    goals of, 20–21
Henry VII, King of England, 39
Henry VIII, King of England, 113
Herjolfsson, Bjarni, 8
Hessians, 246
Hispaniola, 29, 51
Horseshoe Bend, Battle of, 331–332, 333
House of Burgesses, 108
Howe, William, 267, 278
Hudson, Henry, 89, 90–93
Hudson River, 92
Huron tribe, 94
Hutchinson, Ann, 133
Hutchinson, Thomas, 228–229
Hygiene, 181–182, 379–380

I

Immigration, 386
Impressment, 320, 325
Inca empire, 5–6, 40, 46–48
Indentured servitude, 105, 109
India House, 52
Indian Removal Act, 355–356, 360
Indians. *See* Native Americans
Indigo, 168
Industrial Revolution
    in agriculture, 366–367, 370
    in communication, 369
    government assistance for, 364–365
    impact of, on society, 386
    in manufacturing, 363–366
    in transportation, 367–369, 370
Intolerable Acts, 229–231

ALSO AVAILABLE FROM BRIGHT IDEAS PRESS...

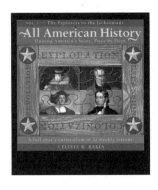 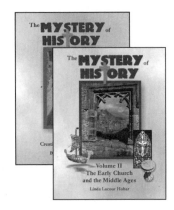 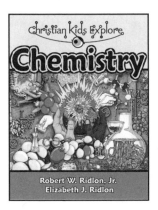 

All American History by Celeste W. Rakes

Containing hundreds of images and dozens of maps, *All American History* is a complete year's curriculum for students in grades 5 – 8 when combined with the Student Activity Book and Teacher's Guide (yet adaptable for younger and older students).

There are 32 weekly lessons, and each lesson contains three sections examining the atmosphere in which the event occurred, the event itself, and the impact this event had on the future of America.

- Student Activity Book — ISBN: 1-892427-11-7
- Teacher's Guide — ISBN: 1-892427-10-9

The Mystery of History Volumes I & II by Linda Hobar

This award-winning series provides a historically accurate, Bible-centered approach to learning world history. The completely chronological lessons shed new light on who walked the earth when, as well as on where important Bible figures fit into secular history. Grades 4 – 8, yet easily adaptable.

- Volume I: Creation to the Resurrection — ISBN: 1-892427-04-4
- Volume II: The Early Church & the Middle Ages — ISBN: 1-892427-06-0

CHRISTIAN KIDS EXPLORE... SERIES

Christian Kids Explore Biology by Stephanie Redmond

One of Cathy Duffy's 100 Top Picks! Elementary biology that is both classical and hands-on. Conversational style and organized layout makes teaching a pleasure.

- ISBN: 1-892427-05-2

Christian Kids Explore Earth & Space by Stephanie Redmond

Another exciting book in this award-winning series! Author Stephanie Redmond is back with more great lessons, activities, and ideas.

- ISBN: 1-892427-19-2

Christian Kids Explore Chemistry by Robert W. Ridlon, Jr., and Elizabeth J. Ridlon

Another great book in this award-winning series! Authors Robert and Elizabeth Ridlon team up for 30 lessons, unit wrap ups, and even coloring pages all about the fascinating world of chemistry.

- ISBN: 1-892427-18-4

FOR ORDERING INFORMATION, CALL 877-492-8081 OR VISIT WWW.BRIGHTIDEASPRESS.COM

Bright Ideas Press books are available
online or through your favorite
Christian bookstore or homeschool supplier.

HEY PARENTS!

Here's a great place to:
Read curriculum reviews
See sample chapters of new books
Sign up for an exciting and useful e-zine
Join our Yahoo groups
Check our homeschool conference schedule
Explore Geography, History, and Science resources
Find great deals on our products!

Secure, online ordering available

WWW.BRIGHTIDEASPRESS.COM

Continue the Story...
All American History
VOL. II
The Civil War to the 21ST Century

All American History, Volume II — The Civil War to the 21ST Century picks up where Volume I left off, continuing this uniquely American story. With the same great features as Volume I, students will journey from the early 1800s to the dawn of a new millennium.

Major topics covered include:

- Civil War and Reconstruction
- Taming of the West
- Influx of immigrants
- Organization of labor
- The Spanish-American War
- The Great Depression
- World War I
- World War II
- The Cold War
- Cultural revolution
- Civil Rights movement
- New technology
- Mass communication
- The Internet

Visit the Bright Ideas Website for Ordering Info
www.brightideaspress.com
or call toll-free: 877-492-8081